Working Hours in British Industry: An economic history

L.S.E. research monographs

This series is published jointly with the London School of Economics and Political Science. It aims to make available research of originality and quality from the whole range of the social sciences, including all the fields and disciplines which are studied at the School. The intention is to provide a continuing outlet for serious scholarly work, and relatively quick publication. The books will be of interest to specialists in the various fields, irrespective of whether they are in universities, government departments, industries or elsewhere, as well as to libraries throughout the world. The following monographs have already been published:

The Politics of Decontrol of Industry: Britain and the United States
Susan Armitage

Students in Conflict
Tessa Blackstone, Kathleen Gales, Roger Hadley, Wyn Lewis

The Business of Banking 1891 to 1914   *C. A. E. Goodhart*

The Share of Wages in the National Income: An Enquiry into the Theory of Distribution   *F. H. Hahn*

Criminal Responsibility   *F. G. Jacobs*

The Nineteenth Century Foreign Office: An Administrative History
Ray Jones

The Criminal Liability of Corporations in English Law   *L. H. Leigh*

The Theory of Customs Unions: A General Equilibrium Analysis
Richard G. Lipsey

Changes in Subject Choice at School and University   *Celia M. Phillips*

Russian Police Trade Unionism: Experiment or Provocation?
Dimitry Pospielovsky

Industrial Demand for Water: A Study of South-East England   *Judith Rees*

The Administrative Functions of the French Conseil d'Etat
Margherita Rendel

Transporting Goods by Road: Policies, Techniques and Distribution Efficiency   *Michael Webb*

Working Hours in British Industry: An economic history

M. A. Bienefeld

With a foreword by E. H. Phelps Brown
formerly Professor in the Economics of Labour
at the London School of Economics and Political Science

London School of Economics and Political Science

Weidenfeld and Nicolson
5 Winsley Street London W1

© 1972 by M. A. Bienefeld

ISBN 0 297 99479 4
Printed in Great Britain by
Redwood Press Limited, Trowbridge, Wiltshire

Contents

Acknowledgements

The author wishes to acknowledge the debts he owes to various individuals and institutions for the help they provided in the preparation of this work. By far the greatest debt is owed to Professor E. H. Phelps Brown who supervised the research on which this book is based, and whose criticisms and encouragement were both invaluable and much appreciated. I could not have wished for a better discussant. Apart from the benefit I derived from our many discussions, his conscientiousness and his incisiveness made it a pleasure to work together.

Dr J. Corina of St Peter's College, Oxford provided some valuable comments on an earlier draft of this book and these were very welcome. In addition I wish to thank the many individuals with whom I discussed at various times particular aspects of this work.

Thanks are due also to those who provided the finances which made this work possible. I wish to thank in particular the Canada Britain Scholarship Foundation and the Canada Council for the assistance they provided at various times. Undoubtedly the greatest contribution on this score was however made by my wife, whose ceaseless toil in the London schools ensured that we had 'shillings for the meter'.

Finally I wish to thank the various libraries and librarians who provided much help. Apart from the university and public libraries special thanks are due to the Trade Union Congress library, and the records sections of the Amalgamated Society of Woodworkers and the Amalgamated Union of Building Trade Workers.

M.A.B.

Abbreviations

ASCJ	Amalgamated Society of Carpenters and Joiners
BTH	Board of Trade (1890), 'Report on Trades (Hours of Work)'
BTW	Board of Trade (1886), 'Report on Trade: Wages (General Report)'
CFW	'Report of the Commissioners appointed to inquire into the working of the Factory and Workshop Acts, 1875'
EFC	see FCR
EMCS	Evidence to the 'Commission on Manufactures, Commerce and Shipping, 1833'
ERCC	see RCC
FCR	'Factory Commission: Report' (1833)
EFC	Evidence to Factory Commission (FCR)
RFC	Reports to the Factory Commission (FCR)
MLG	Ministry of Labour Gazette
MMC	'Midland Mining Commission: Report' (1843)
RMMC	'Report on the Mines of Warwickshire ... etc.' in the Midland Mining Commission (MMC)
MWH	Manuscript of the Webb Collection
OBS	Operative Bricklayers Society
OSM	Operative Society of Masons
OSM-FR	Operative Society of Masons – Fortnightly Review

RCC	'Royal Commission for inquiring into the Employment and Conditions of Children in Mines and Manufactories', 1843

ERCC	Evidence to 1843 Royal Commission
RCC-R1	First Report of 1843 Royal Commission
RCC-R2	Second Report of 1843 Royal Commission
R-RCC	Reports to the Commissioners of the 1843 Royal Commission

RCC-R1	see RCC

RCC-R2	see RCC

R-RCC	see RCC

RMMC	see MMC

RFC	see FCR

SCC	'Select Commission on the Employment of Children' (1816)

SIPEP	Ministry of Labour, 'Statistics on Incomes, Prices, Employment and Production'

WNB	Workers News Bulletin

Foreword

Changes in the hours of work are among the most remarkable and the least investigated occurrences in the whole field of labour.

They are remarkable partly because, since 1850 at least, they have been so great: the normal working week has been reduced from around sixty to forty hours a week, and the extension of holidays has reduced the number of working hours in the year in still greater proportion. If what strikes us most now is the appalling length of the weekly and annual hours from which the reduction was made, we can recognize all the more readily the magnitude of the social change that was brought about by the reduction of those hours by a third. It was a change that was only possible, moreover, because a large part of the total potential improvement in the terms and conditions of employment made available by higher productivity was used up to effect it. In several western countries, in the course of the present century down to the Second World War, the part so drawn upon appears to have been in the region of a half. The reduction of working hours has thus formed a major component of the rise in the standard of living of the workers of the western economies, and of the transformation of their way of life.

But more than this — it is also remarkable that the reduction of hours has not come about fairly continuously, like the rise in pay, through the cumulation over time of small changes made year by year and industry by industry. In most employments it is as practicable to make a marginal reduction of hours at any one time as to make a marginal increase in the rate of pay; but in most of the actual changes of the terms and conditions of employment, hours have not figured at all — they have been changed only at long intervals. When the changes have occurred, they have usually been by substantial amounts, not marginal adjustments, and they have affected wide sectors of employment, sometimes almost the whole field of manual employment, within the span of two or three years.

But the question why these things should have been so has long lain neglected. Dr Bienefeld's pertinacity in pressing that question and, as I believe, his success in answering it, give the present work an outstanding interest. He begins by establishing the facts from the earliest recorded times in Great Britain, and the account that he pieces together, of change both up and down, suggests already one illuminating generalization. He turns then to the effect upon hours of the industrial revolution, and throws on this a fresh light, and one that to not a few readers will be unexpected. From the middle of the nineteenth century onwards, much fuller statistical material becomes available, at the same time as pressure for the limitation of hours begins to be exerted more widely and effectively through trade unions. The stage is now set for the systematic study of the main issues, why through so many changes in pay there were next to none in hours, and what made changes in hours come when they did and then spread them so widely? Dr Bienefeld finds his answers by a powerful combination of abstract analysis or model-building with the application of the hypotheses thereby developed to the sometimes paradoxical evidence of the historical record. What answers he finds it would be as wrong to anticipate here, as to reveal at the outset the solution of a detective story. The reader of the ensuing pages will find his attention arrested and his interest sustained by the systematic working out of a solution to more than one mystery. In doing this Dr Bienefeld has made an original and notable contribution to economic history and economic analysis alike.

E. H. Phelps Brown

Chapter one

Introduction

This study is about the working hours of the British industrial workman. Along with the level of wages this is probably the most important condition of the contract of employment, and yet it is a subject that has been very much neglected in economic literature. Hence although many studies recognize that a substantial reduction of hours of work has taken place since the middle of the nineteenth century, they invariably treat this change on a par with changes in wages. Reductions in hours are treated as ways of obtaining more leisure, and leisure in turn is treated as a substitute for income whose value is measured either in subjective or essentially non-quantifiable terms, or more recently in terms of the net opportunity cost of spending less time at work. This general approach has served to obscure the independent significance of the hours issue through its implicit assumption that hours reductions simply accompany wage rises and therefore do not require separate explanation or analysis. One implication of this position is an expectation of a functional relationship between income increases and hours reductions, though with the more recent 'opportunity cost' approach, account must be taken of changes in the valuation of leisure pursuits including the possibility of secondary employment.

A closer look at the causes of hours reductions demands that these ubiquitous assumptions be investigated. Are hours of work reduced in response to a demand for leisure? Is there a relationship between real wages and hours? Further, it is necessary to reconcile these assumptions with other recurring claims which ascribe hours reductions to quite different causes. Thus it is widely held that hours are reduced to prevent or to eliminate unemployment, or more generally to counteract the employment effects of technological change. At the same time the unions' opponents never tire of claiming that the demand for shorter hours is merely an attempt to raise income indirectly, a conclusion which they derive from the undoubted fact that workmen have generally been willing to work overtime at the same time as demanding reductions in hours. It is the primary purpose of this work to investigate the plausibility of these various claims, and to determine at a macro-economic level which of them is compatible with the historical record.

In the event the marshalling of evidence came to be a major preoccupation of the study, for although there was a great deal of data on hours from the beginning of the nineteenth century, its systematic collection was a slow and painstaking process. Chapters three and four present a reasonably complete and accurate picture of normal hours in the major trades and industries of Britain, based on figures taken from government reports, trade-union records, contemporary newspapers and journals, and books and pamphlets on social and economic matters. As a result these chapters present a mass of highly disaggregated data, accompanied by frequent attempts to explain changes at a micro-economic level. It should be recognized that this micro-level orientation was necessitated by the nature of the data. Chapter five, which deals with the period from 1890 to 1965, is very different in its approach simply because macro-level statistics were already available for those years. In view of the fact that the major focus of the study is on hours at a macro-economic level, this chapter merely summarizes the existing statistics with little digression to a more disaggregated level.

The collection and analysis of nineteenth-century data at a micro-economic level did nevertheless serve an analytically useful purpose, by allowing the more common assumptions about trade-union attitudes to hours reductions to be compared with their actual behaviour in specific instances. At this level it was possible to establish the plausibility of the claim that trade unions seek hours reductions as an anti-unemployment measure; to show the connection between their interest in, and their ability to achieve, such reductions and a variety of institutional factors such as the nature of the unions, the size of firms, or the size of markets; and finally to identify a variety of possible relationships between wages and hours reductions. These findings later helped to indicate the directions in which explanations for the macro-level changes should be sought.

Notably no attempt was made to formulate the relationships suggested by the evidence in precise functional terms. Though such exercises are increasingly fashionable, only rarely are they feasible in the social sciences without the use of highly restrictive and unrealistic assumptions. In this case the data was not sufficiently detailed, accurate or comprehensive to warrant an attempt to quantify the suggested relationships, nor could *ceteris paribus* assumptions have been stretched over the variety of situations analysed. In part this was due to the historical nature of the data, in part it was due to the small number of events to be explained. Nevertheless even with much improved data any attempt to derive formal functional relations would be extremely difficult, for not only would linear functions be totally inadequate, it is probable that no type of continuous function could be used. The relationship between the major variables is most likely of a discontinuous nature, with little correlation below certain thresholds and varying degrees of interaction once these thresholds are reached. In practice the problem of defining such a relationship is worsened by the fact that the thresholds themselves are variable over time, shifting according to the direction and the rate of change of a number of variables. Under these circumstances the present study confined itself to the identification of the major concomitants of changes in hours and to the search for a conceptual framework compatible with the evidence. It is clear that further testing of the hypotheses presented here is both necessary and desirable.

By the end of the fifth chapter the broad pattern of macro-economic hours reductions has been established and the subsequent two chapters deal with the search for an explanation. The pattern to be explained was striking, and consisted of very long periods of total stability in hours, interspersed by brief radical adjustments. From the beginning of the industrialization of Britain there were four such periods of change, and each of them reduced normal hours by something of the order of ten per cent. What finally required explanation was both the pattern itself, and the particular timing of the reductions.

Chapter six provides a theoretical framework that shows that a realistic assessment of the collective bargaining situation should lead one to expect hours to change only rarely under this system. Though workmen with discretion over their time allocation were generally found to change their working hours gradually as their income levels changed, this adjustment mechanism is prevented from functioning under collective bargaining owing to the diverging interests of the parties concerned. Hence the employer's opposition to hours reductions generally outweighs the workman's demand for them, because for the employer such reductions involve not only higher labour costs but also a reduced level of capital utilization. The employer is therefore usually able to 'buy off' the workers' demand for shorter hours, and this may continue indefinitely, unless for some reason the workers' demand for such change increases to the point where a reduction of one hour is valued equally by him with an income increase substantially in excess of his current rate of pay.

Some readers may be put off by the fact that the theoretical exposition makes use of the concept of indifference curves, since these are associated with numerous conceptual difficulties. In fact these were used because they provided a useful way to demonstrate the pitfalls of the 'traditional' labour-leisure analysis, and to illustrate the nature of the conflict of interest inherent in the bargaining situation along with the effect that this has on the establishment of hours. Beyond this the present analysis has little in common with traditional indifference-curve analysis, largely because indifference curves are not regarded as static functions showing simply the rate of substitution between income and leisure. Rather, here such curves are accepted as being changeable over time, if not changing continuously, and much of the analysis concerns the factors likely to cause such shifts. Such an approach makes a 'realistic' appraisal possible because it allows any and all factors to be considered, though often one sacrifices the possibility of rigorous quantification by considering a wide range of variables, some of which are inevitably not meaningfully quantifiable. Nevertheless, those who demand mathematical rigour can achieve it within the framework presented. Hence it is perfectly possible to specify the indifference curves strictly according to some quantifiable dimension. Following one current approach, one could simply assume that the workman's valuation of time away from work is determined strictly by the net income effect, derived by comparing the income foregone by not working with the value of the goods and services 'produced' – for sale or for self-consumption – during this 'non-working time'. It should be clear that the theoretical framework presented here is compatible with a mathematically rigorous treatment of the subject, and that the lack of such rigour in this study is not an inherent result of this approach.

Given this conceptual frame, attempts to explain the timing of the observed reductions first focused attention on the question of whether hours reductions were particularly related to income variations. If they were this would raise the possibility that observed reductions were brought about simply by movement along an indifference curve which indicated an increasing rate of substitution of income for leisure (here meaning time away from work) as income rose. In addition the analysis assessed the possibilities that various factors connected with shifts in the indifference functions were instrumental in contributing to the periodic reductions achieved by the unions.

The evidence shows that real wages were not directly related to the hours reductions. Changes in real wages showed none of the discontinuity of changes in hours, and the periods of hours adjustment were not accompanied by extraordinarily high real-income increases. The possibility that real-wage increases affected the hours-income trade-off cumulatively over time, led to an investigation of the possibility that hours reductions were associated with extraordinary net real-wage increases over the preceding decade. Here too the relationship that emerged was at best inconclusive.

On the other hand money-wage changes were quite clearly related to hours reductions. Ten-year net increases of money wages reached their peaks precisely at those times when hours were reduced and, as with the hours reductions, the peaks in money wages also represented sharp deviations from an underlying trend. It followed from this that 'income' may have had a considerable influence over hours reductions, on the assumption of a money illusion and the assumption that the 'income increases' were cumulative in their effect on the demand for reduced hours.

There were reasons for believing, however, that factors other than the change in money incomes played an important role in bringing about reductions in hours. Thus money incomes do not increase uniformly throughout the economy, but hours reductions were characterized by their uniformity across the organized sections of the labour force. In addition unions were often found willing to work overtime at the very time when 'normal' hours were reduced, suggesting that the reason for the demand was not an immediate demand for leisure to be enjoyed along with an increased income. Accordingly a number of factors were identified which tended to shift upward the employees' relative valuation of time away from work. Most important among these was the workman's fear of unemployment. This issue recurred again and again in trade-union discussion of the hours issue, and had earlier been identified as a likely contributory cause of hours reductions at a micro-economic level. The importance of the employment issue was further established by the fact that in many of the most important early unions the demand for shorter hours first came to the fore at the same time as the earliest introduction of unemployment benefit, and that both of these ·innovations were introduced in the wake of the collapse of the 'tramping' system, which ceased to be the trade-union response to unemployment once slumps in trade became national rather than regional events. Indeed it appeared that the great Amalgamated Societies that dominated the union movement in the latter half of the nineteenth century were established largely in response to these problems.

Even a cursory examination of unemployment at the time of the major hours reductions, revealed immediately a connection between them. Somewhat surprisingly, in every case the adjustment in hours was accompanied by extraordinarily low levels of unemployment. This apparent paradox was resolved by showing that the motive force for the unions was the desire to prevent future unemployment, rather than their desire to deal with its current existence. It was argued that at such times of very full employment both union strength and union fear of unemployment reached a peak and led to the few substantial hours reductions on record. The case that the unions' fear of unemployment reaches a peak just at such periods is made at great length and is based primarily on the fact that at such times of rapid growth and change, fears of the trade cycle and more vague and ominous fears about technological change are most acute.

These findings raise some interesting questions concerning the dynamics of the labour movement as a whole and the book concludes by speculating about some of these possibilities. Thus by showing that the issue of job security has been a powerful factor in trade-union development this study suggests that in future too it could well become the focus for renewed initiatives by the trade unions. The question is not analysed in detail and is raised merely to suggest one direction in which the wider implications of these findings may be sought. To the extent that threats to jobs or to trades or professions develop in future without adequate planning to ease the transition there is every likelihood that this threat will once more lead to moves by employees to organize and will also allow them to achieve a degree of solidarity rarely achieved on another issue.

Finally, to conclude this introduction a word should be said about chapter two. This provides a sweeping historical perspective for the issues under discussion. From this several interesting points emerged. There was a marked coincidence between pressure for reduced working time and rising real wages even on this global scale, and in addition a most interesting adjustment of working hours was shown to have accompanied the Puritan revolution in England. In the course of this, a system with very long working days, but many holidays and a leisurely pace of work, was transformed to become a regimen with more regular and intense work and with few holidays, but also with a considerably shorter working day. Here was a revolution that may have been a prerequisite for the industrial revolution that followed it. Alternatively it might best be considered as part of that later and wider transformation.

This opening chapter also sets the stage for the subsequent analysis of changes in working hours. It therefore throws light on what happened to hours in the course of the industrial revolution. On balance it was found that the 'normal' hours of most of the new industries conformed to the hours of the crafts and industries of a much earlier date. Yet this is not to deny that the industrialization of the economy produced pressures to lengthen hours, nor that on balance hours were lengthened by it. Thus, in spite of the basic stability of 'normal' hours, actual hours increased. These increases came about primarily in one of three ways: normal hours themselves did increase in certain industries — notably in the textile mills; the hours in factories were generally longer and the work more intense than had been the case in the domestic trades, so that the massive move into the factories lengthened the hours of the majority of the working population; and finally the normal hours were often transgressed in practice and this led to the excesses that have been extensively documented by numerous social historians. Indeed, it is a monument to the importance which the workman attached to the issue of hours that he prevented the extension of normal hours in most trades and industries even during the disruptive years of the early nineteenth century, when he was often on the defensive before a new system which ran roughshod over his traditional practices and forced him to seek new ways of defending his interests.

Chapter two

The early history of hours of work: before 1820

1 Introduction

In history there are no beginnings and no ends. Each point in time is but a meaningless abstraction without the context of its past, and so it is that this work whose primary aim was to identify and analyse changes in working hours in British industry begins some centuries before industry came to play a significant role in the British economy. The great sweep in time is necessitated by the fact that a fundamental aspect of a man's life, such as the amount of time he regularly spends at work, changes but rarely but when it does the roots of that change can be traced far back through history.

The significance of the hours of work that were established in the early British industries depends on the hours that were being worked elsewhere in the economy at that time. This requires an assessment of the uniformity of hours at that time and, more important than that, it requires an investigation into the way in which these hours were established; the length of time they had been observed; and the sanctions that were in existence to enforce them. This chapter is therefore primarily concerned with establishing the foundation on which later working arrangements were built.

If the establishment of a norm or a base line is the primary purpose of this chapter, it is not its only function. Since most of this volume is concerned with the changes in hours under industrial conditions it was of obvious interest to attempt to establish the major patterns of changes in hours during the pre-industrial phase of England's history. Though the evidence that could be collected on this score was necessarily sketchy it was sufficient in the end to piece together a coherent picture, which quite apart from its intrinsic interest allowed some of the features of the later changes to be more clearly understood.

At the most general level the long sweep of history revealed an inverse relation between the number of hours spent at work and the real-wage level of the working man. Thus from the time of the Black Death to the end of the fifteenth century the workman's real wages were on the rise and at the same time there is unmistakable evidence that he was also reducing the number of hours spent at work. Both of these trends reversed themselves with the advent of the Elizabethan age and the erosion of the working man's leisure which set in at that time culminated in the seventeenth century with the total abolition of holidays by the Puritans. Since most of the earlier increases in leisure were taken in the form of additional holidays this was a serious development from the workman's point of view. With the coming of the eighteenth century real wages resumed an upward trend and it was at this time also that the hours of work were once more reduced. It is interesting to note that by this time the reductions were effected through a shortening of the working day rather than through an increase in holidays. It was in the process of these reductions that the ten-hour day was established as the generally accepted normal working day, and this concentration on regulating the daily hours of work was undoubtedly an indication of the increasing intensity and regularity of work.

The identification of these trends as general to the economy invites the misconception that they involved the majority of the working population. This was not true for the entire period here under discussion. At all times these trends were general only to that small part of the population that hired out its labour and therefore any attempt to assess the total significance of these changes must consider the changing size of this sector of the population. But in order for this to be done a viable definition of what constitutes 'hiring out one's labour' must be found and it is this need that focuses attention on the extent to which the significance of the hours issue depends on the nature of the inducement to work or, more narrowly, on the nature of the contractual relationship between employer and employee. The general trends identified above must be seen against the background of the changing patterns in these relationships which also characterized this stretch of history.

The nature of the inducement to labour ranges from the largely self-imposed discipline of the self-employed to the total coercion of the narrowly confined slave. Between these there are various degrees of dependence best illustrated by the domestic worker who began as a self-employed producer but who in time came to work for particular buyers, thence became dependent on them for the provision of his raw materials and later his machinery, and who finally followed the machinery into the workshops and the factories of his employer. When he arrived there the degree of his dependence was differentiated from that of the slave only by his 'freedom' to seek alternative employment. In the face of massive unemployment, an enclosed countryside and colluding employers this 'freedom' must often have seemed a questionable boon to those who were supposed to enjoy it. From the perspective of a study of the hours of work and their determination, the most significant stage in this transition from producer to wage labourer came somewhere between the workman's move into the employer's workshop and the transition of that workshop into a factory, because it was at this point that the contract of hire either explicitly or implicitly stipulated rigorously the hours that were to be worked. There is evidence that it was precisely this aspect of the coercion of the factory that accounted for the reluctance of numbers of domestic workers to consider the move into this kind of employment even though their own position was often deteriorating rapidly.

The above picture is clearly a heuristic one and it is not intended to suggest that all workers or even all domestic producers moved through all of the stages of dependence. Rather this 'ideal type' is considered as useful to illustrate the various degrees of a workman's dependence, and to assist in describing some of the changes in the nature of contractual relationships that accompanied the trends in wages and hours described above.

It appears that it was the disruption of the Black Death which first forced the hours of work out of the anonymity of customary observance and led to their explicit definition in the gild statutes of the time. It is not surprising that hours should first have been defined in this way, for at the time the urban crafts would have accounted for a substantial proportion of the contractually employed working men; though the conflict of interest inherent in that relationship was very much modified by the fact that every employee was a future employer and this distinguishing feature only disappeared very gradually.

At about this same time the breakdown of the feudal contract of service was accelerating in the countryside and wage labour contracts became much more common there. Still the numbers working on these terms were small but in retrospect we know that a trend had begun which would not cease until it had changed the face of the earth. Thus as the trends we have identified unfolded over the next four centuries they affected primarily a slowly changing sector of the working population comprising the craftsmen in the towns, certain special industries like the building industry, and a slowly growing number of rural wage labourers.

For most of this period what formal definition of hours there was occurred in the 'statutes of the realm' whose primary concern was the protection of customary practice as far as hours of work were concerned, and it was only with the coming of the eighteenth century that the issue came to be defined at a more micro-economic level. This shift in focus was clearly related to the breakdown of traditional restraints on the pace of work and to the increasing sharpness of the conflict of interest between master and man as the latter's chances of advancement grew progressively smaller. With the breakdown of old regulations new ones had to be established and the workman proved himself in quite a strong position by successfully establishing the ten-hour working day. This was achieved with relatively little conflict, which is truly impressive when one considers the fact that the previous definition of the working day had existed for at least four centuries without being effectively challenged. But if generally in this period the workman was able to assert his interests successfully in the reformulation of working arrangements there was at least one major industry where this was not the case. The exception was to be found in the cotton mills and it was an exception that boded ill for the future.

The changes that were revolutionizing manufactures in Britain at this time were primarily based on changes in the size of markets and on related changes in technology. Whereas in most trades these changes were gradually eroding traditional structures and practices the cotton industry underwent in some areas a fundamental transformation that revolutionized its technology, shifted the industry geographically and changed the composition of its labour force. A concomitant of these changes was the establishment of a working day ranging from eleven to thirteen and a half and fourteen hours per day. The seriousness of this development lay in the fact that the changes which had overtaken this industry were almost certainly precursors of changes that would soon be experienced by many other industries and there was reason to believe that a similar fate would befall the workman in these other areas.

In the end this did not happen to any great extent. In most industries a more traditionally rooted labour force alerted to the impending threat was able to hold the line on this issue, though of course almost all of them experienced a great quickening in the pace of work. Indeed the anomalous position of the cotton mills, and later of the textile mills in general, led to a rallying of forces which in the end re-established the ten-hour day and thus brought even this industry back into line.

While the hours of the wage labourer were thus slowly adjusting themselves to a changing mode of production the great bulk of the working population were still self-employed and they naturally worked what hours they liked. Such hours were not subject to agreement between different parties and hence they are rarely documented. Nevertheless the major characteristics of the work habits of this part of the population were established and they provide an interesting backdrop to the changes that are the focus of this study.

The most striking feature of the hours of the self-employed was their irregularity. Leisure was enjoyed in the form of holidays frequently taken at the beginning of each week, and almost as frequently the time so lost was 'made up' at the end of the week. It was the often incredible hours worked at these times that form the basis of the erroneous but common view that the domestic worker generally worked fantastic hours that usually exceeded the hours worked in the factories. Though this was true of many one- or two-day periods, on a weekly, monthly or annual basis it was the factory worker who worked many more hours than his self-employed brother. Thus from the point of view of the hours of work the major impact of the increasing industrialization of industry was not the lengthening of the daily hours of the wage employed, though this did happen in the textile industry and later in some of the smaller sweated trades. Rather the real significance lay in the increasing proportion of the working population that were subjected to the increasing regularity and intensity of work that formed part of this process.

A further feature of the hours of the self-employed that emerged from the findings relating to the latter part of the period here under review, was their distinct tendency to fluctuate inversely with the incomes being earned. Here then was support for the view that income and leisure truly are substitutes, for under circumstances where their substitution was entirely at the discretion of the working man an unmistakable inverse relation appeared. When one adds this to the finding that on a broad historical view reductions in the hours of the wage employed were associated with rising trends in their real wages a strong presumption is established that reductions in hours should be closely associated with rises in real wages, and our analysis of subsequent changes begins by investigating this possibility.

Finally the simultaneous existence of two important sectors in the economy observing distinctly different patterns of work allocation should lead to a certain degree of interdependence. This was found to be true in this case. Hence in the domestic trades there is evidence that the ten-hour day which came to be generally accepted in the wage employment sector, was also regarded by this sector as a 'full' day's work. Conversely the attempts of the new industrial system to introduce regular work throughout the year were constantly hampered by the refusal of the employees to stop 'playing' one or two days of the week, in accordance with the practices observed by their neighbours in the domestic trades.

2 Hours of work: 1300 to 1700

In considering the number of hours worked at some point in time it is necessary to consider in turn the number of hours worked per day, per week and per year, and hence, in attempting to establish an approximate picture of working hours over this long historical period, hours will be discussed separately for these different periods.

The amount of time spent at work is an issue which primarily concerns three interest groups: the public, qua consumer; the employers; and the workmen themselves. It is these three forces that must strike a balance between them, and any result so achieved must be seen to be to the mutual advantage of all three parties if it is to survive. If it does so survive for any length of time it will pass into the realm of custom, and the privileges enjoyed by its terms will take on the attributes of 'rights'. It is only if such a balance is then upset, either by a change in the strength of one of the parties, or by a change in the way one of the parties sees its interests, that the issue will be 'forced out into the open'. This means that it will be formally defined and will thus pass out of the realm of custom, whence it can return only through a long period of mutual acceptance.

In Britain the earliest formal definition of hours of work took place in the gild statutes of the thirteenth century. It appears that after 1200 the towns began to take a greater interest in the affairs of gilds, and 'it became the custom to demand that their current regulations be reduced to writing in a common form', and it is said that this 'transition from oral to written rules forced a clear and hence a novel definition of many customs that had previously been left ambiguous'.[1]

In most cases one of these rules concerned the hours of work. 'Nominally, to insure the good quality of their wares, the Gild Statutes always ordain that no one "shall work longer than from the beginning of the day until curfew", nor "at night by candle-light". But doubtless the real ground for this ordinance was rather regard for the well-being of the Gild-brothers; it was the wish to give them leisure for fulfilling their domestic and political duties, and to prevent the collective body from being forced to over-exertions by the competition of a few too zealous for gain, and from being deprived of every enjoyment of life'.[2]

Although the view that gilds were purely restrictive bodies has been successfully challenged,[3] it is accepted that a large number of them, especially those supplying local markets, practised various forms of restriction. While 'the key restrictive policies were those that bore on the supply of skill ... competition was farther limited by regulation of hours of work',[4] and these were set at 'about twelve during winter days and up to fifteen or sixteen in summer'. This reckoning clearly includes the meal times as part of the 'working day', though this practice will not be followed in this volume.

In general the freedom of the gilds to regulate their own affairs was limited by the requirement that their rules 'tende not to the hurte of the common weale of this towne'.[5] Although this requirement led to many conflicts between the gilds and the public authorities, the almost complete absence of disputes over the issue of hours indicates that the length of the working day continued to be mutually accepted.

Then in the fourteenth century the Black Death overtook the nation and left its deep imprint on almost every aspect of society. Among other things this catastrophy greatly changed the balance of forces in the then embryonic labour market. 'While the plague was by no means confined to the labouring classes, the consensus of opinion is that the death rate was highest among the poor', and 'complaints as to the scarcity of labour of all kinds, especially agricultural' and 'of the exorbitant wages demanded by the labourers fortunate enough to survive . . . have been recorded by all commentators'.[6]

Under these circumstances all manner of customary practices were being swept aside and in response the public authorities intervened, attempting to reaffirm customary observances. Hence the towns reasserted the power of the gilds to regulate their crafts on condition 'that the said masters must properly treat and govern their serving-men in the trade, in such manner as the serving-men in like trades in the city have been wont to be properly treated and governed',[7] while the state issued the Statute of Labourers even while the plague was still in progress, requiring that workmen 'shall receive only the wages, liveries, hire or salaries which used to be offered in the places where he should serve in the twentieth year of our reign of England, or in the five or six common years last preceeding'.[8]

Once again one is struck by the almost total absence of dispute over the hours to be worked. Even in the aftermath of this 'great economic upheaval'[9] when a very wide range of customary practices were challenged successfully, the hours of work rarely appear as the subject of dispute. The Statute of Labourers for all its comprehensiveness does not even explicitly mention hours and court records of the Statute's enforcement reveal not a single instance of litigation over this issue.[10]

The absence of conflict over this issue, either before or after the Black Death, suggests that the number of hours to be worked in a day continued to be a mutually accepted quantity. Hence one is not surprised to find that hours in the latter half of the fourteenth century conform to those laid down in the much earlier gild statutes. Thus at this time hours are variously reckoned as from 'sunrise till the ninth hour', or from 'sunrise to 30 minutes before sunset', which we are told makes a working day of 12¼ hours in summer.[11] Moreover this acceptance appears to have continued for some time yet since independent sources suggest that these were still the hours worked, at least in London and in Coventry, in the second half of the fifteenth century.[12]

Only as the fifteenth century drew to a close were there unambiguous signs that the period of mutual acceptance was coming to an end. By 1495 the issue had become sufficiently controversial to require explicit definition of the hours of work in a Statute of the Realm.[13] This Act had become necessary because a situation had arisen 'where diverse artificers and laborers retained to work and serve waste much part of the day ... sometimes in late coming unto their work, early departing therefrom, long sitting at their (meals) ... and long time of sleeping after none'.[14] The Act intended to rectify this situation and thus specified a working day from five in the morning to 'between seven and eight of the clock in the evening', with two and one-half hours for meals and sleep in the summer.

The passage of this Act reflects the obvious concern of the authorities with the apparent erosion of the traditional working day. Clearly neither the problem nor the concern of the authorities disappeared with the passage of this Act, as is emphasized by the need to reiterate these limits in a further Statute twenty years later.[15] The trend towards shorter working days is also corroborated by the hours of the builders which in the years 1474 and 1537 and in diverse places were found to vary between 10½ and 11½ hours per day.[16]

As the sixteenth century proceeded it became clear that the high tide of the workman's fortunes was drawing to a close. The real-wage trend turned sharply downwards,[17] and comprehensive geographic and occupational shifts in the economy meant that 'the effective organization of large masses of wage-earners for self-protection was impossible'.[18] 'Systematic overtime' became the rule of the day 'to bridge the gap between wages and rising prices'.[19] From this time there is also no longer any evidence of a downward pressure on the hours of work.

The statutory history of this period suggests no further changes in the definition of the working day. The Statute of Artificers of 1563, the most comprehensive piece of labour legislation up to that time, confined itself to the reaffirmation of the hours set down in previous statutes. However, this does not reflect a particular concern with the issue; its inclusion reflected merely the fact that the Statute was designed to consolidate and clarify previous labour legislation.[20]

The working day did not again become the subject of legislation until the eighteenth century and this suggests that for a time the issue had ceased to be contested. The few independent pieces of evidence relating to hours at this time also suggest that the statutory hours were being generally observed,[21] and there is reason to believe that this stability continued unabated for a very long time. When evidence as to hours becomes plentiful again in the eighteenth century, the great majority of working men worked precisely those hours that had been laid down in the statutes of the Tudors.

The issue of the working week turns on the subject of the Saturday half-holiday, and its history complements that of the working day. Initially its observance appears to have been universal, but it too was challenged in the course of time and by the eighteenth century it had become a rarity.

In the fourteenth century, gild statutes regularly prohibited work 'on Saturday or the eve of a double feast when noon has been rung', and this custom was said to have been 'common to all countries' and to have 'had its origin in the custom of the Roman Catholic church to solemnize the eve of festivals and Sundays by religious services'.[22]

It appears that from a very early date there were efforts to shift the burden of additional leisure to be enjoyed by the workman, to the latter's wage packet. There were therefore moves to introduce payment by the day which are strikingly similar to the efforts by employers of the nineteenth century to counteract the effects of reduced hours by introducing payment by the hour.

At first such departures did not receive official sanction and so a London regulation dated 1362 laid down that workmen were entitled to a 'full day's pay' for Saturdays.[23] Later the authorities were clearly becoming convinced of the wisdom of such a change and so as early as 1402 a statute specified a number of trades where men could not be hired by the week and for whom the half days should be paid as such.[24] By the end of that century and in the face of the workman's pressure to reduce hours this view had won the day. It became statutory law that 'no artificer nor laborer working but the half day take no wages but for the half day, and nothing for a holiday'.[25]

These later statutes are concerned not only with the half day on Saturday, but more generally with the half days preceding all holidays and this concern reflects the fact that the major variant in the hours of work at this time lay in the number of days that were worked. The proliferation of holidays was far more significant than any of the changes so far discussed and it brought with it a proliferation of half-holidays on the eves of these feasts. The concern of the legislators can undoubtedly be better understood when one recalls that the King's masons at this time stopped at 3 pm on Saturday and before fifteen holidays; stopped at 11 am before thirteen further holidays; and worked until 7 pm on the eve of the remaining nine feasts.[26]

That the primary focus of variation in hours should have been an increase in the number of holidays is not surprising when one considers that 'regularity, consistency and intensity of work ... were quite alien to the worker of the seventeenth century, and indeed of Tudor England'.[27] The pattern of change is the same as that found for the daily hours except that it is more pronounced. Once again from the time of the Black Death to the end of the fifteenth century as the workman's situation improves he comes to enjoy an ever greater number of holidays. This increase is halted in the sixteenth century, and sharply reversed by the Puritans in the century to follow.

A word is in order here concerning the definition of the term 'holiday'. Periods during which no work is done range from the enforced idleness of unemployment to the institutionalized provision of leisure through paid holidays, and between these two extremes lies a range of alternatives that are not always clearly distinguishable. So the idleness apparently imposed on some trades by the climate or by some other consideration was often at least partially transformed into a positive means of restricting supply or of providing leisure, as was clearly the case with numerous trades who prohibited all work over Christmas for periods sometimes extending over several months.[28]

In any event the extensive availability for many of secondary employment in agriculture always tended to dilute the meaning of the term unemployment. Indeed, to the extent that casual labour plays a significant role in an economy, the definition of unemployment becomes virtually impossible since in such a situation work is often regarded as an intermittent phenomenon. People not only move in and out of employment, but also in and out of the labour force. One might say that under such circumstances the entire labour force displays many of the characteristics now usually associated with the secondary labour force.

In order to avoid much of this difficulty the holidays observed only by particular trades, often extending over longish periods, will not be considered here. Rather only the public holidays will be dealt with. This normally entails festivities common to all trades in an area, commemorating a particular religious or secular event and normally restricted to a few days at a time.

Abstentions from work enforced by various individual trades at diverse times are not dealt with because with most of these it becomes impossible to distinguish enforced idleness from the needs of secondary employment, leisure preference or the desire to restrict supply. Indeed in most cases these motives tended to be inextricably interwoven. In addition of course such regulation was usually the result of agreements between masters in a trade and is thus rather different from the changes that are of primary concern to this study.

Also excluded from this analysis is the common practice of many trades to suspend work for a period of about a month to allow members to participate in the harvest. This was a widespread and an ancient custom clearly rooted in the highly seasonal demand for labour in agriculture. To the townsman this was clearly not a time for leisure initially, but in fact as the rural ties of townsfolk weakened the custom was often maintained long after it had ceased to serve a purpose in agriculture. At that point it often served to provide the workmen with leisure or to restrict the output of the trade.[29]

Bearing in mind these exclusions it is possible to identify some very distinct trends in the number of specific holidays enjoyed by wage employees in general.

Early in the fourteenth century the number of holidays taken by the masons at various building sites in the kingdom ranged between twenty and twenty-seven, the exact number depending on the number of festivals which in any given year fell on a Sunday. The majority of these were connected with the four major festivals: Christmas, Easter, Whitsuntide and the New Year, and anywhere from fifteen to twenty-four of the total were directly connected with these four occasions.

By the middle of the fifteenth century, after almost a century of rising real wages, the masons had considerably increased the number of their holidays. Now they were found to celebrate[30] forty-six holidays, of which anything from thirty-eight to forty-three fell on days other than Sunday.

As has been noted, the sixteenth century brought a reversal of the workman's fortunes. Wage trends turned downwards; the statutory working day was reaffirmed and enforced; the cost of the half-holidays was shifted on to the employee; and now the proliferation of holidays was also stopped and previously gained privileges began to be eroded.

A few of the most powerful trades in certain areas had begun to demand payment for holidays and it was this threat which first became the subject of statutory regulation. An Act passed even before the end of the fifteenth century outlawed this practice,[31] and once again sought to curtail the workman's enthusiasm for holidays by ensuring that it was he who felt their economic burden.

Soon this determination to prevent further gains by the workman turned into a movement to reverse the privileges he had obtained. In 1539 the Bishop of Exeter gave voice to this trend when he 'observed (that) . . . artificers and labourers . . . still needed "spiritual instruction", backed up by punishment, to persuade them to work on saints' days'.[32] By 1552 this trend had triumphed and in that year Parliament passed an Act limiting holidays to those specifically so named, and ordered that 'none other Day shall be kept and commanded to be kept Holy-day, or to abstain from lawful bodily labour'.[33] It is significant of the great gains which the workman had made in the previous period, that this Act still enumerated twenty-seven such 'holy days', and stipulated that a half-holiday should precede fifteen of the major festivals.

But this was only the beginning. The puritan ethic was in the ascendant. For a short spell under Queen Mary, during the last years of the sixteenth century, the limitation on holidays was repealed for a time, but the reversal could not last. By 1604 the Act limiting holidays was re-enacted amid redoubled efforts at enforcement.

In the second quarter of the seventeenth century the revolution came and placed the Puritans in power. Rather surprisingly one of their first acts was to increase the number of holidays by introducing a monthly fast.[34] This was soon followed, however, by the more characteristic decree ordering that 'all Festival dayes, vulgarly called Holy dayes, having no Warrant in the Word of God, are not to be continued'.[35] Moreover, in 1649 the monthly fast went the way of these earlier observances when the new rulers realized that the religious aspects of these fasts had been 'wholly neglected', and abolished them forthwith.[36]

Henceforth the slate was wiped clean as far as statutory holidays were concerned and, although in practice the observance of holidays displayed a remarkable persistence at times, their numbers were finally reduced to a paltry few. By the end of the seventeenth century the majority of working men enjoyed but a very few holidays around Christmas, Easter and Whitsun. The days of regular and intense labour were clearly on the horizon.

3 Hours of work: 1700 to 1820

a introduction

The eighteenth century brought with it a return to prosperity for the working man. Wages once more assumed an upward trend and as the century wore on a new working day extending from 6 am to 6 pm gradually replaced the day that had existed since the Tudor statutes extending from 5 am to 7 or 8 pm, or more latterly from 6 am to 8 or 9 pm. The newly established working day was generally associated with a two-hour provision for meals, so that effectively it represented a ten-hour day.

The day from 'six to six' had existed in some of the early heavy industries since their inception, since many of these worked twenty-four hours a day for technical reasons. In this century it spread to the traditional crafts and to some of the smaller-scale industries, and even in the domestic trades where hours were by their nature irregular the ten-hour day came to be widely regarded as 'a day's work'. It came, in time, to be generally accepted as a normal working day and hence formed the base line or the norm as the pace of industrialization quickened and as the industrial revolution took shape and swept the working man into the mills and factories, into the cities, and into the proletariat.

In this upheaval traditional defences were brushed aside and working conditions were changed on all fronts. The earliest indications were that the newly won working day would also be lost in this maelstrom. The textile mills that sprang up in the last quarter of the century ran roughshod over the customary hours of employment and introduced working days of thirteen, fourteen and even more hours. As these mills were precursors of the new industrialism this was a bad omen indeed.

Fortunately for the working man the experience of the textile workers did not turn out to be typical. In most other major industries the working day from 'six to six' was maintained, though many other privileges were lost. However in the small unstable trades whose labour force did not have a strong traditional base, the sweat shops developed. Here the suffering imposed on the working man, and more often the working woman and child, matched and at times even surpassed the worst excesses of the 'satanic mills' of the textile industry.

The effectiveness with which the working day was defended in all those industries where the labour force was not totally uprooted and 'replaced', speaks of the great importance attached to it. It was socially important since it defined the limits within which any social life was possible, and it was economically important to those who for centuries past had learned that wages fell when prices fell, and that prices fell when supply became excessive. This lesson lingered on in the minds of men who had lived and worked in local markets as independent producers.

Largely because other industries did not follow textiles in the establishment of their working hours, it became possible to challenge the hours being worked in the textile mills. This challenge began before the end of the period discussed in this chapter, but its success had to wait until the middle of the nineteenth century. Only then did the textile mills return to the ten-hour day.

For the sake of clarity of exposition the hours of work and their variation over this period will be discussed separately for the traditional crafts,[37] the industries, the domestic manufactures, and finally the textile mills.

b traditional crafts

The evidence for these trades suggests that until the middle of the eighteenth century most of them continued to work the same hours as they had done in previous centuries. Those that had achieved reductions below that level, primarily the building trades, seem to have done so around 1720. Of the others most seem to have reduced their hours shortly after 1750, although at least one trade, that of the bookbinders, achieved their reduction gradually over the last quarter of the century. By the beginning of the nineteenth century the day extending from six to six was 'normal' in this sector. Although a large part of the evidence for these trades stems from London there is some indication of comparable hours in the provinces.

Specific evidence of the pressure for reduced hours around 1720 comes from the tailors and the masons. The London tailors formed a combination through which they were able to reduce the hours of work by one hour per day, although their combination was subsequently outlawed and further such trade policies were curtailed for many years.[38] Meanwhile in Sheffield 'the Tailors' Society . . . was founded on the 20th September 1720, by a combination of tailors not to work for an unreasonable length of time for their employers'. At this time 'from 6 am to 8 pm were the usual hours, which they considered too long, and in future resolved to work no longer than six in the evening for any man, anyone doing so to be fined 5 shillings'.[39]

That these demands for shorter hours were not confined to the tailors is made clear by a petition of the master tailors to Parliament[40] in which they warn that the confederacy of journeymen tailors to reduce their hours of work is a bad precedent and can already be seen to be affecting other trades, such as the 'Journeymen Carpenters, Bricklayers, and Joyners (who) have taken some steps for that purpose'. Some years later we find the building trades of London virtually the only trade working a day from six to six, and it is not unreasonable to assume that they achieved these hours about 1720. Indeed, from Edinburgh we have evidence that the builders there achieved just such a reduction of hours at this same time. Thus in 1764 the master masons of that city were petitioned for a rise in wages as 'these have not been increased for a hundred years past'. They refused, however, on the grounds that it would be bad precedent and that wages had been at their present level 'within memory . . . and . . . they then began work at five o'clock in the morning, whereas now they do not begin till six, their stated hours being from six to six of which time one hour is allowed for breakfast, and another for dinner'.[41] Thus 'within memory' of 1764 the day from 6 am to 6 pm had been established among the Edinburgh masons.[42]

However general this reduction of hours in the first half of the century may have been, in London it was of modest proportions. A comprehensive survey of hours in 118 London trades is fortunately preserved from the year 1747,[43] and it shows that of these 118 trades, 100 were working a day which corresponded exactly to that laid down in the statutes of the fifteenth and sixteenth centuries.[44] Of the remaining eighteen, thirteen had established a working day extending from 6 am to 6 pm and of these thirteen, nine were connected with the building trades,[45] with millwrights, flax dressers and coppersmiths among the others.

It appears that soon after the publication of this list renewed pressure for reduced hours arose. Once again it was the tailors whose agitation provides the remaining evidence. A pamphlet[46] issued by the journeymen of that trade in 1752 demanded shorter hours since their hours were from 6 am to 8 pm, while 'the hours of work, in most handicraft trades, are from six in the morning till six at night'. Even with allowances for the partisan nature of the source this indicates a spread of the 'six to six' custom. Consistent with this finding is the report that 'in or about 1750 "there were in some shops (bookbinders) Day-men or Night-men, each party working from six to six" '.[47]

The middle fifties were years of continued depression but by the end of that decade there are once more signs that pressure over the issue of hours was building up. Thus in 1761 'the London cabinet-makers were indicted for having combined to raise wages and shorten their hours of work, and there were similar reports of this "growing evil" among the shoe-makers, tailors, and peruke-makers'.[48]

A further strong presumption that hours had been reduced at some time around the middle of the century stems from the passage of an Act in 1768, to reduce the hours of tailors by one hour per day – to a day extending from 6 am to 7 pm.[49] It is extremely unlikely that such an Act would have been possible unless the hours in most other comparable trades extended from 6 am to 7 pm or some shorter period.

A pamphlet written in 1770 gives further support to the view that hours had generally been reduced between 1747 and that date. It suggested the establishment of workhouses for 'extirpating idleness, debauchery and excess', and for these to represent effective threats they could not be places where the poor would 'do but little work'. Rather they must be ' "Houses of Terror" where the poor shall work 14 hours in a day, allowing proper time for meals, in such manner that there shall remain 12 hours of neat labour'.[50] Since these would have been rather moderate hours in the London of 1747, one might assume that the hours in that place had been reduced since that date.

If, therefore, there is reason to believe that the hours of labour in the handicraft trades were generally reduced between 1747 and 1768 – and probably around the early 1750s or 1760s – there is at least one exception to this, although it is an exception to prove the rule. In 1772 the bookbinders were still working the same hours they had worked in 1747, namely from 6 am to 9 pm with but one and one-half hours for meals.[51] By 1806 after four separate reductions they had achieved a day extending from six to six with two hours for meals.

Between 1772 and 1779 'there had been a ... strike in favour of finishing at 8 pm ... and ... the men had won their point'. Then in about 1782 the social clubs of journeymen, which existed 'for the purpose of "taking a social pint of porter together" ', were transformed into trade societies by the issue of the hours of work. Their hours – extending from six to eight – 'were felt to be an intolerable grievance ... when many trades worked from six to six'.[52] By 1786 they were ready to strike over this grievance, and although their leaders were imprisoned a reduction of one hour per day was accomplished. In 1794 they established the day extending from six to six, and finally in 1806 they extended their meal hours from one and one-half hours to two hours and thus established a ten-hour day.[53]

Other evidence further corroborates the widespread acceptance of the day extending from 6 am to 6 pm towards the end of the years discussed in this section. Thus the coopers of London worked a day extending over this period in 1820[54] while the experience of the London painters is particularly indicative. In order to induce the men to accept the provisions of the Combination Act of 1799, the employers of that trade agreed to pay journeymen 'at the rate of one guinea per week for good and able workmen — a day's work being reckoned from 6 o'clock in the morning till 6 o'clock in the evening'[55] and in return the operatives agreed 'that the Act to prevent unlawful combinations of workmen be enforced'.

On balance the evidence for the traditional crafts suggests a significant reduction in the hours of work, leading from a day extending from 6 am to 8 or 9 pm, to one extending from 6 am to 6 pm. This reduction was achieved by the building trades, as well as a few others, some time around 1720. For the great majority of the rest the reduction came either around 1750 or around 1761. Of those that were not able to share in this reduction, at least one, the bookbinders, was able to 'catch up' through a progressive reduction in hours over the fourth quarter of the century.

The most significant thing to notice about these findings is that once again these successful pressures to reduce hours coincide with a rising trend and a peak in the real-wage series of the building trades.[56] Here the evidence once more suggests that inverse relation between real wages and the hours of work that was such a prominent feature of the previous period. In this there is some tentative support for a backward sloping individual supply curve of labour, though of course the supply to an industry would depend in addition on participation rates, mobility and population size and age structure.

It is interesting to speculate why the builders should have led this movement for shorter hours, while the bookbinders lagged far behind. Even at this distance it is possible to identify some of the major factors responsible. The major advantages of the building trades lay in their traditionally strong organization;[57] the fact that the industry had undergone few technological or organizational changes; the fact that buildings are stationary — which facilitated the monopolization of markets; and finally the relative mobility of the labour force which brought them into contact with a variety of work practices. Finally it is important to recognize that periods of prosperity do not benefit all trades equally and it is therefore of interest to notice that 'the period from the spring of 1716 to the end of 1721 had . . . seen an upward swing of general activity, then depression in one section of the economy (weaving), offset by prosperity in others'. But of these 'others' none was more prosperous than building and 'the boom in building and construction was borne on the wave of optimism that culminated in the bubble of 1720'.[58]

For the slow reaction of the bookbinders there is no ready explanation except perhaps the complete absence of any trade organization and the extremely small amount of capital required to set up in this business, which prevented the masters from colluding easily to restrict competition and induced the journeymen to see their masters' point of view more readily as they could look forward to being masters themselves.[59]

In closing it may be relevant to point out that the two dates, 1751 and 1761, or which there is evidence of general pressure on hours of work, were both periods of great activity. Thus 'between 1748 and 1751 a strong upward movement developed' in the economy, while all the available indices 'suggest conditions of boom in 1761' and there are 'many indications that the prosperity extended to the wage-earners'.[60]

c industries[61]

There is little evidence of any change in hours for any of the industries in this category for which we have information. The day extending from six to six seems to have been all but universal, and it was often used in connection with shift working.

Both the iron and the glass industries were induced by technological considerations to work their factories continuously. In the iron industries this was done by using two twelve-hour shifts — each working from six to six — while in the glass houses the men worked alternate six-hour stretches.

Although the iron industries — i.e. blast furnaces, forges, and rolling mills — maintained this system until the twentieth century, there was at least one startlingly early experiment with three eight-hour shifts. Thus in 1785 one of the largest iron-works in South Wales reported that they 'have altered the Plan of work so as to have three hands to work Eight hour shifts'[62] but no more was heard of this system in subsequent correspondence from this works. Except for such unusual experiments the hours were universally determined by two twelve-hour shifts.

In the glass industry the almost incredible split-shift system, in which men worked six hours on and six hours off, had existed at least since 1624 and was to remain in many works until the twentieth century. When the cutting of glass was introduced around the middle of the eighteenth century, the workmen in this trade were set to work from 6 am to 6 pm with two hours for meals.[63]

In the pottery trades the hours were 'ten, for a day at that season of the year when day-light will allow of it' and these 'have been the hours ... for forty years' before 1816.[64] This means that these had been the hours virtually from the beginning of the industry, since before 1763 it had been 'of the rudest kind, pursued in wretched hovels, and confined to a few potters'. After this it developed rapidly so that by 1793 it employed fifteen to twenty thousand people.[65]

Although all the potteries worked a similar day from 6 am to 6 pm, this was a purely nominal quantity, and when 'half-nights or half-days, or out of time' were being worked the day ended at 9 pm. Furthermore it seems that these extra hours were extremely common and were withdrawn only during a slump in demand. Indeed the custom seems to have been to work until 10 pm until well into the nineteenth century, and this was changed only a few years prior to 1816.[66] Nevertheless the very fact that all time beyond 6 pm was termed extra time is an indication of how general the working day ending at that hour had become.

Engineering did not emerge as a separate industry until well into the nineteenth century, but it appears to have worked the day extending from 6 am to 6 pm from its inception.[67] Thus the millwrights, who are one of the most direct forerunners of this industry,[68] were one of the few trades who were working from 'six to six' in the middle of the eighteenth century, and the same was of course true of the carpenters who are also mentioned as one of the antecedents of the engineers. Thus it is not surprising that when we meet with evidence as to the hours of engineers in the early nineteenth century they are uniformly working the ten-hour day.[69]

In the coal industry, which 'was one of the earliest fields of modern capitalist enterprise'[70] the hours seem to have been short, even at this early date. Three separate estimates of their hours vary between six and eight hours per day. Adam Smith speaks of the colliers working eight hours per day,[71] while an engineer reported that in 1765 the Scottish miners worked two shifts of from seven to eight hours, and those of Newcastle from six to seven hours.[72]. Another account of their condition in 1771 confirms these reports for Yorkshire by stating that the colliers there still had half the day left after performing their stated tasks.[73]

The explanation for these surprisingly short hours in the coalmines can be found in a number of special conditions under which production takes place in this industry. The extreme irregularity of wages and employment to which this industry was subject[74] led to early attempts to control output so as to minimize these fluctuations. The actions of the owners in this respect, including their establishment of the 'vend' in the north-east are well known, but the same incentives that existed for the owners to restrict supply existed also for the miners, particularly in view of the close relationship between wages and prices in this industry.[75]

The same pressures therefore that later led to the creation of the 'vend' among the coal owners, led to the establishment of the 'stint' among the men. The stint was defined in terms of a certain amount of output, and this together with a daily wage amounted to a piece-work system with a limitation on an individual's earnings — in short a regulation of supply, or, looked at another way, a work-sharing arrangement.

If this was clearly in the interest of the men, why were they able to have their way? Partly because they 'had been employed together in large groups'[76] for a long time and were thus able to exert considerable pressure at the pit-head, but much more important was the fact that this system suited the employers in their efforts to control supply. Since coal in different seams is of different ease or difficulty of working, to fix miners' hours would result in widely differing daily outputs per man, and the owners preferred to fix this output. Doing so, moreover, stabilized the unit labour cost of coal; removed to a large extent the need for supervision — possible because quality control was hardly necessary; and, possibly most important, enabled the use of two day shifts, which conferred all the above advantages as well as increasing the rate of return on capital.

d domestic trades
This system of manufacture had been much extended over the previous two centuries, so that by the eighteenth century it included the second largest group of participants, after agriculture.[77] It is for this reason that we shall spend some little time in looking at the hours worked by this group, for it is they who form the back-drop to the picture we are describing.

The evidence regarding this sector of the economy uniformly bears out the experience of the economy as a whole in the sixteenth and seventeenth centuries. The hours of work varied inversely with the level of real wages — i.e. prices — although there was a certain reluctance to extend hours when these (prices) were falling. While work tended to be irregular and reduced hours were more likely to be reflected in the number of days spent idle than in the number of hours worked every day, there is nevertheless evidence that even here there was a tendency to regard a day extending over twelve hours, including meals, as a normal or reasonable working day.

In these trades a tendency to spend less time at work began to manifest itself in the seventeenth century, when, in the second half of that period the trend of real wages was once more upward. High wages often meant that 'the men have just so much more to spend in tipple, and remain now poorer than when their wages were less. . . . They work so much fewer days by how much more they exact in wages'.[78] It was the predominance of the domestic system together with this attribute of it which accounts for the general acceptance of the backward-sloping supply curve of labour at this time, and for the great preoccupation with the problem of idleness, although this was also a concomitant of Puritanism.

The association of high wages with short hours is documented extensively throughout the eighteenth and into the nineteenth centuries in the industries organized in this manner. Thus in 1745 the framework knitters around Nottingham 'never wrought more than ten hours a day for five days in the week and always kept Saturday free for going into Nottingham with their work, or for gardening, or any other thing they had to do',[79] while in 1759 'the check-weavers of Manchester "were never in better humour in their lives"; their pieces were shortened,[80] their wages raised . . . provisions . . . plenty, and work enough to be had'.[81]

By far the most extensive description of the work practices in these trades comes from the parliamentary commissions which inquired into these matters in the early nineteenth century. Thus the metalworkers of Liverpool stated that the hours which they keep are 'sometimes eight, ten, and sometimes twelve' and in addition they are in the habit of drinking 'a day or two' each week. Extra time to make up for this loss 'is not necessary, (as) their wages are very good'. The hand-loom weavers of Lancashire also conform to this pattern as 'when their wages are good they work very little, when they are bad they must work longer', indeed at that very time 'the wages of the weavers are so very low . . . that I believe they are obliged to work longer hours than they do in the cotton factories'.[82]

The second dominant feature of these trades was the irregularity of their hours. 'In the old domestic industries, and indeed in all trades in which the workmen had command of their own time, it was the too common practice to work very long hours one half of the week and go hand-idle the other'.[83] But if this was a dominant feature it was not universal, and we have a good number of references which indicate that many of these trades had a conception of a certain number of hours which made up a normal full working day. Apart from the frame-work knitters, who we have seen never worked more than ten hours around 1745, the shoe-makers around Preston worked 'twelve (hours) . . . including meal times'[84] on a regular basis, while the hand-loom weavers, even when they are extremely depressed, 'admit that ten hours and a half a day is considered by them "hard work" '.[85]

While evidence concerning the resistance of the domestic trades to the extension of hours refers almost exclusively to the hand-loom weavers in the 1830s, there is one instance which falls within the present period. Thus in 1818 it is said that 'the weavers ... some years ago were so extravagantly paid that by working three or four days in the week they could maintain themselves in a relative state of luxury ... (but) when the change took place, and it became necessary they should lend themselves to habits of increased industry and frugality, some discontent arose'.[86] The discontent in question had led to some disturbances which had finally been put down by the use of troops.

Once again the inverse relation between wages and hours worked is evident. There is now, however, a suggestion that longer hours in response to lower wages are not as readily provided as is the case with shorter hours when wages rise. Especially if hours threaten to extend beyond what is normally considered a day's work the workman may be induced to challenge the validity of the circumstances forcing him to such practices.

It appears likely therefore that the hours of work, like wages, may be subject to a ratchet effect, though the point of downward inflexibility may drift upwards more slowly in the case of the hours ratchet since readjustments in what is considered a 'normal' day are likely to operate more slowly than similar adjustments to an income level. Finally, from the workman's point of view, the hours ratchet has the advantage that gains made by its operation cannot be eroded easily by the employers since they do not have the power to extend the number of hours in a day, in the way they can increase the number of shillings that will buy a 'normal' basket of goods. In the nineteenth century the working man became increasingly aware of this difference and this change is of great importance to our analysis.

An important element in the situation of the domestic worker is the complete freedom which the operative has to change hours of work, which results in hours being irregular, extremely varied as between trades and regions and even individuals, and responsive with only a short time lag to changes in the economic situation of any particular trade. Thus general trends become impossible to identify — as, indeed, they would be for the 'actual' rather than the 'normal' hours worked in most industries during this period.

Finally, when discussing the hours worked by these trades one must take into account the fact that most of those working in this sector pursued farming as a primary or secondary employment.[87]

This interdependence with agriculture would affect the labour supply function of these industries in three ways. First, the relatively short hours which were being worked in agriculture in the eighteenth century[88] would have tended to shift the entire curve to the left, in the same way that the hours in other trades affected those of the farm workers, as is illustrated by a report from Hampshire towards the end of the eighteenth century, which stated that the farm workers could not be induced to work past 5 pm (presumably from 5 am), because they 'could not be got to work longer at daywork on a farm than other labourers wrought at task-work in the forests, or at the salt-pans, or on the canals, or at the variety of jobs to be found at Portsmouth'.[89] Second, the existence of such secondary employment would make the supply curve above any existing wage less elastic if it sloped backward, or it might even make it slope upwards to the right, since a rise in the price of the produce of the domestic manufacture might well induce the individual to increase the time spent at that trade as well as increasing his leisure – both at the expense of the now relatively less attractive or remunerative farm labour. Third, the supply curve below some wage rate would certainly slope downwards to the left, since more and more time would be allocated to farming as returns from manufacture fell – assuming that returns in farming were not diminishing rapidly. This last phenomenon may well explain why it is only in the nineteenth century that we have the most compelling evidence of the need to extend hours in response to falling prices.

The effect of considering agriculture as an alternative employment is of course the same as the effect of any alternative employment for which entry and exit are entirely free.

This brings us one step closer to an industrial labour supply curve, which would be an aggregation of the individual curves, taking into account all the possibilities of entry into and exit from the market in question.

e textile mills

In this industry in general, but in the cotton mills in particular, we find a trend towards increased normal hours. This begins in the fourth quarter of the eighteenth century and extends into the next century. In this process it begins to meet opposition almost immediately and this builds up until the trend is arrested by legislation, partially in 1802 and more generally in 1819, although even this latter Act was not equipped to prevent evasion. While examining this trend and the reaction to it one should note the repeated references to the existence of a general working day extending from six to six, which corroborate the general findings of earlier parts of this chapter and highlight the unusual position of the textile mills.

The cotton industry which provides the major element in this story began to employ centralized production after 1770,[90] but even for the spinners, who were the first to be affected, the move into the factories took a long time to be completed. Thus as late as 1804 we are told that spinning is done in the 'country villages . . . by women and children'.[91]

During these early years two different kinds of mills for spinning cotton were established: those powered by water which were located in remote places and staffed largely with parish apprentices, and those powered by hand, being merely large workshops established in some cities like Manchester. In the former 'it frequently happened, in different parts of the country, that the machinery was employed the whole four-and-twenty hours; but . . . the time of working was then much less than it is now (1816), because it is well known that you must divide the four-and-twenty hours into two sets; that you cannot work the children more than eleven hours, which is much less than they work at present'.[92] The employment of shifts seems to have been quite general in these mills although they were not always arranged simply on a six-to-six basis.[93] The large workshops equipped with hand-looms and located in the cities were open long hours. Thus in Manchester in 1790 the 'mills . . . all worked from six to eight . . . and (were) worked by hand at that time'. Since these mills were employing adults drawn from the surrounding domestic industry the habits of those people persisted and hours in these shops were by no means regular, and 'it was too generally the practice to drink the first day or two of the week, and attempt to make it up by working very long hours towards the close of the week'.[94]

With the introduction of steam the mills moved into the towns; parish apprentices were no longer used on any scale; and the employment of local women and children, who made up at least three-quarters of the work-force, led to the abandonment of night work in all but some rare exceptions.[95] Thus the 1816 Commons' Select Committee asked one of the witnesses whether 'children are employed now a greater number of hours since night-work has been abolished',[96] indicating that this change was a generally accepted fact by this time.

These changes 'produced a complete revolution in the spinning manufactures of cotton, of wool, and of flax' through which 'adults were superseded by children, whose wages were lower, and who soon acquired a great dexterity . . . (while) the very moderate exertion of the children, and the great expense of the mechanism, *introduced the custom of working twelve hours per day in the mills*'[97] (my emphasis). In other words the cotton mills adopted a working day lasting from 6 am to 7 pm with one hour for meals, making twelve hours of work, and this was a new departure made 'necessary' and possible by the expense of the mills and the hypocritically alleged light physical exertion of the work.

This came to be regarded as the generally accepted working day for textile factories throughout the country. The hours of work 'with respectable manufacturers do not much exceed ... thirteen per day, from six to seven, deducting one hour for meals'.[98] But if this was the general rule there were exceptions on both sides. In some of the major centres of the cotton industry, i.e. Manchester, Preston, Glasgow, it seems that the pressure to increase hours was sustained and led to working days of up to 13½ hours, while in the woollen mills of the south-west a ten-hour day was retained.

Fortunately a comprehensive picture of hours in the textile mills is available for the year 1816.[99] This shows that the Lancashire mills worked the longest hours in England. For 26 Manchester mills the modal and median 'day' extended from 6 am to 8 pm and involved 13 hours of work. Some other Lancashire centres such as Bury, Ashton, and Preston, worked similar hours, with most of the Preston mills working 13½ hours per day. These very long hours were, however, worked only in the larger centres clustered around Manchester. In most of the rest of Lancashire the working day in the mills extended from 6 am to 7 pm and, with a one-hour meal break, this amounted to a twelve-hour working day, though there were a few exceptional mills even here that had followed the lead of the Manchester mills, and had introduced longer hours.

The Scottish mills exhibited the same features, though slightly different hours. Thus of 41 cotton mills reported on, 26 worked 12½-13 hours per day, while 15 worked 11½-12 hours. The distinction lies, as in Lancashire, between the large centre and the peripheral area. Thus 'the works in Glasgow, and the immediate vicinity are about the same', working usually 12½ hours per day, while 'those in the country are an hour shorter'. Indeed, there was some evidence that the hours of the Glasgow mills had been lengthened relatively recently since one manufacturer stated that 'we once wrought an hour shorter' and they changed in his mill 'because we found it our interest, and it was generally done'.[100]

A third group of mills is striking in its difference. The establishments in the woollen industries of the south-west had retained by and large the ten-hour day, though a number of places had been able to retain only the day extending from 'six to six'. In these few the meal hours had been reduced to one and hence the working day had been extended to eleven hours. The stability of hours in this area was underlined by the statement of a witness that he had 'known the business (of Wiltshire wool) from a child, my father having been a manufacturer; and they (the hours) were the same in his time'.[101] Other parts of the woollen industry that had moved into factories elsewhere in the country, were less fortunate and seem generally to have been working a day extending from 6 am to 7 pm. This was true of the mills in Nottinghamshire and those of Leeds,[102] and later evidence suggests that most of the West Riding accepted this as the standard day. The one woollen mill for which we have information in Glasgow worked 12½-hour days in conformity with the hours in the dominant cotton industry of that city,[103] while there is some suggestion that some woollen mills in the far north of the West Riding, around Skipton, worked thirteen-hour days.[104]

In the other textile and allied trades the day extending from 6 am to 7 pm predominated, although again those working in the south-west tended to have shorter hours while those working close to a place like Manchester tended to adopt the longer hours of the dominant trades in those cities. Thus the silk mills worked these long hours in Derbyshire,[105] while in at least one town in Cheshire they worked these hours but with 2½ hours for meals. In the south-west the hours were once more shorter ranging between 10½ and 11 per day.[106]

In the dyeing, bleaching and flax-spinning trades the same pattern prevailed. There was a general acceptance of the day extending from 6 am to 7 pm and the occasional case of longer hours, especially when the factories were located in those centres where hours in the dominant industries were long.[107]

There is one exception to this pattern. The textile printers of Scotland maintained a uniform ten-hour day throughout their trade – working 'six to six' with two hours for meals. It is interesting to notice that of the six textile and allied trades for which statistics on hours were available, the textile printers had by far the shortest hours and also by far the highest proportion of males in the labour force.[108] This tends to confirm our earlier supposition that hours were more likely to be lengthened in an industry where a traditional labour force was non-existent or where it was replaced by a new labour force, often composed largely of women and children.

It appears therefore that by this time the textile mills had substantially lengthened their working day beyond the limit generally considered acceptable. Some reasons for such a development have been hinted at and it is time to consider these more closely.

A desire for longer hours was created in this industry because 'in establishments where there is a large fixed capital, it is a very serious injury to the proprietors of those establishments to suspend the working of them'.[109] This clearly was the explanation of the shift systems employed in the early cotton mills, and indeed in the iron and glass trades. With the abandonment of shifts in the textile mills a pressure for longer hours resulted.

The fact that shifts were abandoned in this industry has already been documented. The reasons why they were discontinued are unclear. Two major causes suggest themselves: the move into the towns made the use of shifts difficult or impossible owing to the social disruption caused by their use, and the fire hazard and increased wastage made night work unattractive. The first point is suggested by the fact that it was after their move into the towns that the shift system was abandoned by the mills, and that the industries that did use shifts such as the glass and iron trades tended to exist in smallish communities almost entirely dependent on this industry and hence amenable to its needs.

If the abandonment of shifts created a demand for longer hours, why were the employers able to impose these hours on their workers? Apart from the fact that under normal circumstances employer interests controlled the legislative and repressive apparatus of the state, it is suggested that they were able to do this for three major reasons: the geographic shift of the industry which often accompanied the move into the factories; the predominance of women and children in these mills; and, in certain centres, the possibility of collusion among employers.

The geographic shift of the industry removed the protection usually afforded by customary practices, which are often hard to change. Thus we find the south-west, one of the traditional centres of the wool industry, still working a ten-hour day when most of the other areas were working twelve and even thirteen hours per day.[110] The employment of women and children naturally weakened the bargaining strength of the operatives because of the great difficulty of organizing these groups. The role played by collusion among employers is rather ambiguous, but seems to have been a real factor in the very long hours established in some of the major cotton centres. Normally one might expect active competition among many relatively small employers to lengthen hours, while collusion would often be used to restrict supply. In this case however certain centres who were faced with active competition from outside seem to have employed this tactic to give themselves an advantage over their competitors. Thus we have seen that a Glasgow employer increased hours 'because it was generally done', while in Preston 'there was a general agreement among the proprietors of factories . . . to fix the hours of labour to thirteen and a half' and a witness stated to the 1816 Committee that 'if the masters wished twelve hours only to be worked it would be so'.[111]

Finally this extension of hours in the textile mills resulted in active opposition which by the end of this period (i.e. by 1820) had led to legislation intended to arrest this trend at a twelve-hour day. A brief look at some of this controversy both further documents the extension of hours and confirms the general acceptance of 'the ten-hour day' in the rest of the economy.[112]

Since the operatives in the mills were often not in a position effectively to represent their interests, the early opposition to these changes came from people who represented the 'public interest', that third party to any bargain. Direct opposition from the operatives did not become important in England until after 1828, and until then the opposition was led by medical men and philanthropic employers who had taken it upon themselves to define and defend the public interest in this matter.

The first sign of such opposition came as early as 1784 and came naturally from Manchester.[113] An outbreak of fever at one of the early mills led to an investigation under Dr Percival of Manchester and among other things this inquiry 'recommended a longer recess from labour at noon and a more early dismission from it in the evening, to all those who work in the cotton mills'[114] and this led the Manchester magistrates to pass a resolution 'that in future they would refuse to allow "indentures of Parish Apprentices whereby they shall be bound to owners of cotton mills and other works in which children are obliged to work in the night or more than ten hours in the day" '. In 1795, another inquiry, headed by the same doctor, again deplored 'the untimely labour of the night, and the protracted labour of the day' in the cotton mills, and called for 'a general system of laws for the wise, humane, and equal government of all such works'.[115] This time the call found listeners in London and in 1802 an Act[116] was passed which prohibited the employment of parish apprentices at night or for more than twelve hours per day in the cotton mills. Though this Act was never enforced[117] it was symbolic of the opposition which had grown up to the long hours in textile mills.

In 1815 the issue was re-activated through the efforts of Robert Owen. The law clearly needed changing because 'owing to the use of steam power in factories . . . large buildings are now erected . . . in the midst of populous towns, and instead of parish apprentices being sought after, the children of the surrounding poor are preferred'.[118] Owen's efforts resulted in the Select Committee of 1816, and eventually in the passage of an Act of Parliament in 1819,[119] restricting the hours of all children to twelve hours per day, exclusive of meals.[120]

This Act has been imbued with an undue significance by some major analysts of this period and the matter bears some looking into. It has been claimed that this Act was a significant legislative milestone because 'it broke down the barriers', since now 'the state had intervened between employer and employed'. It had established its right 'to regulate the conditions of labour engaged in the ordinary market'. In actual fact the principle of non-interference in the affairs of the market was maintained by the government into the twentieth century. The issue here concerned the classification of 'free agents' in the labour market. Whereas the government had previously regulated the conditions of parish apprentices because these were not considered to be 'free agents', it now extended this definition to children below the age of sixteen. It would later extend this definition to women and children under the age of eighteen, but at all times it maintained the principle that it would not regulate the condition of free agents in the market. Indeed Peel had made this quite clear when he introduced the Bill in 1818. He stated that 'he had been an advocate of free labour . . . when he brought in the Bill of 1802 . . . (and) he had not changed his views in this respect, but he could not think that little children, who had not a will of their own, could be called free labourers'.[121]

This Act, like its predecessor, could not be enforced and on balance its importance is again merely as a symbol of the continued pressure to arrest the hours of work in the textile trades at twelve hours per day. Its extension from parish apprentices to 'free' children was simply a reflection of the fact that now it was the latter who worked the long hours of the mills.

f the working week

For much of this period there is very little evidence concerning the working week. Naturally the predominance of the domestic trades meant, as has been pointed out, that the working week would be irregular, fluctuating with the wage (or price) level. The greatest tendency of these trades was to 'play' early in the week, hence often doing no work on Monday and this was sometimes extended to Monday and Tuesday. On the other hand this enjoyment of leisure early in the week often prejudiced their chances of enjoying the Saturday half-holiday since the work lost early on had to be 'made up' later in the week.

In the great number of other trades which adopted the day extending from 6 am to 6 pm, it appears that a six-day week was common. However, enforcement of this practice was often difficult, especially in those industries which drew their labour force from former domestic workers. These were generally forced to put up with the irregular habits of their employees. This was especially true of trades which moved into large workshops — such as the potters, some early cotton spinners, many metal-working trades, and the woollen mills in the south-west of England — where work was less capital intensive, power usually provided by hand and operatives much less interdependent. The other industries that were moving into large factories, with heavy fixed capital expenditure, made a much more determined effort to do away with irregularity, although even they did not always succeed. Moreover in those textile trades where daily hours were extended the Saturday was usually exempt from such extension, continuing in most instances to end at 6 pm, while in a few instances, and interestingly enough in many where daily hours were particularly long, it came to be shortened by one or two hours beyond this.

The irregular habits of the domestic workers need no further documentation, while the six-day week in the old crafts is largely inferred from the adoption of this custom in the seventeenth century and its re-appearance in the nineteenth century when evidence once more becomes available. The retention of irregular habits by domestic workers when they moved into the workshops of certain trades was described in the case of the early cotton spinning establishments and the potteries;[122] it certainly persisted in the metal-working trades, for it was still quite general there much later in the nineteenth century, while in the woollen mills of the south-west of England the workers in the new mills had not only retained the ten-hour day, but also left 'their work at two o'clock . . . on Saturday' thus working 'only . . . seven hours' on that day.[123]

In the heavy iron industry we must rely on inferences from a slightly later date, and these suggest that in some cases the blast furnaces began to work a seven-day week, though it is not possible to say just when the system began or how widely it spread. In the forges and rolling mills on the other hand a six-day week was common, while certain groups worked only five days. There is also some evidence that irregular working remained a problem even in this industry.

The glass trade with its curious split twelve-hour shift continued to work from Monday morning until Friday morning, as it had done since the earliest days.[124] This explains in part why the split shift was found acceptable for so long.

The textile, and in particular the cotton, mills progressed fastest with their efforts to enforce regular work. Although 'it must always be of importance that workpeople should be steady and attentive to their work . . . as the capital occupied by a hand-spinner was so much less than that which is now occupied by a power-spinner, it of course was not of the same importance'.[125] Accordingly, by 1816 'idleness, or absence from work, on the part of parents employed in cotton mills, cannot take place without occasioning their dismissal from their employment'.[126] Thus not only were hours lengthened in these industries but regular work was also enforced. Their practices as to Saturday closing varied considerably but under the circumstances a surprising number stopped work early on Saturday. Thus in the Derbyshire and Nottinghamshire mills they finished at six on Saturday nights, though they worked twelve extra minutes on each of the five other days for this privilege; in the Glasgow area, where hours were long in general, it seems that 'every second Saturday (they) stop at six o'clock',[127] while in Lancashire the practice varied from a good number of towns which worked six equal days every week to a number that stopped some time around four o'clock on Saturday. It is interesting that of this latter group most firms were located in Preston, where daily hours were particularly long.

On balance, in most trades and manufactures, work ceased on Saturday at 6 pm, and this practice was maintained by most of the textile mills even when they extended the hours on other days. Of those that stopped one or two hours earlier on Saturday the greater part were in the domestic trades or in some of the workshops dependent on these trades for their labour, but this group also included a number of Lancashire cotton mills in areas where hours were particularly long on other days. The major incentive for stopping early on Saturday was that it was market day and early attendance meant better shopping. This may explain in part why the textile mills generally refrained from working past 6 pm on that day.[128]

g annual hours

The rule of the Puritans in the seventeenth century had reduced the number of holidays drastically and, although there is some faint indication that a few of these festivals were revived after the Restoration,[129] it is clear that this did not change the fact that by the end of the seventeenth century only a few holidays remained to the working man. This continued to be the case throughout the period here under review, so that in 1820 it was undoubtedly true that the working man enjoyed only a few holidays clustered around the three major feasts of Christmas, Easter and Whit Sunday.

It must be stressed that this refers only to official holidays for in fact it is clear that people managed to enjoy a considerably greater number of days away from work in most trades. In the domestic trades this was standard practice and it has been shown that in most industries 'playing' on Monday and/or Tuesday continued to be a problem.

By the beginning of the nineteenth century, holidays in the textile mills, where regular working had been most firmly established, varied on the whole from five to twelve days per year. In many cases this did not however reduce annual hours since the holidays were 'made up' by working overtime without extra pay before and after the event. Detailed records on weekly hours in a Manchester cotton mill in 1815 suggest that nine or ten holidays were given. Though the 'normal' working week was 76 hours, overtime was worked in 34 weeks of the year, 'principally for the convenience of the people, who prefer occasional holidays, especially at Whitsuntide, for five days, when a great number avail themselves of the opportunity and season to visit friends and relations in the country from whence they come; and all enjoy the fair and the races'.[130]

While the exact distribution of days varied, the number of days given by this mill seems quite typical of Manchester. Of twenty-five mills for which information is available, twenty-one granted something between eight and twelve days per year for stoppages and holidays.[131] In Preston the number of days was somewhat less than this, though it appears that in general the number of holidays given in Manchester was indicative of their number elsewhere. Thus a Kent mill-owner found 'it . . . necessary to give . . . holidays at Easter and Whitsuntide, two or three days at a time' as well as 'Christmas-day, particular fast-days, or anything of that sort'. In the south-west also the same approximate number of holidays was granted though here the labourers 'are never required to make up lost time for . . . holidays'.[132] In the final analysis it is the presence or absence of this practice of 'making up' the time for holidays that seems to differentiate one area from another. Hence social pressure forces the employers to give nominally approximately the same number of holidays, but many shift the burden of this on to the employee's shoulder by forcing him to make up the time thus lost.

On the whole, in those trades where regular working was the rule, holidays were reduced to a minimum at this time, and they were to remain at that level for more than a century.

4 Summary

This chapter has brought the history of the hours of work to the threshold of the industrial age and has provided a base from which to measure the changes that followed. The most important aspect of the situation existing just prior to the final push into the age of steam was the general acceptance of the working day from 6 am to 6 pm as the 'normal' day. This was combined with two hours for meals to make a ten-hour day in practice.

Thus a witness before the Select Committee of 1816, who was facing some very hostile questioning could state that the 'employment of children in cotton mills . . . working so many hours, was a system of oppression incompatible with the principles of the Constitution' because their hours are 'contrary to the usual and acknowledged hours of daily labour in England',[133] without being asked to elaborate on this assertion. There must indeed have been such a thing as the 'usual and acknowledged hours of daily labour'. All our evidence suggests that these were the ten hours per day, worked between the hours of 6 am and 6 pm.

Though this day was universally recognized it was not always observed and the most systematic extension of it took place in the cotton mills. Since this extension was intimately connected with the industrialization of that trade it is of some significance and raised the expectation that a similar fate would befall the workmen in other trades when these were similarly transformed.

The extension of hours in this industry was hence of interest because it created pressures which might either lead to such an extension in other industries or to a reversal of this aberration. Even before the end of the period here under review there appeared an active opposition to the hours in this industry. This opposition achieved some modest successes before 1820, but more significantly it raised a degree of support that made it the major focus of the hours issue over the next thirty years.

Though the primary concern of this chapter was to establish the *status quo ante*, the process of doing this threw up some interesting observations about the change of hours over time.

The most important of these was the coincidence, at a global level and over a wide historical period, of rising real-wage trends and pressures for reducing the time spent at work. At a more precise level this inverse relationship appeared also in the trades where the hours of work were entirely at the discretion of the working man. Here too hours were reduced when prosperity reigned.

On the other hand there was an indication that in order for hours to lengthen beyond the traditional concept of a full day's work, a ratchet had to be overcome. It appeared that this was most easily accomplished when capitalization in an industry was high; when an industry underwent a geographic shift, hence moving away from its traditional labour force; and finally when an industry relied heavily on woman and child labour. Without such special circumstances an extension of hours past the accepted norm appeared unlikely.

There is thus a benchmark against which the changes of the next period can be measured. There is also some tentative evidence that wages and hours are inversely related and that the extension of hours past a certain point requires an extraordinary set of circumstances, though it appeared that these might be provided by the process of industrialization. The much more detailed analysis of subsequent periods will throw more light on these issues.

Chapter three

Hours of work: from 1820 to 1850

1 Introduction

It was during this period that the working men in most industries were able to begin the creation of institutions to represent their interests which would be able to operate relatively effectively in the economic landscape of England after the industrial revolution. Just what kind of institution would best serve these needs while being tolerated by the powers that be was ascertained only in the course of the struggle as attention was focused alternatively: on fundamental political changes by the Chartists; on changes designed to restore the economy to its former condition by the Builders' Guild and the Owenites; on direct industrial action through general unions; and finally on industrial action in certain more or less narrowly defined crafts. By the end of the period it was clear that the last of these alternatives had won the day for the time being. This had certain implications for the issue of the hours of work, which became one of the foremost issues in the industrial arena as each craft quite naturally attempted to regulate the supply in its particular market. However, during this period, the hours of work remained virtually unchanged, since most of the time and energy was spent on building up the respective unions. In those cases where it was possible to begin to consider the regulation of supply it was first necessary to ensure that the market was surrounded by effective barriers to entry. These foundations for a shorter hours policy were laid during this period by a number of trades and in these the results began to become apparent in the late 1840s.

In the meantime the textile workers exerted much of their energy in an entirely different direction, namely the use of political pressure to gain the particular industrial benefit of a reduction in the hours of work. Their success in this endeavour is well known, and we shall examine below some of the reasons why this strategy could succeed in this industry. In any event, by the end of this period, the textile trades had adopted the working day extending from 6 am to 6 pm that was generally accepted as a full day's work.

It must be remembered that 'as late as 1840 the new industrial wage-earners were still only a minority . . . among the British working-class as a whole',[1] and a large, though a declining number, of wage-earners were still employed in manufacture under the domestic system. For this sector of the labouring population the evidence continues to show an inverse relationship between the amount of time spent at work and the price level of their products, which determined their rate of pay.

In general we are able to identify a number of separate trends in the hours of work[2] over this period. In the bulk of the manufacturing sector[3] the period was one of consolidation of hours with the working day from 6 am to 6 pm continuing to be generally accepted as the normal working day, although there is evidence of distinct pressure to extend hours in a number of trades, and in a very few this pressure led to an actual extension of normal hours. The considerable reduction of normal hours achieved by the textile trades may be viewed as part of the consolidation of hours since it changed their hours to conform to the general practice. The domestic trades made up the third group and here hours varied with the state of trade although even here there is again evidence that a day of ten or ten and a half hours tended to be regarded as a day's work.

2 Textile mills
By 1820 hours in these mills had generally been extended so that the working day lasted from 6 am to 7 or 8 pm with but one hour allowed for meals in most cases, and with the longest hours being worked in some of the major centres of the cotton industry. A slightly shorter Saturday was common in most places, although this was often 'made up' on the other days of the week. The opposition engendered by this change had resulted in legislation which restricted the hours of work to twelve hours per day,[4] although the enforcement provisions of this legislation were woefully inadequate.

In 1825 the cotton mills once more became the subject of legislation when an Act was passed confirming the twelve-hour day and limiting work on Saturday to nine hours.[5] This established a working week of 69 hours, but again the provisions for enforcement were neglected. The passage of such legislation without adequate provision for enforcement produced a situation where hours in the large centres, instead of being relatively long, came to be relatively short, because enforcement and supervision in these large centres was relatively easy while in the country and the smaller towns it was extremely difficult.

Meanwhile the number of people subjected to the long hours of the textile mills had increased rapidly and the problem had also ceased to be one almost exclusively of the cotton industry with the rapid growth of mills in other sectors of the industry, especially in woollen and worsted.[6]

Around 1830 a strong reaction against this trend developed, in part because of the great increase in the number of people affected by it, but also because (in the absence of any legislative restriction) the sectors of the industry outside cotton were extending their hours beyond the twelve per day that had been fixed as the maximum for the cotton mills.

The history of this reaction and its eventual success not only in preventing a further extension of hours but also in establishing a ten-hour day in this industry needs no repetition. We shall, however, look briefly at the economic circumstances which made the success of this movement possible.

By 1830, then, the situation with regard to the textile mills was that there were a few who had maintained a working day of ten or eleven hours; there were a very large number working the twelve-hour day, and among these were the cotton mills of Manchester and Glasgow; and finally there was a further substantial proportion that worked something between 12½ and 13½ hours per day on a regular basis.

This was the situation described by the Report of the 1833 Factory Commission.[7] It stated that 'there are many places in the western district, as at Coventry and Birmingham, in which the regular hours of labour do not exceed ten' and although this included many domestic workers it also included 'some of the factories in the great clothing district'. In addition there were a few factories in the north-east and in Scotland where 'the regular hours of labour do not exceed eleven' and 'eleven hours is called a day at Leeds' but 'in general, both at Leicester and Nottingham, they are not less than twelve', while 'in Manchester the regular hours of work are twelve', and in Scotland 'in general they are from twelve to twelve hours and a half, while in several districts they are not less than thirteen'.

Although the twelve-hour day was predominant in the cotton industry, it was by no means universal. Thus in 1833 in the Stockport cotton mills 'thirteen hours is the regular run . . . now, and nine on Saturday' and the witness, who owns a mill in this town, does 'not know when they ever worked less upon the average'.[8] Indeed, even these long hours were established only recently since the issue had aroused a good deal of public interest through the 'Ten Hours Movement'. Thus, although the hours 'are not confined within the law', they 'are very much reduced compared to what they used to be' because 'public opinion exercises an influence upon it'. Furthermore, such hours were said to be not unusual although 'in Manchester . . . they work more regularly and less'.

Precisely the same pattern seems to have been evident with regard to the hours of work in the West Riding of Yorkshire, the heart of the woollen and worsted trade. Here too the hours seem to have been greatly extended by 1830. After this their extension was checked and even reversed because of the public reaction to these events. This reaction was sparked off by Oastler's now famous letter on 'Yorkshire Slavery' which appeared in 1830[9] and which charged that hours in the Bradford worsted mills were 'from six o'clock in the morning to seven in the evening . . . with only thirty minutes allowed for eating and recreation' and these hours, which except for the short meal break are familiar to us by now as the standard hours in the factories, were confirmed by a hostile employer's reply.[10] The same employer charged that hours in the cotton mills were longer than this, and although this would confirm our suggestion that the twelve-hour limit was not enforced in these mills away from the major centres, it cannot be accepted at face value because of the obvious bias of the writer.

One week later an editorial in the 'Whig' *Leeds Mercury* showed that these estimates somewhat understated the actual length of hours of work. 'Oastler had denounced the thirteen-hour day with but a single half-hour's break. Yet this was the normal day in only the best Bradford mills. In the worst establishments . . . it stretched (i.e. extended over) at least 14 to 15 hours. And in the remoter villages the normal day was from five in the morning until nine at night, not counting the time taken in going to and from the factory. Nor was this condition of things confined to Bradford (as Oastler had seemed to suppose); it was general "throughout the manufacturing district" '.[11] Since this was a 'Whig' newspaper, primarily representing the interests of the new industrialists, this evidence can be regarded as not overstating the case. Indeed the description is confirmed by an independent witness who reported that in 1830 in Halifax 'no mill worked for less than thirteen and a half hours' — i.e. from 6 am to 8 pm with half an hour for meals, while 'some went on until eight-thirty or nine'.[12]

By 1833 when the Factory Commission collected its evidence it reported that 'there appears to be a general tendency in all manufactures to settle down the extent of the labour of their operatives to about twelve hours daily. All the witnesses agree, that during the last twenty years great improvements have been made in the operation of the larger branches of our manufactures, by which the severities in the mode of performing the labour, as well as the duration in time, have been considerably reduced'. These reductions extended back for twenty years only in the cotton mills, however. In the other trades if hours had shortened at all this seems to have been, as in Leeds, only very recently, in response to public pressure.

Thus 'quite lately, since the agitation of this question, some have had rest for breakfast and drinking, as well as dinner' and 'within the last eighteen months several mills have considerably shortened their time of labour' in Leeds,[13] and we have noted the same process in the Stockport cotton mills.

In general it appears that the mills in the West Riding largely accepted the working day from 6 am to 7 pm, differing only with respect to the amount of time they allowed for meals. The only exception to this seems to have been the worsted mills, which worked a day extending over more hours than this. Thus the fact that 'eleven hours is called a day at Leeds' stemmed from the fact that originally two hours a day were allowed for meals, and indeed in 1833 'at Leeds they sometimes stop half an hour for breakfast, one hour for dinner, and half an hour for drinking; but this is very unusual'.[14] These were also the hours proposed by a meeting of forty mill-owners from the West Riding woollen and worsted mills who met to discuss the issue of hours following the publication of Oastler's letter.[15]

The only mills not to have adhered to the day extending from 6 am to 7 pm were those in the worsted trade. Thus it was said of the entire north-east that 'the flax-mills (worked) ordinary hours (of) . . . about eleven and a half; . . . the woollen-yarn mills and cloth-dressing mills, about twelve; (and) the worsted-mills alone . . . (worked) ordinary hours amounting to thirteen'.[16] It should therefore not be surprising that the major impetus for further restrictive legislation immediately after 1830 came from the West Riding.

In Scotland where there was a further concentration of textile mills those not subject to legislation showed a distinct extension of hours beyond twelve hours a day. Thus of a sample of 44 flax-spinning mills — almost the only other kinds of textile mill outside cotton mills found here — 37 observed working days of between 12½ and 13½ hours.[17] On the other hand, in the cotton mills, heavily concentrated around Glasgow, the 69-hour week laid down by statute was almost universally observed, although there were some very few cotton mills outside Glasgow which had not conformed to this legal limit. It is interesting to note that the day from 6 am to 7 pm could no longer be observed by those mills complying with the legal limit, since they required twelve hours of work to be combined with one and one-half hours for meals. Thus in Glasgow a day extending from 5.30 am to 7 pm had become common in the cotton mills.

With the publication of Oastler's letter in 1830 the interests opposing these long hours began to articulate their complaints and to press for a restriction of hours. By 1833 they had brought about the passage of an

Act[18] which restricted hours in every 'cotton, woollen, worsted, hemp, flax, tow, linen or silk mill or factory' to 69 hours per week, and thus halted the lengthening of hours which had marked the quick growth of the worsted and flax-spinning mills. More significantly this Act included extensive provisions for enforcement, and although there was some difficulty with this in the beginning it is true to say that from this date onwards the normal working week in the textile mills was 69 hours.

But the limitation of hours at twelve per day was not considered sufficient, and the demand for a ten-hour day persisted. Only in 1847 was it finally successful. In that year an Act[19] was passed which established in the textile trades that ten-hour day which had long and widely been regarded as 'a day's work'. At the same time the Act provided for an eight-hour Saturday and thus established a normal week of 58 hours. This meant that suddenly this industry was working fewer hours than most others, but this sudden reversal was not to last long because in 1850, because of administrative difficulties,[20] the Act was amended to provide for a 10½-hour working day, a short Saturday and a sixty-hour week. The working day was to extend from 6 am to 6 pm and so, finally, the textile mills had drawn even with the bulk of the manufacturing sector.

There are many factors which contributed to the success of this movement; and some of the economic ones will be discussed in detail in the final section of this work, but we shall look briefly at the most important of them at this stage. Support for the movement to reduce hours in these industries came from four major sources: from moral reformers like the Rev Bull and Richard Oastler who were working for their definition of the public interest; from a large number of medical men who were dealing with the public interest from their point of view; from the philanthropic and far-sighted employers like Sadler and Fielden; and finally it came from the workmen themselves.

The moral reformers were in a good position to exert considerable influence on this issue because the moral sensibilities of the time were very prominently displayed; because the textile mills did work longer normal hours than most other trades; and because women and children did form the bulk of the labour force of this industry. In the case of Oastler the moral fervour was allied with a political view that made this issue a major party-political one. The fact that some Tories used this issue to try to counteract the effects of the Whig Reform Bill agitation gave it a political importance which it could not have attained otherwise.

The medical men were treating the problem from the point of view of public health, and their appeal was powerful so long as the causal relation between mill and public health hazard was as direct as it had been in the early outbreaks of fever in the Lancashire mills. Their influence receded in proportion as this causal relationship became more and more indirect. Their major weapons during this controversy were references to the occurrence of visible physical deformities, and attempts to document the rising or relatively high death rate of the cities.[21] On the whole their influence was small, except with reference to the very early legislation.

The influence of the group of employers that was pressing for a reduction in hours grew in proportion as the common-sense notion that output was simply a constant multiple of the hours of work was shown to be mistaken, and as the industry emerged from its early highly competitive stage and came to be made up of larger units, many of whom began to develop an interest in restricting competition and in protecting the *status quo* in the industry.

The influence of the workers themselves increased as their organization improved, while their interest in reduced hours increased as their economic position improved and as their fear of unemployment increased.[22]

While all of these factors undoubtedly played a role in determining the end result it must be borne in mind that since this struggle was being carried on in the political arena a purely economic explanation is not possible. It is surely significant that the three major Factory Acts were all passed at times of tremendous political upheaval: 1819 was the year of Peterloo; 1833 was wedged between the Reform Act of 1832 and the Grand National Consolidated Trades Union; and 1847 was the year preceding the Continental revolutions and the last great push of the Chartists in England. The evidence supports the view that the threat implicit in the deep discontent of the working classes which gave rise to these periods of unrest contributed to the passage of the Factory Acts, or, to view the matter from the other end, that the government used concessions on this issue as a means of reducing the pressure in these explosive situations. Indeed, there is reason to believe that the 1847 Act did achieve this end. Thus when 1848 brought revolution to the Continent, and the revival of Chartism in England, Lord Shaftesbury wrote that 'amidst all this contempt and desertion . . . the operatives of Lancashire and Yorkshire, suffering as they are, remain perfectly tranquil thanks, in no small measure, to the boon of the Ten Hours Bill'.[23]

These circumstances attest to the great importance placed on the issue by the employees. The fact that action on the issue was in every case delayed until truly extraordinary political upheavals forced the government's hand, indicated on the other hand the strength of the opposition to such change.

3 Industrial sector
In the great majority of industries which had moved into factories or had established 'regulated' workshops, the normal day continued to extend from 6 am to 6 pm although a small number of them introduced a day from 6 am to 7 pm. While the ten-hour day was maintained in most of the largest industries, even in these a distinct tendency towards longer hours made itself felt during this period, in the shape of a widespread reduction in the number of hours set aside for meals. These were reduced from their original two hours to 1½ or one hour in many cases, and in some they were reduced even below that level. A very few groups, like the bookbinders, experienced an actual extension of the total working day inclusive of meals, while others like the tailors and the dressmakers simply continued to observe longer hours than were general.

The working week was almost universally one of six full days, although in Scotland an early Saturday was common, and towards the end of the period the practice was introduced into a number of the larger centres in England. In addition there were a good number of trades that maintained the custom of the domestic trades of 'playing' one or two days of the week, while at the other extreme there were a few shift-working industries that worked a seven-day week.

In spite of some variety in hours worked, the day extending from 6 am to 6 pm continued to be the 'normal' day in the manufacturing sector. But, although the 'ten-hour day' was still widely regarded as the standard full working day, in many industries it had been extended to 10½ or even 11 hours. In what follows we shall present the evidence for this finding, and discuss the experience of various industries briefly, having regard to the economic circumstances of each.

a metal industries
This group, which in 1851 comprised about 572,000 people, may be subdivided into three major sectors: the heavy iron industry, which includes the blast furnaces, the foundries and the rolling mills; the engineering and allied trades, which includes the various types of machine manufactures; and a third group, which includes the metal-working trades making tools and implements and some small groups like the coachbuilders.[24] This ignores a few small trades, but these three groups make up the great bulk of this sector.

In the heavy iron trades the evidence is quite unanimous as to the universal observance of the day from 6 am to 6 pm either by itself or in connection with two twelve-hour shifts per day. Thus a report to the Royal Commission of 1843[25] stated of the iron trades in the West Riding that 'hours of work are, as respects iron-works, from six in the morning till six in the evening. They do not vary with the seasons',[26] and indeed they did not vary from region to region since exactly the same hours were reported to be worked in all the other industrial areas of the country. Indeed the only exception to this chorus of unanimity came from Wolverhampton where it was said the iron-works 'work from five, six, or seven in the morning, till seven at night'.[27]

Though occasionally only one and one-half hours were set aside for meals, two hours predominated, so that the ten-hour day was most commonly worked. It should be noted that with shift-working trades, such as the blast furnaces, the hours of work were often expressed as twelve hours, even when the source in question normally referred to working hours exclusive of meals.

The practice as regards the working week was more varied, and ranged from the use of Sunday labour in the blast furnaces, to the persistence of the 'playing system' in parts of the industry.[28]

'For the same reasons that the furnaces are kept working during the night, they are also kept in work during the Sunday',[29] and it appears that this practice was of long standing. In spite of the fact that 'efforts have been made by several of the iron-masters in all the districts to dispense with the attendance of the people employed at the furnaces during a certain number of hours on the Sunday' and 'that these efforts have been attended with complete success in every one of the iron districts' there was no sign that the practice was about to be adopted generally. The most concerted attempt to make this practice unanimous had been made in South Staffordshire around 1839, but it had collapsed and by 1841 only one-third of the works stopped for some time on Sunday.[30] By 1843 we still hear of 'the great injury done to the working classes of South Staffordshire by the uninterrupted smelting of iron in blast furnaces throughout the Sunday in the majority of works', though by this time 52 out of a total of 129 furnaces suspended their operation on Sunday,[31] while also at this time 'the furnaces at the Govan works in Scotland were run two weeks with a twelve-hour break'.[32] Sunday labour in the blast furnaces continued to obtain generally throughout this period, since even the instances of cessation from labour on that day normally involved only a stoppage of from six to eight, or at most twelve, hours.[33] Although there is some evidence to suggest that some furnaces worked only six days, or six twelve-hour turns a week,[34] the evidence of the 1842 Royal Commission is easily the most reliable source of information on this issue.

Finally it is interesting to note that the major impetus for the restriction on Sunday labour came from the largest iron-works,[35] which is not unexpected in view of the widespread efforts in this industry to restrict competition at all times, and to restrict supply during periods of bad trade.[36]

In the rolling mills and the foundries, where shift work was uncommon the question of the working week turned on the issue of the short Saturday, and in some cases on the problem of 'playing' the first days of the week.

There is no evidence of the existence of a short Saturday, except in the iron-works of the West of England, where 'on Saturday afternoon the boys are commonly set at liberty about two or three o'clock'.[37] In addition it is probable that the practice was observed in the Scottish works, since the observance of the short Saturday was quite general there,[38] and the same thing was true in a few Lancashire towns.[39] These places apart, the practice seems to have been quite unknown in these trades.

A report that towards the end of this period, in the second half of the 1840s, the ironmoulders introduced the short Saturday in London and 'other large towns'[40] could not be verified and seems doubtful in view of the fact that in 14 centres for which we have information in 1850 all the ironfounders were still working a sixty-hour week or more.[41]

On balance the evidence suggests that it was quite general for 'the rollers . . . in a works in full operation' to be 'kept constantly employed, day and night, during six days of the week'.[42] In addition the capital intensity of the industry had made regularity of attendance an important issue so that the six-day week in question was not just a nominal quantity. Thus in 1826 an iron-master could write that 'there is no good reason why the Colliers cannot work every day in as regular a Manner as Puddlers or any other class of Men'.[43]

Nevertheless, in certain areas and establishments even this industry did not entirely succeed in breaking the irregular habits of the workmen. Thus in a Leeds iron-works 'on Monday little work is done', while in a large London brass foundry the workmen 'frequently . . . do not come on Monday',[44] and in the whole of Staffordshire 'almost all classes of men work only five days a week in "good times" ' though the 'enginemen, blacksmiths, carpenters, and labourers . . . generally have a six day week'.[45] Hence it appears that as in the domestic trades themselves the irregularity of the workmen increased with the coming of 'good times'.

On the whole this industry worked a sixty-hour week, with the exception of the blast furnaces where men usually worked seven twelve-hour shifts for a working week of between seventy and eighty-four hours.

Finally it is interesting to note the existence of a certain amount of pressure for the introduction of eight-hour shifts coming from the Staffordshire employers, who, it seems, wished to bring about such a reorganization in order to get rid of a number of restrictive practices which had been established by the men. Thus 'with the furnaces nine heats can readily be worked by one man in twelve hours; and if, as is sometimes the case, the furnace is provided with three sets of men, instead of two, ten or even twelve heats may be finished in the twelve hours'. But it seems that the men opposed the system and 'generally prefer the usual mode of working, and make about seven heats in twelve hours, a quantity which they seldom exceed'.[46] The same point was put to the 1843 Royal Commission by two employers who spoke of 'a great improvement in puddling iron immediately from the smelting furnace . . . which . . . affords additional facility for making the proposed change in the hours of work . . . for the produce of the puddling furnaces is expected to be so much greater in the same time that higher wages can be given to the workmen, thus compensating them for the reduced hours of work' although 'the exertion required will be more continuous and exhausting'.[47]

It appears therefore that the tendency to restrict supply noted among the employers of this industry had its counterpart in the workmen, as in the coal industry. The interesting point about this situation is that their restriction concentrated mainly on the pace of work which would not be given up in return for some more leisure. While this attitude reflects the extreme physical hardship of the work, which made frequent breaks important, it may also reflect a greater interest by the men in the restriction of supply than in an increase in leisure. So strong was their opposition that one of the witnesses who had adopted this plan 'some years ago' had been forced to abandon it. He now proposed that 'if a few works would combine to enforce the practice they would soon find it answer (their problems)'.[48]

In the engineering trades 'the hours of work . . . are 10 per day, and this is never departed from'.[49] While this statement is made with particular reference to Lancashire it is also generally applicable to the industry. Thus in Birmingham, where this industry was strongly represented, 'the regular hours of work . . . are 12, out of which two are usually deducted for meals' and 'this may be considered the rule'.[50] There is evidence that this was the case also in all other major industrial areas.[51]

This is confirmed by the widespread and general assumption that these were the hours worked by 'mechanics'. Thus a witness to the 1833 Factory Commission stated 'that he thinks that the hours (in textile mills) should be ten, for "how is a woman to stand more hours than a labouring man or a mechanic" ',[52] and another deplores the long hours of the mills as 'all mill labour (is) family labour; the present plan being for children and wives to go to the factory before their husbands, if they happen to be mechanics or labourers, and to leave later'.[53]

Some difficulty arises when occupational groups conflict with industrial groupings. Thus it appears that at least some of the engineers working in the textile mills had little choice but to work the hours which prevailed there. In Glasgow such 'mechanics ... blacksmiths, turners, filers, machine-makers and fitters-up' were said in 1833 to be working 69 hours per week, and to have worked 74 hours during the 1823/4 boom, and before the passage of the 1825 Factory Act.[54] It is quite reasonable to assume, since these hours correspond exactly with those being worked in the textile mills, that these 'mechanics' also achieved the ten-hour day when it was introduced into the textile mills in 1847.

During the 1830s there were some pressures to undermine the traditional ten-hour day in this industry, and in 1836 the London engineers struck to restore the ten-hour day and the sixty-hour week, and enforced the payment of overtime rates for woik done beyond these limits.[55]

The working week in this industry was a sixty-hour week which extended over six full working days, and before 1840 there is no evidence that a short Saturday was worked by any portion of the trade. With the coming of the great prosperity of the middle of the 1840s[56] the engineers began to press for a short Saturday. On 26 February 1846 they were granted the four-o'clock Saturday in London,[57] and by 1850 they worked from 57½ to 58½ hours per week in 14 of 41 cities and towns for which we have information.[58] The reasons for the success of this industry in reducing the hours of work in a few places at this time included the relatively strong position of the trade, because entry was restricted by barriers of skill; the relatively high earnings; the size of the boom in the instruments and construction industries;[59] and the extraordinary extent of the slump in these two sectors which had just occurred in 1843. Since high unemployment rates attend a depression like that of 1842[60] this tends to strengthen the demand for shorter hours as a means of spreading employment, a phenomenon to which we shall return.

A summary of hours in the remaining metal-working trades is considerably more difficult because of the great variety in hours which prevailed. The difficulty arises largely because this was an industry in transition, moving from the domestic system into workshops and factories at very different rates. Much of the industry was still working under the domestic system, while a substantial proportion was working in what one might call unregulated workshops. These shops were open, say, from 6 am to 8 pm, and within those limits the workman was quite at liberty to allocate his hours. 'In a state of prosperity it is rare that they work as much as they do now (1833)'[61] so that we can take it that in prosperous times they worked less than this twelve hours (assuming two hours for meals) maximum. The regulated shops on the other hand showed a heavy preference for the ten-hour day, although there were cases of eleven hours being worked.

Here it is relevant that the hours of work in Birmingham were almost universally ten per day, since this included a substantial number of metal-working trades. In Sheffield the grinders had long had a union, which in 1843 restricted the operation of the grinding wheels to the hours between 7 am and 7 pm: this attempt to maintain the traditional working day was however not entirely successful, for in many cases the time allowed for meals had by 1843 been reduced to one hour per day.[62] In the hafting and cutlery branches of the trade the few shops that had introduced regular hours worked a ten-hour day, although at least one shop had introduced a day from 6 am to 7 pm with two hours for meals. By the middle of the century the 'large factories and steam-wheels' where 'hours were more regular . . . worked about ten hours a day on the average' although the hours of the grinding wheels seem to have been reduced further.[63]

While in general the introduction of regular hours into the workshops brought with it a week of six full days, there were a few instances of short Saturdays,[64] and some indication that as in other industries there was difficulty in disabusing the former domestic workers of their habit of 'playing' on Monday and/or Tuesday.[65]

The only other trade in this category for which we have information as to hours is that of the coach-builders, and their hours conform to those prevailing elsewhere. Thus in 1850, of 25 cities and towns, 21 were working 60 or more hours per week, reflecting a general acceptance of the ten- or the 10½-hour day and the six-day week.[66]

This general acceptance by the metal trades of a normal day which extended over twelve hours when considered together with the fact that

provision for meals was usually ample in these industries,[67] implies that
the normal daily hours of work in this sector of the economy were ten
hours per day. To this some of the smaller metal-working trades were the
only exceptions. The working week was less uniform, although the
sixty-hour week predominated. Those working less than this by the end of
this period were mainly engineers who had obtained a four-o'clock
Saturday in a number of large cities; those working longer hours were
largely the men in the blast furnaces who worked a seven-day week, and
those whose meal hours had been cut down to 1½ hours per day.

b mining and quarrying

In 1851 this sector employed 394,000 people, the overwhelming majority
of whom worked in the coal-mines. The remainder worked in ironstone,
tin, copper, lead and zinc mines, and included some others engaged in
processing the products of these mines.

Because of the great dispersion of the coal industry and a considerable
variety of work practices, a summary of hours in this industry is extremely
difficult. Nevertheless the 1842 Royal Commission gives us a very
complete picture of conditions as they existed at that time. Its dominant
feature was the widespread adoption of the working day extending from 6
am to 6 pm, or some equivalent twelve-hour period. The condition of the
hewer seems to have deteriorated from the time when he was able to
enforce the working of the 'stint', limiting his labour to between seven and
nine hours per day. The Commission did not find this system operating in any
of the mining districts, except as a nominal unit of accounting for piece work.

Worse still for the workman, the loss of the stint and the consequent
extension of the working day had not been accompanied by the
introduction of regular meal breaks in most cases. Thus while the industry
adopted the day from 6 am to 6 pm in conformity with general practice,
most of the miners worked these hours with only one meal break of
twenty minutes or less.

The majority of the coal-mining areas were reported by the 1842 Royal
Commission to be working a twelve-hour day, and all the largest areas
conformed to this practice. Admittedly, these hours included the time set
aside for meals, but 'of all the coal districts of Great Britain there are only
three in which any regular time is usually set apart for the rest and
refreshment of the work-people during the day',[68] so that all the mines in
the country, with the exception of those in South Staffordshire, the
Forest of Dean and some of those in North Wales,[69] were working twelve
hours per day.

Of the remainder a few areas still worked a day of less than ten hours;[70] two had adopted a day of more than twelve hours;[71] and some were found to work a day of approximately ten hours, with some variation on either side.[72]

How did this situation arise? It arose because only rarely had the miners had a normal working day. They originally had observed the 'stint' which was a direct limitation on supply independent of the time worked, and it was accepted by both employers and employees because of the peculiar situation of the industry. When the coal market became a national instead of a local market the restriction of the supply of coal no longer made economic sense, and was abandoned to a large extent; the stint went with it. It often remained as an accounting unit but it ceased to have any other meaning. Thus the Midland Mining Commission of 1842 explained that according to a wage table they give 'it would be imagined . . . that pikemen (hewers) were the worst off, whereas the fact is that, as they are paid by piece-work, they can often accomplish more than one task or stint in a day' while 'the bandsman (transit worker) . . . being paid by the day of twelve hours cannot earn more than his day's wages'.[73]

The stint had disappeared from the coal-mines because the nature of the industry had changed. Markets had widened and undermined the old policies of supply restriction at the same time as increasing the degree of competition. But competition had also increased because of the entry of large numbers of small firms into the industry, though of course this itself was partly the result of the widening of markets. In any event this influx was so severe that in some areas it alone would have sufficed to disrupt traditional work practices based on supply restriction. Hence the Royal Commission investigating the hours of work was led to observe that it had been 'the misfortune of the (Midlands) coal district, as compared to that of the north of England . . . that many men can save enough, say £1,000 to open a pit'.[74]

The result was an oppressive system of sub-contracting under which the mines were turned over to 'butties' who paid according to output, and who used their power over job allocation to lengthen the day and to cut piece rates progressively. As a result there was a great deal of unrest in the pits and it was this that eventually led to the appointment of the Royal Commission to which reference has been made.

There is much evidence concerning the progressive extension of hours under this system. One estimate placed the 'addition (at) . . . nearly a quarter of a day', and numerous others confirmed that the extension had been substantial.

The reasons why men were forced to accept these hours are not far to seek. Thus one witness reported that 'with the butties you're forced to go down a quarter before six or half-past five of a morning, and I lost my place . . . for speaking out about going down too soon'.[75] But apart from such crude pressures the workman was induced to accept these conditions because of his own deteriorating economic position. Wages had been reduced by 12½ per cent in 1842 and again in 1843 and hence the men were sorely tempted to take a little more income over a little more leisure. This was particularly true because their leisure requirements were largely satisfied by the fact that at this time 'the few days worked in the week . . . is the great complaint'.[76] There were thus many cases where the men attempted to enforce the stint amongst themselves but were unsuccessful because the men often preferred to 'go for the big shilling'. In some cases where the output per man was fixed they went as far as to take small boys into the pits with them hence entitling them to two daily quotas.[77]

Under the butties the men were not given the option of whether or not to restrict their hours. The stint had arisen under circumstances where the men had been paid by the piece but they had been in a position to decide the amount of work they would do in a day. Now under the butties this discretion over time was removed and they were required to work a specified number of hours. They were still paid by the piece, but apparently only because direct supervision of underground work was not possible even by the butties. Hence there were instances of 'pits being sunk on time-wages for the first few hundred feet, while supervision was possible, but on piece-rates thereafter'.[78]

The question of the working week scarcely arose at this time, since no one could get even five days' work a week. Even in good times mining work was irregular, for even then 'mining labour is subject to many interruptions . . . so that perhaps five days work per week is as much as in the best of times a pit's company can be working'.[79] It was hence not surprising to find that the Saturday half-holiday was virtually unknown in this industry though there were a few exceptions even here.[80]

It was natural for the miners to combine to resist the extension of their hours. In 1842-4 a number of attempts were made to restrict hours, but all were unsuccessful. Some of these were attempts by regional unions to reach agreements with the employers; others were merely attempts by miners to impose restrictions on themselves; but neither policy met with any success.[81] At this time too it came to be realized that the problems of national markets could not be solved by local or regional organizations.

Hence the workmen formed the 'Miners Association of Great Britain and Ireland' (MAGBI) and attempted to launch a legislative movement to limit their hours, but the movement ran into militant opposition from the beginning and died an early death.[82]

While conditions in the ironstone mines were very similar to those in the coal-pits, the metal mines presented a sharp contrast. In these the traditional mining hours had clearly been maintained, and the working day consisted of eight hours or less;[83] hence in the tin, copper, lead and zinc mines of the Cornish district 'the regular hours of work are, under certain circumstances, six in number, but generally they are eight', and the same hours were observed in the Alston Moor mines. In this latter area, moreover, these hours were worked for only 'five days in the week'.

The explanation for this state of affairs must be sought in the great stability surrounding these mines even at this time of general change. The concentration of these mines in several small areas, together with their long history and the consequent strength of traditional work practices sufficed to protect their hours of work. This was made easier by the fact that they were not being challenged to any great extent, as this industry was not experiencing any substantial technological change, nor the rapid growth, and consequent competition, of much of the coal-mining sector.

c building and construction

This sector employed about 497,000 people. In general it merely maintained throughout this period the working day, from 6 am to 6 pm, which it had established more than a century before, although there is evidence that a 10½-hour day was introduced in a good many places. The working week was one of six full days, although the last five years of the period saw the beginning of a movement for shorter hours on Saturday among the masons of certain areas. The experience of this industry at this time is less interesting for the changes which actually took place in its working arrangements than for the manner in which a threat to increase hours in the early 1830s was averted, and for its pursuit of trade policies which placed it in a position to become a spearhead of the short hours movements of later decades.

Since very few women and children were employed in construction the Royal Commissions did not investigate its conditions, and there exists no comprehensive summary of the hours before 1850. It is virtually certain nevertheless that the normal working week was one of from sixty to sixty-three hours, made up of six ten-or 10½-hour days throughout.[84] The prosperity of the mid-1840s brought pressure for reduced hours from the masons, but, although in 1846 they struck for a nine-hour day in South Lancashire, they were in the end able only to substitute a ten-hour day for what had come to be a 10½-hour day.[85] In the next year the London masons held a public meeting 'to promote shorter hours' in spite of the fact that trade was getting worse. They sent a memorial to the employers requesting a four-o'clock Saturday without reduction in wages, something which they claimed was 'already conceded in many other towns, and in other trades in London'. Rather surprisingly 'most of the builders agreed' to this request, although the men were not in a position to force the recalcitrant ones to fall into line.[86]

A brief look at the building trades over this period will suggest why the masons turned to such a policy at this particular time. In the building trades generally the rise of the general contractor had increasingly threatened the traditional structure of the industry, and with it the traditional work practices of the trades. The unease caused by this gradual erosion exploded into action with the formation around 1830[87] of the Operative Builders' Union (OBU), which in 1833 'made a general attack . . . upon the new system of "general contracting" ' and because it was an alliance of workmen and small masters 'met with phenomenal success'.[88]

Having 'abolished' the general contracting system in the south of Lancashire early in 1833, the workmen proceeded to take the next logical step in their drive to reaffirm the traditional customs of the industry. They proceeded 'to impose on their masters a set of regulations respecting the Equalising of wages . . . the making of overtime, the performing of work in any other manner than by the day'.[89] As a result the community of interest between the workmen and the small masters soon collapsed. Now the masters went on to the offensive. Trade came to a halt in Lancashire and the men were presented with the notorious 'Document', under the terms of which they had to sever all connection with the union if they were to be employed. From the beginning there was little chance that the men could defeat the masters in this struggle. Worst of all, while they were locked in battle their mutual 'enemy' the general contractor grew and prospered.

It soon became obvious that the general contractor could not be simply outlawed since he served a need *vis-à-vis* the client in organizing and co-ordinating the work of the various trades. Under Robert Owen's leadership the men came to realize this fact and attempted to usurp the function of the general contractor through the establishment of the 'Grand National Guild of Builders'. Unfortunately this body suffered from severe administrative and financial difficulties from the outset and its demise was hastened by the fact that before the strikes then in progress were settled Owen induced the men to add a demand for the eight-hour day to their conditions.[90] Though this demand proved to be quite unrealistic the existence at this time of the National Regeneration Society, an Owenite body whose main aim was the establishment of the eight-hour day, may have misled the participants as to its feasibility.

With the collapse of the Guild and the euphoric hopes on which it had been built, together with the more or less total collapse of general unionism,[91] it came to be accepted that the task at hand was to live with the new system and to strengthen one's position within it. While this was obviously not true of the Chartists, an increasing number of skilled craftsmen adopted this attitude.

Those that were in a position to do so set about trying to isolate some small sector of the labour market in which they could exert some influence. Thus the masons who even four years after the collapse of 1834 were the only building trade that 'possessed a genuine national organisation, strong in membership and financially sound' concentrated in the 1830s on the establishment of effective barriers to entry into the trade and attempted to put a stop to 'the system which existed till of late, allowing anybody to learn our trade and to serve what time they please'.[92] At the same time such practices as payment by the piece were attacked because they made the orderly regulation of working conditions more difficult.

As the 1840s drew near it appears that the union leaders decided that the barriers around their trade were now effective enough for a reduction of hours to play an effective role in restricting supply. Apparently this view was shared by the rank and file, for the 1838 Delegate Meeting declared: 'That this Meeting conceiving that a reduction in the hours of labour would be of permanent advantage to the members of our society inasmuch as it will be *the only means of maintaining a high rate of wages,* recommend all our brethren to carry so desirable an object into practice'.[93]

Thus by the 1840s the masons conceived themselves to be in a position to utilize a restriction of the hours of work as an effective restriction of supply. That this was not the case of the other building trades emerges from the Lancashire strike of 1846, for while the masons were engaged in this dispute trying to get a nine-hour day, the other trades were attempting to establish a more rigid enforcement of their apprenticeship regulations.[94] Clearly they were one step behind the masons, but moving in the same direction.

The adoption by the Lancashire masons of the demand for a nine-hour day and a fifty-four hour week, rather than some mere modest proposal, is probably due to the fact that the city of Manchester had in 1843 adopted a Saturday one o'clock closing which had become universal by 1845, and thus included the building trades.[95] The reason for this remains obscure, but 441 bankers, merchants, manufacturers and calico printers signed the original statement which declared that 'at the respectful solicitation of those in our employment (we) agree to close our places of business at 1 o'clock every Saturday afternoon'. The document appeared in 1843 and would seem to have had some connection with the fact that this was the peak of the agitation for the Factory Bill which centred in this area, and that it was just the end of a very severe depression.

d paper, printing, etc.
This sector comprised about 78,000 employees and we have information regarding the three major industries that make it up, namely the paper mills, the printers, and the bookbinders. It is difficult to give a general summary of hours in these three sectors, except to say that the ten- or the 10½-hour day were usual, although there was a good deal of dispersion about this mode. A six-day week was general, though in the English paper mills, a short Saturday was common.

The paper mills can be divided into three groups. Those in the south-east and outside London generally worked from eight to ten hours a day, exclusive of 1½ or two hours for meals, although overtime was common and appeared at times to be compulsory.[96] The others were divided into those that worked ten-hour days, many of which worked two twelve-hour shifts, and those that had adopted textile-mill hours and worked twelve hours per day. With regard to the working week, 'in general, at least in England', the majority of workers in these mills 'leave work on Saturday at two pm but in the East of Scotland "many mills, for the purpose of making up seven days work in the week, the younger hands as well as adults labour eighteen hours on the Saturday and eighteen hours on the Monday" '.[97]

For the printers it appears that 'the ten-and-a-half-hour-working day, and a six-day week, remained the norm in the printing trades for more than fifty years'[98] after the early nineteenth century. But this norm was subjected to considerable upward pressure in the 1830s. In 1835 the London union decreed that establishment hours were to be twelve, including the time for refreshment, 'Overtime' was to be paid extra, and together with some renewed apprentice regulations, they had this schedule of hours accepted by their employers. Only the very large shop of Messrs Spottiswoode refused to accept these conditions[99] and it is on the basis of evidence from this shop that the 1843 Royal Commission stated that printers' hours were eleven per day, although almost all of the other shops mentioned in the evidence worked from 8 am to 8 pm with 1½ hours for meals. At the same time the hours in Liverpool and Glasgow were eleven per day, while those in Edinburgh and Belfast were still ten per day.[100]

The upward pressure on the hours of London printers was explained by one witness who stated that 'there are many men out of work' and that this was due to 'the introduction of a great number of apprentices, who are employed by some printers to do the principal part of the work'.[101]

By 1850 their position seems to have improved, and in most cities and towns for which we have information they worked between 59 and 63 hours per week, indicating a ten- or 10½-hour day and a six-day week. Of the others, most worked slightly less and a very few worked slightly more than this (see figure 1).

In 1849 the Provincial Typographical Association succeeded the National Typographical Association. It had branches in seventeen major cities, though not in London, Manchester or Birmingham, and its rules stated that 'the hours are limited to fifty-nine per week (which is counted as sixty, nine hours on Saturday being charged and paid for as ten), as a maximum'. At the same time the hours of the London compositors were confirmed at 'ten hours and a half per day' while 'in Scotland they worked sixty hours per week'.[102]

The bookbinding trades who had finally adopted the ten-hour day in London in 1806 seem by 1843 to have lost it again. It is in the late 1820s that the problem first appeared as it had become the practice to work two hours extra each day among printers and bookbinders, and while the former prohibited overtime in 1827[103] the latter were in no position to do so. By 1843 they were generally working a day from 6 am to 8 pm in London, while the females that had come into the industry in large numbers generally worked a day extending over eleven or twelve hours, with 1½ to two hours for meals.[104]

The most probable cause of this extension of hours is to be found in the fact that 'many girls and women . . . are employed' and that 'now the binding of the book is subdivided into many branches, and each man does only one of them. . . . Thus an apprentice now learns only exceeding little, and is unfit to get his living setting up for himself; or to work anywhere, except in the large shops'.[105]

Indeed, it is clear that as with the building trades, the major concern of these trades in the 1830s was the protection of their markets from outsiders. Thus in 1839 a struggle between the bookbinders and their employers, which 'was the climax of all the quarrels ... of the past ten years' ended with an agreement that stipulated 'that the Employers acknowledge the Society and will not in future employ any person but what is legally entitled to the trade', and 'that when the Apprentices now in their employ are out of their time, they will not fill up their places until they are reduced to a reasonable number'.[106]

By 1850, the bookbinders in eight out of nine towns for which we have information worked six days of ten or ten and a half hours, so that they had recovered their former position by that date.[107]

e clothing and skins, leather, etc.
Although these two sectors occupied about 969,000 people in 1851, they will be looked at only briefly in this section since the great majority of these people were then still working under the domestic system. The major trades to have established themselves in regulated shops were the tailors and the dressmakers and we shall deal mainly with these.

In the London tailoring trade it appears that the hours in those shops where regular hours were worked were still those decreed by the 1768 legislation, namely from 6 am to 7 pm with one hour allowed for meals,[108] although there were a good number of irregular shops as well as many domestic workers engaged in this trade. In general the trade was in a state of flux; 'the men principally come from the country', presumably to work during the season. The irregularity of this trade was its greatest disability since it made necessary either excessive hours during the season, or heavy unemployment at other times. This problem could be avoided if 'the season' in one place could be timed so as to coincide with the off-season in another, and this was true to some extent in the tailoring trade. Alternatively, to the extent that its skills were easily acquired a trade might in the season be able to draw on part-time workers who would not be a 'burden' to the trade in the off-season. The actual solution seems to have been a little of both.

That the long hours were felt to be a grievance by the men is shown by the fact that during the time of the Grand National Consolidated Trades Union, when hopes were raised everywhere, the London tailors took the opportunity to strike for shorter hours of work, but their strike, like the giant union, collapsed having achieved nothing.[109]

Neither do these long hours seem to have been peculiar to London, for in 1850, of nine cities other than London for which we have information, six work 72 hours, one works 66 and one 60, and only in Leicester have the hours been reduced to 55. Thus the twelve-hour day is by far the most common, although a very few towns have gone below it. The six-day week on the other hand would seem to have been universal.

The trade of millinery and dressmaking suffered the same irregularity as the tailors, but here the effect seems to have been over-working in the busy season rather than unemployment in the slack. In the busy season hours in this trade were 'almost incredible', with those few establishments who had made a 'praiseworthy attempt . . . to lessen the evil' working 'for 15, 16 or 17 hours *per diem'* of which about one hour is allowed for meals. These were clearly 'actual' hours and not 'normal' hours, however. It appears that even in this trade the normal hours worked outside the season were '13, 12 or less, inclusive of meals' and 'in the country towns the hours of work, on the whole, are shorter than in the metropolis' though 'the hours are frequently as long' even there.[110] There is in general no question of a short Saturday in these trades, and the week is one of six full days, which in the season was occasionally extended into the Sunday.

The machine lace industry was concentrated in two areas: one around Nottingham, Leicester and Derby, and the other in the west country, around Tiverton, Chard and Barnstaple. In the former the machines were worked by two shifts for 16, 18 or 20 hours per day, which made a working day of from eight to ten hours inclusive of meals. In the latter area the factory hours were from 6 am to 6.30 pm in Tiverton, and from 6 am to 7 pm in the other towns.

The only other industry for which there is any indication of regular working hours is that of hosiery, and here the 'regular hours of work are from ten to twelve, exclusive of meals', but these were frequently exceeded.[111]

That hours in this industry were extremely irregular reflected its still very close ties with the domestic industries. Where regular hours had been introduced they tended to be long, because of the difficulty of organizing these trades and the fact that many were in the transitional stage just at this time.

f food, drink and tobacco

Though this sector employed 401,000 people in 1851 we have very little information regarding hours in it. One of the larger industries in it would have been baking, where hours were notoriously long and where attempts at reform were unsuccessful for a long time. The only substantial industry for which we have detailed information is the processing of tobacco, and here the ten-hour day seems to have been the average, though eleven and nine hours were the most commonly worked. Thus London and Lancashire worked eleven, the East of Scotland ten, and Northumberland and Durham with the West of Scotland nine and one-half hours per day. In the first three the day was spread over twelve hours while the last two extended over only eleven hours.[112] Figure 1 reflects the considerable diversity in hours in this industry. The working week consisted of six full days, except in the West of Scotland where it was customary to stop early on Saturday.

g bricks, cement, glass, pottery, etc.;
   chemicals, oil, etc.; wood, furniture, etc.

Between them these sectors employed 296,000 people in 1851. We shall examine the pottery and glass trades in detail. We also have some information for the cabinet-makers, probably the largest single group, and the chemical industry. In addition we shall look briefly at the calico printing and the bleaching and dyeing trades.

In the potteries the regular working day was still only being introduced, but in every case the intended normal day extended over twelve hours, though in England only 1½ hours were usually set aside for meals, against two hours in Scotland. Nevertheless in most establishments the work continued to be rather irregular, with much overtime worked towards the end of the week. Furthermore, the working week practically never consisted of six days, and 'often no work is done from Saturday noon till the following Tuesday or Wednesday morning',[113] though some of the larger shops were pressing hard to introduce regular hours.

Hours in the glass houses depended on the kind of glass being produced. Thus in the flint glass-works, hours were 'uniformly the same in all parts of England' in 1843, and they consisted of the split twelve-hour shift, six hours on and six hours off, which had existed in this trade from its inception several centuries before. Since the six-hour spells were not broken for meals, which was probably the reason for their existence, this meant twelve hours of work a day. Weekly hours were considerably more moderate, however, since the workmen 'seldom work more than from four to five days in the week' so that weekly hours would never exceed sixty, and would usually be below fifty.

Although in the other branches of the trade the hours varied considerably they also did not usually exceed sixty per week. Thus the crown glass-works worked 'three journeys in a week, and a journey varies in duration from ten to sixteen, or even more hours', while glass-bottle manufacturers worked 'for five journeys per week, of ten or twelve hours each',[114] though this was greatly exceeded at times.

The glass cutters and polishers, who worked independently of the furnaces, worked 'generally ten hours a day'.[115] Their custom as to Saturday work is not clear.

For the cabinet-makers we have only the report of their hours in eleven cities in 1850, and it would appear from this that a week of six ten-hour days was the most common arrangement, although some places seem to have extended their daily hours to eleven. All seem to have stopped on Saturday at 6 pm, even those who on other days were working eleven hours or more.[116]

In the chemicals industry in 1850 eight out of nine cities worked between 58½ and 62 hours per week, indicating the acceptance of a ten- or 10½-hour day in most places, and of a short Saturday in some.[117]

Calico printing was concentrated in Lancashire and Cheshire, and in the West of Scotland, with a few works in the East of Scotland and in and around London. Of all these areas it can be said that 'the regular hours of work for block and machine printers in all the print-fields are, in summer, from 6 am to 6 pm', while for meals 'throughout the trade, two hours are generally allowed'.[118]

It appears that Saturday was a full day in the print fields of England, but in the West of Scotland the workmen 'being on the whole an intelligent class of men, have had the wisdom (though paid by the piece) to resist long hours of work, and especially to reserve to themselves some leisure on the afternoon of Saturday' when they 'drop work at three pm, working on that day eight hours'.[119]

It must be recognized, however, that while these were without doubt the normal hours in this industry, extremely irregular hours were often worked, so much so that 'there can scarcely be said to be any regular hours' in the Lancashire grounds. The difficulty in this industry seems to have been the fact that like the dressmaking trade it depended on fashion and on 'working to order' and although many employers disliked the practice they declared themselves unable to resist it owing to competitive pressures. The result was the adoption of twelve-hour shifts in many places during the season. The really excessive hours were worked primarily in those places which did not employ such a system, though these 'are exceptions to the general practice of the trade'.[120]

4 Domestic trades
This very numerous body of working people was heavily concentrated in

the clothing sector, although a good number were also to be found in the smaller metal-working trades. The dominant feature of their hours, then as before, was their irregularity, and this was so extreme that any summary even of any one trade is all but impossible. Indeed, we shall not attempt such a summary but shall briefly present some of the evidence concerning these trades in order to reaffirm the three major features of the hours of work, where there are no institutional constraints on the individual workman's allocation of his time between leisure and income. These features are: the inverse relationship between the amount of time spent at work and the wage rate which was often determined by the product price; the tendency among these trades to regard a twelve-hour day, inclusive of meals and other breaks, as a full working day; and also the tendency, when economic pressure forced these trades to work longer hours, to sacrifice the twelve-hour day rather than give up the one or more 'idle days' which they enjoyed each week.

The extension of hours when the price of products fell was a general phenomenon. In 1833 the silk weavers of Cheshire and Lancashire 'who all weave by hand' as 'there is no powerloom weaving' as yet, were faced with a situation where 'the value of silk goods (had) generally much decreased within the last few years'. As a result they 'must work 12 and 14 hours a day at their own houses'. The fall in the piece rates of the hand-loom weavers in Lancashire meant 'that in order to obtain a subsistence at present they are obliged to labour more constantly, and for a greater number of hours' and to make matters worse, 'in consequence of this excessive labour, those people produce a fourth more goods than they would otherwise do if they got better wages'. Similarly for the metal-workers who work in their homes in Wolverhampton. 'In a state of prosperity it is very rare that they work as much as they do now',[121] while in the Sheffield trades in which 'the workman determined his own hours ... hours were short ... in boom years, when wages were particularly high ... workmen apparently preferring leisure to income after reaching their normal earnings'.[122]

In spite of the basic irregularity of hours in these trades, there prevailed a certain conception of what a full working day was and when economic pressures eased a little this was often the day that was adopted. In almost every case where such a 'day' was recognized, it was the day extending over twelve hours, inclusive of breaks, that was so regarded. Thus in 1843, 'in the western district, as at places like Coventry and Birmingham, where there is no factory labour properly so called, for the operatives, with few exceptions, work at their own houses ... the regular hours of labour do not exceed ten; while it appears that some of the workpeople labour upon an average not more than nine hours daily'.[123]

Similarly two hand-loom weavers from the area around Preston, Bolton and Chorley in Lancashire, where fine goods were woven and where people were not nearly so depressed in 1833 as they were in other areas, assumed throughout their evidence that the working day was one of 10½ hours. Thus their estimates of wage rates in this trade were based on 10½ hours of work per day, and in another place they state that they work 'about ten and a half hours, (beside) one and a half for meals'. It is true that they stated in another instance that work continued from 6 am to 9 pm, but it is clear that this referred to the hours a man was forced to work 'when he has payments to make'.[124]

By the same token, the families of the lead miners of Derbyshire, who worked at the hand-loom at home pursued this task for twelve hours a day, inclusive of meals.[125]

Indeed there is some evidence of this limit to the working day being maintained even in the face of considerable economic hardship. Thus the hand-loom weavers around Oldham, who a witness thought would in 1833 be 'obliged to work more or starve', answered his question as to whether they 'do not . . . work 12 hours, the same as the factory hands' by saying 'that they did not, that they work now about 10½ hours', and this in spite of the fact that the witness agreed that 'extreme distress' has 'a tendency to force people to work more'.[126]

Equally, in Sheffield, although 'the trade has been languid the last year . . . twelve hours a day is considered the usual day's work, including two hours for meal times, so that the hours of working are ten hours';[127] while for Wolverhampton, where there were many domestic workers and workers in unregulated workshops in 1843 and where trade was then 'in a very depressed state' the Royal Commission of that year concluded that 'in none of these trades are the regular hours less than twelve, and in some they are thirteen'.[128]

Nevertheless, when adverse economic circumstances forced an extension of hours, it was usually this daily limit that was first transgressed. It was this that produced the situation in the hand-loom weaving trades where they 'work fourteen or sixteen hours per day . . . (for) . . . two or three days in the week, and they generally, notwithstanding their poverty, spend one or two days in idleness'.[129] Indeed this practice is so widely documented that it hardly needs further support. Suffice it to say that there is evidence that this practice prevailed also among the draw-boy weavers of Kidderminster, the hosiery trades in general, the pin makers of Warrington, the domestic workers of Sheffield, and the nailers of Willenhall.[130]

If then the domestic trades reacted to falling prices by increasing their output, the obvious remedy was an agreement to restrict supply. But such agreement was uniquely difficult in an industry made up of large numbers of small producers, dispersed over wide areas, with virtually no barriers to entry such as might be provided by large capital requirements or the need for extensive training. Therefore the usual experience of these trades in this respect is summarized by an exchange before the Committee on Manufactures which met in 1833. 'Do combinations exist among the hand-loom weavers about Glasgow? No, they have attempted them, but they cannot; it is too much extended'.[131]

Nevertheless some trades in the domestic sector which were less 'extended' were better able to help themselves in this respect than others. Thus the bobbin net trade, relatively concentrated around Nottingham and using relatively expensive machinery, when faced with falling prices and lengthening hours, was able to make 'a remarkable attempt . . . in 1828-9 to regulate the hours of working universally throughout the trade': an attempt particularly noteworthy for 'the success with which it was temporarily attended, and the almost absolute unanimity of the machine owners on the subject'.

Two aspects of this event deserve particular attention. One of the reasons for its success was obviously the fact that both masters and journeymen saw it in their interest, so much so that when the agreement broke down there was 'an address to the committee from the journeymen . . . requesting them to continue their superintendence'. The other is that the day was restricted to one extending over twelve hours, which it was declared was 'the natural period to be considered as *permanently* desirable'.[132] The special needs of the larger factories were catered for by giving them special permission 'to work their twelve hours, with an interval for an hour for dinner', thus extending their day over thirteen hours.

Another instance of a domestic trade which was able to combine occurred among the weavers around Huddersfield who worked in the woollen cloth and the fancy waistcoat manufactures and whose condition 'had been gradually deteriorating from that time (1819)'. They were able to reverse this trend by combination. In 1832 'they formed trades' unions, and they have forced an advance of their wages, both in the fancy trade and in the woollen trade'.[133] Such direct raising of the wage without bothering about the restriction of output was sensible if their wage rates had been set in an unequal bargain between large merchants or factors and individual producers, a likely situation. Further evidence of domestic trades who were able to form effective combinations came from Sheffield, where some of the metal-workers had regulated their trades for a long time.

When such recourse to collective action could not be had – as was the case with most hand-loom weavers – the condition of the worker deteriorated progressively. This apparent failure of the market mechanism deserves some further attention.

While it is true that an inverse relationship between the amount of time spent at work and the level of the price of the product raises the possibility of an unstable equilibrium, this would be offset on the individual's level through the operation of diminishing returns past some optimal point, and on the industrial level by entry into and exit from the industry. This mechanism had been effective when the weavers were in a very strong economic position at the end of the eighteenth century:[134] high wages attracted new entrants and the wages fell. 'The sole cause of the fall in wages was the over-crowding of the labour market. At first there were too few weavers, but then their numbers increased out of all proportion' and to make it worse 'among the new-comers were many country labourers, used to low wages'.[135] On the other hand when their wages began to fall, the reverse mechanism operated only very slowly, because a number of obstacles to leaving the trade had developed. Most important among these was the disappearance of agriculture as a secondary employment, together with the rise in many of the other trades of strong workmen's associations which were able to maintain effective barriers to entry. Finally even their way into the woollen mills, the logical place for them to go, was obstructed partly because of combinations in the mills and partly for other less obvious reasons including the preponderance of children and women in the mills.[136] This often meant that whereas the children of the hand-weavers could get places in the mills, the adults themselves could not.

In addition to these difficulties there was the problem that in many cases the regular and long hours of the mills proved a strong disincentive to the old domestic workers: with their irregular working habits the number of hours they worked every week was rarely equal to the number worked in the mills, although they did work very long hours on some days. An employer in the north of Lancashire who had made a careful survey of the conditions of the four hundred hand-loom weavers whom he provided with work reported in 1833 that their condition was extremely wretched, that 'upon the average, there were three persons in each family working 60 hours a week' and this was true only 'in bad times'. Little wonder then that though 'many of those weavers were employed (in 1826) at 10s and 12s a week' at day labour, 'as soon as there was work in the loom at 6s or 7s they went back to it' as 'the labour (in the mills) was too severe for their habits'.[137] One of the most comprehensive statements of the strength of this feeling among the domestic workers came from an authority who was usually an apologist for the mills. Yet he wrote that a

'cause for the low wages of the weavers is, that their employment is in some respects more agreeable as laying them under less restraint than factory labour. Being carried on in their own cottages, their time is at their own command; they may begin and leave off their work at their pleasure; they are not bound punctually to obey the summons of the factory bell: if they are so disposed they can quit their looms for the public-house, or to lounge in the street, or to accept some other job, and then, when urged by necessity, they may make up for lost time by a great exertion . . . (which) helps to account for many continuing at the loom, notwithstanding the wretchedness of their circumstances'.[138]

In general we can say that the influx of labour into the hand-loom weaving trade in response to the high wages of the turn of the century had been rapid, but that the exit from it in response to the low wages of the 1830s had proven much more difficult, not least because the hours worked by the domestic trades, even when they had been extended as a result of the low wages, were on the whole shorter than those worked in the mills.

5 Holidays and the short Saturday
Once we have established the normal day, the question of the working week becomes one of the short Saturday, except in the domestic trades or those still enjoying the 'playing system'. The Royal Commission of 1843 concluded that 'it is in many districts a common practice to leave off work at an early hour on Saturday afternoon';[139] but their evidence shows that the practice was confined to Lancashire and the West of Scotland where it was no doubt influenced by the fact that the textile mills had been working a short Saturday at least since 1825.[140] Beyond this it appeared only in the paper mills and in parts of the West of England. Apart from this it was still a rarity.

In the 1840s the interest which developed in the hours of work in some of the stronger trades, like engineering and building, tended to focus on this issue, and by 1850 some small gains had been achieved, though (as is shown in the selection of industries in figure 1), they were confined to a few trades in a few areas of the country.

Holidays continued to be virtually negligible throughout this period. Paid holidays were extremely rare, and the general practice was similar to that of the coal-mines where 'there is no instance in the whole kingdom of rest from colliery labour for a single day or even half a day, the wages going on . . . but in most districts nothing is done in the pits on some of the principal fasts and festivals'.[141]

There were a very few instances of paid holidays. Thus in Scotland New Year's Day and in England Christmas Day were often paid without being 'made up', and there were some very rare instances where more days were paid, as in some Kentish paper mills where there were as many as eight such holidays. These were, however, exceptions to prove the rule and the rule was very few holidays and virtually none of them paid.[142]

6 Summary

The detailed account of the normal hours of work which has occupied this chapter is important because it is the earliest such description possible. As such, it allows one to verify various hypotheses concerning the hours prevailing before 1820, and provides a starting point from which to assess the changes of subsequent decades.

It warrants a number of generalizations about the working day. The most important of these is that the 'normal day' was generally accepted as extending over a twelve-hour period, which was usually from 6 am to 6 pm. These limits were common to the great majority of industries working regular hours, and were observed even in a good number of the irregular and domestic trades. The only important exception was in the textile mills, whose most usual normal day extended from 6 am to 7 pm. These mills allowed only one hour for meals, and therefore worked a twelve-hour day; but the great majority of other industries allowed either 1½ or 2 hours, so that actual working hours were ten or ten and a half.

Generally it was the ten working hours that were considered 'normal' even though a number of industries worked ten and a half. That this was so appears from the statements of numerous witnesses before government bodies of various kinds. Thus a witness from the textile mills 'thinks ten hours, the usual time of working in this country, long enough for the mills also', while a number of others feel that hours in the mills should be ten, as they are for 'mechanics and labourers'.[143] Other commentators made the same point by referring to the 'long' hours of the textile mills — meaning 'long' relative to those worked in other sectors of the economy.

Thus Baines, who was no enemy of the mills, wrote that 'it must be admitted that the hours of labour in cotton mills are long, being twelve hours a day on five days of the week',[144] while a witness before a government commission who was asked what he meant by 'long' hours, explained that he meant 'twelve working hours'.[145] Another who was asked to consider the problems a 'Ten Hours Bill' would present to a man who may have built a textile mill never dreaming that such an Act might be passed, replied that such a man 'ought to have sufficient foresight to have known that it was *unnatural* to work persons *unreasonable* hours'[146] (my emphasis).

If we look beyond this static picture at the changes which took place during the thirty years between 1820 and 1850 we find a number of different trends. In the textile trades working hours were first stabilized at twelve per day in 1833, and were then reduced to ten per day in 1847, only to be extended to ten and one-half per day in 1850. This reduction established in the textile trades a working day which extended over twelve hours, from six to six, and thus made the observance of these limits all but universal.

In the rest of the manufacturing sector, the day from six to six continued to be regarded as a full working day, inclusive of meals, for the whole of these decades. However, in spite of the stability of these outer limits, there is some indication of pressure to extend the working day in the early 1830s. In most cases these pressures were met by strong opposition, which prevented their becoming effective.

The engineers, the builders and the printers took action in the middle of the 1830s to reaffirm the day from 6 am to 6 pm as the normal day, and it is significant that 'the skilled mechanics and the printing and engineering trades had ... held aloof from the general movement (of 1834) and their trade clubs were unaffected either by the Owenite boom or its subsequent collapse'.[147] The bookbinders, however, seem to have been unable to protect their hours effectively at this time, and were found to be working a day from 6 am to 8 pm in London in 1843. They did, however, re-establish the day from six to six by 1850, as is shown in figure 1. In the domestic trades hours continued to be variable, though even these trades tended to regard the ten-and-a-half-hour day as a full day's work. In the coal-pits there was a distinct extension of hours; just when this took place is not clear, though it was probably during the 1830s. In any event the stint system which had previously prevailed in this industry had prevented the establishment of a normal day, so that this was an extension of actual rather than of normal hours.

The difference between actual and normal hours deserves some comment. First it must be realized that during the years now being discussed the two were often very different. The 'practice of working extra hours is peculiar to no district, and to no description of factory; but it is more or less common to all'. This state of affairs was more serious when as 'in the clothing districts, both masters and men agree in stating that if extra work were refused when a press of business comes, the workmen so refusing would lose their situations'.[148] In such circumstances the normal day is in danger of becoming irrelevant, though it always maintains its relevance as the determinant of the point at which overtime pay begins. Indeed, since written agreements were all but unheard of at this time[149] we are usually dealing with what in fact are 'customary' hours; though in so far as the unions had enshrined these in their rules, the difference between them and specified normal hours becomes negligible. In either case the only obstacle to an attempt to change either customary or normal hours comes from the power of the workmen or their union to oppose it.

Figure 1 is a summary of the data provided by a government report on hours in 1850.[150] The figures refer to towns, cities, and occasionally areas, with the number in each trade varying between six and forty-one, and averaging nineteen. While these figures can pretend to no great accuracy, they can be used as indicators of the dominant characteristics of normal hours in the various industries. The conversion of the figures into percentages may be misleading where the number of towns enumerated is small, but it has been necessary in order to make the groups comparable in the graphs. The result confirms the picture of normal hours we have drawn, in that it shows the heavy preponderance of the sixty-hour week, an impression borne out by table 1, in which the statistics of figure 1 are expressed as unweighted mean averages.

If these were the changes which the normal hours of work underwent, does the evidence suggest what caused them?

The explanation of the reductions achieved in the textile trades, and this was easily the most significant change during these thirty years, is complicated because the reductions were achieved through political channels, so that the number of non-economic variables is greater than usual. Nevertheless, we can identify a number of economic considerations as having played a part in bringing these reductions about. Both of the significant pieces of legislation affecting this industry, that of 1833 and 1847, came at times of bad trade. But a distinction must be made, for the Act of 1833 was primarily a response to the extension of hours beyond twelve per day in textile mills outside the cotton industry, and merely

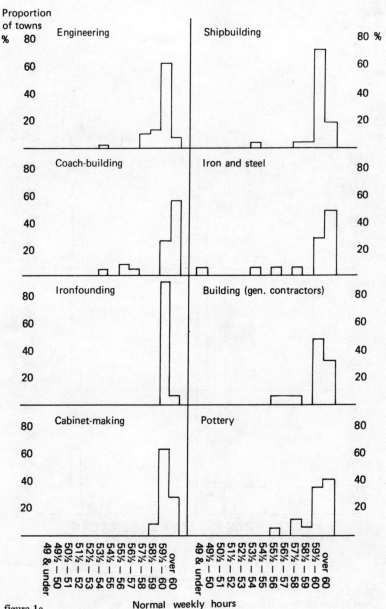

figure 1a
Great Britain 1850: certain industries
Frequency distributions of normal hours
(unweighted per cent of total sample of towns and areas)
Source: *see* Notes to figures and tables

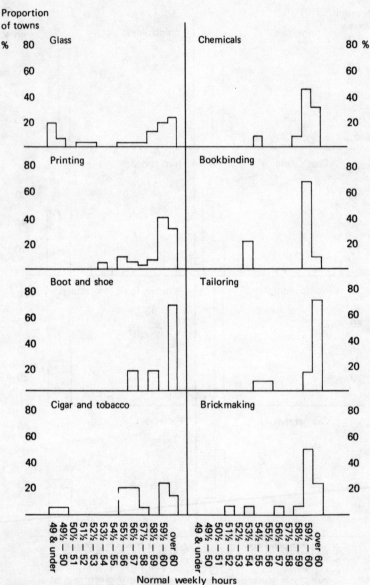

figure 1b
Great Britain 1850: certain industries
Frequency distributions of normal hours
(unweighted per cent of total sample of towns and areas)
Source: *see* Notes to figures and tables

table 1
Great Britain 1850: average normal hours in certain towns in certain industries
(figures in parentheses refer to the number of towns and areas on which averages are
based)

industries	average normal hours
engineering	59.5 (41)
shipbuilding	59.9 (23)
coach-building	60.4 (25)
iron & steel	59.5 (15)
ironfounding	60.1 (14)
building (general contractors)	60.1 (15)
cabinet-makers	60.5 (11)
brickmaking	59.3 (16)
pottery	60.3 (17)
glass	56.5 (30)
chemicals	59.9 (9)
printing	59.8 (44)
bookbinding	58.9 (9)
boot & shoe	60.6 (6)
tailoring	60.8 (14)
cigar & tobacco	57.6 (19)

Source: *see* Notes to figures and tables

imposed the same twelve-hours limit on these. The Act of 1847, on the
other hand, substantially reduced hours in the whole of the industry, and
we are not surprised to find that this action was finally taken when the
political threat of Chartism was growing rapidly, but also, and perhaps
more significantly, in the year of the most severe slump in the textile
trades in almost forty years.[151] As has been suggested, the timing owed
something to the Acts being used to defuse the discontent among the
working classes, but it is also relevant that the demand for shorter hours
had always been put forward as one means of reducing unemployment.
This points to a factor that did not affect the textile trades alone, for in
evaluating the condition of the working man at this time 'it is necessary to
take account not only of both prosperous and depressed years but also
perhaps of the new insecurity which the changing character of the business
cycle brought with it'.[152]

If these general economic circumstances did much to bring about the reduction of hours in the textile trades, an equally important element was the changed attitude of many of the employers. This manifested itself in two major ways. First, the employers began to consider much more seriously the possibility of productivity gains resulting from a reduction of hours. Hobsbawm has made this point on a more general level when he concluded that in Britain 'the mid-century (19th) brought the beginning of the substitution of "intensive" for "extensive" labour utilisation'.[153] Second, some very large firms had now arisen, and an increasing number of employers had an interest in the maintenance of the *status quo* and in the restriction of competition from small firms.

It may be added that since the normal hours in the textile mills were longer than those in most other manufacturing industries their reduction was more likely. It is significant that when hours were reduced the new ones conformed to the general practice in two of their most important aspects: the newly established working day extended from 6 am to 6 pm, and the working week consisted of sixty hours. The combination of a ten-and-a-half-hour day with a short Saturday to achieve this incorporated two practices which were also widespread, though not as universal as the day extending from six to six or the sixty-hour week.

The pressure for longer hours which became apparent in many other industries in the early 1830s was seen to coincide in most cases with periods of rapid change in industrial organization, characterized by the rise of the general contractor in building, or the extension of the division of labour in the bookbinding trades which diluted skills, made upward mobility more difficult and allowed the introduction of women and unskilled workers into the industry. The occurrence of such changes suggests the existence of intense competition in these trades, since they would take place only when men were competing sufficiently intensively to ignore traditional ways of doing things. This same competition would have led to the extension of hours, or to pressures in that direction, particularly while employers were concerned 'to exhaust the possibilities of cutting labour costs by extending hours and cutting money wage-rates'[154] and while the largest employers in an industry did not have the power or the desire to restrict such competition in the interest of the *status quo*.

The relative lack of success of the efforts to extend hours reflects the tenacity with which the workman held to these traditional practices. Indeed it is almost certain that the upsurge of unionism of the early 1830s was to a large extent due to the threats to traditional practices determining the amount of work to be done in a day, and this included the pace of work, as well as the amount of time spent working. We saw this to be the case with the building trades in particular.

In any event many trades managed through combined action in the later 1830s and the 1840s to reaffirm most of their traditional privileges, including the sixty-hour week. By the second half of the 1840s we found those unions who had successfully maintained their privileges and protected their markets from outsiders turning to efforts to improve their position, and chief among these was the effort to reduce the hours of work. This was a natural development since the whole rationale of the craft unionism that had grown up was based on the desirability of restricting supply. The leaders of the better educated trades had accepted the economic axiom that 'wages must inevitably depend upon the relation of Supply and Demand in each particular class of labour' and among the flint-glass makers 'the scarcity of labour was one of the fundamental principles laid down at (their) first conference held in Manchester in 1849' and the ironmoulders declared in 1847, that 'all men of experience agree that wages are to be best raised by the demand for labour'.[155]

During the boom of the middle forties some of the strongest of these unions were able to achieve some minor reductions in weekly hours by obtaining a short Saturday. But the later extension of this movement owed something to the Factory Act of 1850, which made the textile mills cease work at 2 pm on Saturday, and it is not surprising that it was only in Manchester, the English centre of the cotton industry, that the short Saturday was obtained generally by all trades.

The changes in hours experienced in the domestic trades were of course much more continuous, and varied inversely with the wage rate, though there was often a great reluctance to extend hours beyond the accepted working day or week. Indeed, this reluctance may paradoxically have compounded the problems of the hand-loom weavers because it made them reluctant to move into other employments where the hours were longer or the work more intensive, and thus helped to prevent an exit from the trade which might have improved the position of those who remained. But other evidence suggests that many of those hand-loom weavers who were willing and anxious to move into the mills could not do so.

In the coal-mines, where hours had become very long by 1842-3, a combination of the above factors was operating. The falling wages and irregular employment of the early 1840s made the men willing to work very long hours on those days on which they could obtain work, as the idle days meant that they had ample leisure but little income. As a result, efforts by the unions to get the men to restrict themselves in the amount of work they would do were unsuccessful. On the other hand the very rapid expansion of the industry[156] witnessed the opening of countless small pits and led to very active competition, in the course of which a sub-contracting system was adopted which was entirely inimical to the restriction of supply in general, or in particular. The result was the extension of hours which has been described.

These then were the normal hours of work in the period 1820-50, and it is of interest to compare these with the hours which were found to exist previously. This discussion deals with the question of what happened to the hours of work during the industrial revolution.

The dominant finding is the great stability of the normal daily hours of work in most industries. It appears that in most trades the normal day extended from 6 am to 6 pm and that these limits remained unchanged for the whole of the period normally referred to as the industrial revolution. Within these outer limits of the working day, working hours varied between ten and ten and a half, and the increases in the regularity and intensity of work of course implied increases in annual hours for most men.

While this was true of most men who worked regular hours in the manufacturing and construction industries, the major exception was the textile industry, in which in the last quarter of the eighteenth century the normal working hours were extended from ten or ten and a half to twelve. Indeed, they were even further extended first in cotton and then in the other textile trades, but in each case the extension was curtailed by legislation. Before the middle of the nineteenth century, moreover, the working day extending from 6 am to 6 pm returned to this industry.

The domestic trades adjusted their hours to their economic fortunes so that they were more variable than in other trades; and since their fortunes progressively declined during the first half of the nineteenth century, their hours became progressively longer. Yet even at their longest they were usually less, on a weekly basis, than those worked in the mills: indeed the difference was usually sufficient to provide a significant disincentive to move into the mills. There is evidence that the hours in these trades were rarely extended beyond sixty a week, though they were often very irregular. To the extent then that the industrial revolution represented a shift from the domestic trades into other forms of industrial organization it brought with it an increase in the number of hours worked.

In the coal industry hours had originally been short, at least for hewers, and it is probable that hewers' hours remained unchanged in the early part of the century. But in the 1830s this industry began to undergo some dramatic changes, and it was at this time also that the hours of work were extended.

This short summary emphasizes the danger of speaking of 'an industrial revolution', since it is clear that different industries underwent their 'revolutions' at different times. It is also clear that in almost every case rapid changes in the structure or in the processes of an industry led to or were accompanied by intense competition which at this time led to a pressure to extend hours. Thus this pressure was experienced by the textile trades in the last quarter of the eighteenth century, by the building trades in the 1830s, by the coal-mines in the late 1830s and the early 1840s.

The extent to which such pressure resulted in the actual extension of hours depended on the ability of the labour force to organize to protect its interests, and this tended to be least feasible when the changes in question involved a substantial geographic shift of the industry. This was the case with textiles in the late eighteenth century and coal in the second half of the nineteenth century, but not with such trades as bookbinding, printing and building. At the same time the pressure to extend hours could be eliminated by the employers, if they were in a position to restrict competition. This, too, was least feasible when an industry was undergoing a geographic shift. In either case, a change in hours became the more likely the lower were barriers to entry facing new competitors.

Chapter four
The course of normal hours: 1850 to 1890

1 Introduction

This period witnessed a substantial reduction in the hours of work. It was during these years, moreover, that the normal hours came to be explicitly defined in large numbers of collective agreements between employers and employed, though for some time past hours had been enshrined in the rules of the trade unions.

The first half of the period was dominated by the rise of strong, and in some cases national, craft unions whose ability to isolate their markets from the general pool of labour earned them the name of the 'aristocracy of labour'. It was these trades, dominated by the builders and the engineers, that were first able to induce their employers to sign collective agreements formally defining the conditions of employment, and including a definition of the normal hours. They were the same trades that had concerned themselves with the building of barriers around their labour markets, and with other such 'narrow trade interests', ever since the collapse of the general union movement in 1834. By the 1840s they had gained so much control over supply that they could begin to take an active interest in the reduction of the hours of work as the only 'permanent means of improving their position'. Hence it has been said that 'the whole point of the classical craft union was to keep the trade, and the entry to the trade, restricted'.[1]

The result was a continuing interest in the reduction of hours throughout the first twenty-five years of this period. This interest resulted in some minor changes in normal hours in the 1850s; some more significant reductions in the 1860s, concentrated in the building trades and, within the building trades, in the masons; and in a general and comprehensive reduction of normal hours in 1872-4, which included the vast majority of the unionized trades,[2] and therefore also the vast majority of the trades that had established a regular working week. Although the part of the labour force that might be defined as the aristocracy of labour would not have accounted for more than about ten per cent of the total working population excluding agriculture and female domestic service,[3] the changes in normal hours brought about at their instigation affected a much larger proportion of the working population, since all the lower paid employees in the industries dominated by the 'labour aristocrats' were equally affected by any change in hours. Nevertheless it is important to remember that what follows does not apply to the working classes as a whole.

This chapter and the one that follows will confine themselves primarily to a description of the nature and the extent of the changes in normal hours that occurred in Great Britain between 1850 and the present day. The analysis of these changes follows in the last two chapters of the book.

The dominant feature of the changes in the normal hours of work readily emerges as their discontinuity when they were determined by collective bargaining. Apart from examining these changes in hours on a macro-economic level, a detailed account of such changes in two of the major building trades will be presented for most of the second half of the nineteenth century. Even in this very decentralized industry changes were found to be concentrated in a few periods of great prosperity.

The years from 1875 to 1890 were dominated by a falling secular trend in prices which began just after the boom of 1871-3. The unions, which had grown and prospered during the previous period, were weakened by the depression of the late 1870s, and for much of the 1880s they were on the defensive, although most of them were able to obtain steadily rising real wages by keeping wages from falling as rapidly as prices. The last years of this decade saw the fanning into flame of the smouldering discontent of the unskilled who had been left without the means of representing their interests after the collapse of Chartism. They could not join the craftsmen whose whole policy depended on the exclusion of outsiders, and they could not copy them, since they had no one to exclude. By the 1880s two changes had made union activity by the unskilled more feasible. The conservative and moderate unionism that had grown up in the fifties and sixties had served to legitimize the union as an institutionalized expression of the interests of the workmen acceptable to the government; this acceptance resulted in the legislation of the 1870s which gave the unions legal protection. Secondly although the plentiful availability of blacklegs meant that the unskilled could still not threaten a long stoppage of work, the increasing capital intensity of many industries had conferred greater importance on the one threat of which they were capable, namely the temporary disruption of work through a withdrawal of their labour.

The years that followed were in many ways remarkably similar to those between 1830 and 1850 when the workmen had sought institutional channels through which to exert their influence in a changed environment, and had vacillated between industrial action, political action, and merely

legislative pressure within the existing system. They had then emerged
with the craft unions as the effective institution – albeit for only some of
them. Now they were to emerge with the industrial unions, the Labour
Party, and the industry-wide bargains of 1918-20.

2 Hours of work: 1850 to 1860[4]

Essentially this decade saw very little change in the normal hours of work,
as is made clear by figure 3.[5] What changes there were concerned the
shortening of the Saturday hours, save only that a very few masons in
Lancashire and the West Riding were able to establish a nine-hour day.

From our perspective, the period was dominated by three events. A
large engineering strike was lost; public interest in the issue of the
Saturday half-holiday revived; and the London building trades tried in vain
to establish the nine-hour day. Though little was achieved, it was not for
lack of interest in the issue by the unions.

We had left the 1840s with the craft unions poised to exploit their
position in the market by a reduction of hours. In the early 1850s they
continued to move in this direction, and it is not surprising that the
masons and the engineers took the lead.

By 1850 the London masons complained that many who had granted
the four-o'clock Saturday at their request in the late 1840s had withdrawn
it during the following years of slack trade and in 1851 there was a strike
of 1,500 masons against one employer who refused to concede the
privilege.[6] In December 1853 *The Builder* reported without qualification
that among masons the '4 pm Saturday (was) . . . recently introduced'. In
London the bricklayers were by this time in a position to take similar
action, and in the same year, 1851, they obtained the four-o'clock
Saturday, but only after a sixteen-week strike.[7]

Meanwhile the engineers had met at Birmingham in 1850 to condemn
systematic overtime and to pass a resolution to use 'all reasonable means'
to make hours of work uniform so that 'on subsequent occasions, if
circumstances require a further reduction in the hours of labour, such may
be accomplished without one district having to make greater advances than
another'.[8] In the following year they formed the Amalgamated Society of
Engineers (ASE); by December they had almost 12,000 members in 121
branches, and when polled as to whether the Society should take
immediate action on the question of hours the members voted 8,986 to 16
in favour. But before the Society could take action it was faced with a
lock-out, in January 1852, and was defeated to the extent of having to

accept the 'Document'.[9] Although the union survived it was cautious with regard to the issue of the hours of work for some time to come.

Shortly after this some events in the London building trades indicated that the demand for a wage increase might grow to overshadow the demand for shorter hours when prices rose as rapidly as they did from 1853 to 1855. Early in 1853 the London masons continued their pressure for reduced hours. In March it was reported that they had 'declared the practice of overtime injurious' and that 'after March 26th, 1853, all overtime must be paid time and a half, or abolished altogether'. It was claimed that the employers at once agreed to abolish it and that as a result 'many more masons are taken on'. In May this policy was pursued further when a committee was set up at the instigation of the masons, but including the carpenters and joiners, to agitate for the nine-hour day.[10] The movement was overtaken, however, by the price rises of 1853, which induced the carpenters to desert the cause because they 'preferred receiving an increase of wages'.[11] The event is corroborated by a description of it which appeared some years later and which stated that 'as to the advance of 6d per day, in 1853, the masons had commenced an agitation for nine hours' labour per day, instead of ten, and when the question was becoming ripe, some of the employers took the wind out of it by voluntarily advancing wages' which 'of course had the effect they anticipated, of setting aside the nine hours' question'.[12]

By 1856 the issue of shorter hours was once more prominent, but now it had ceased to be primarily a preoccupation of the craft unions. *The Times* letter column began to reflect an awakening of public interest in the issue. Lord Shaftesbury wrote to urge the adoption of the Saturday half-holiday and to warn that 'if Saturday were reduced to the condition of an ordinary working day' Sunday worship might be impaired, and his letter elicited replies from two large employers who highly recommended the Saturday half day. They had both adopted it — one as early as 1853 — and had found it beneficial to themselves and their employees.[13]

At a more practical level there appeared at this time a renewed enthusiasm for the traditional holidays. Hence in the same year of 1856 the Whitsun holiday in Lancashire was observed 'to an unprecedented extent', and there were reports of little work having been done in the industrial towns for five days of that week. In Leeds and Manchester 'the whole industrial population of these districts have been giving themselves up to holyday making and pleasure seeking to an extent almost beyond precedent' while in Leicester and Nottingham it was the feeling that 'never before, was enjoyment more unanimously participated in'.[14]

Clearly the prosperity of the early fifties had brought with it a substantial demand for leisure, and this reinforced the pressure for reduced hours being exerted by the craft unions for other reasons. The cause for this growth of the demand for leisure must be sought in the high levels of employment and the substantial wage increases of 1853-5. Although these had been more than offset by the dramatic price rises of the same years, the likely operation of a money illusion would make such a causal relationship plausible. A further cause of the increased interest in leisure, and in the Saturday half-holiday in particular, may well have been that it was now that 'the railways ... for the first time made cheap travel a reality for the poorer classes'.[15] While this became of importance only very slowly, it was significant enough to induce the bricklayers' union to hail the weakening of the sabbatarian spirit, since 'one great result of this change in public opinion is the cheap Sunday excursion in the summer season'.[16]

In Manchester and Salford the Saturday half-holiday which had been introduced generally in 1845 had certainly lapsed in the building trades by the early 1850s. By 1856 there had 'for some time' been a movement 'for shortening the hours of labour' and this movement 'began with the retail shopkeepers who had brought to their assistance the mayors' of the twin cities and had held public meetings over this issue. The masons had taken it up and had requested 'the Saturday half-holiday, as now before the public' in a memorial signed not only by them but also by the 'Bricklayers, Carpenters, Plasterers, Painters, Paperhangers and the Masons' Labourers'. The system was to begin on the first Saturday in March 1857, and many employers 'expressed themselves favourable to the movement'. In spite of this promising beginning the masons found it necessary to enforce their demand by a strike early in 1857, though the other building trades all obtained the concession without a strike.

This reduction of hours in Manchester called forth high praise from the Central Committee of the Masons, who stated that the 'Manchester members have signalised themselves as pioneers of a good work — that of shortening the hours of labour'.[17]

For the remainder of the decade there was a constant stream of applications for permission to strike to enforce reductions of hours. The great majority of these requests were made in conjunction with efforts to establish a recognized 'code of working rules' in the various localities. The need to define the hours of work formally in such a document led to many attempts to remove numerous practices which had grown up over the past years. In many cases this involved a return to the ten-hour day from one of ten and a half hours, either by increasing the meal times from 1½ to 2 hours, or by reducing the working day from one extending from 6 am to 6 pm to one extending from 6 am to 5.30 pm. At the same time there was a wide-spread adoption of the Saturday four o'clock closing, so that by September 1859 the Lincoln employers in conceding this to all their building trades could say that they did so 'because they believe that it is right, and in accordance with the custom of the country in most large towns and large mercantile concerns', and as early as 1857 Hull had demanded the concession 'in common with most towns in England'. Even so the four-o'clock Saturday was often combined with a 10½-hour day, so that in spite of the short Saturday the working week still extended over 61 hours.[18]

The adoption of 'codes of working rules', to which the employers were to agree, had been a novelty at the start of the decade. By the end of it they were common among masons. In 1849 the practice was so novel that the union explained to its branches that 'the employers and men of Manchester are subject to a printed agreement between each other for the regulation of the hours of labour'.[19] After this more and more lodges adopted them, and by 1857 the Central Committee warned that 'the question of lodges forming a local code of rules is one of very grave consideration, inasmuch as it involves sweeping demands upon employers'. Their appeal for moderation in this respect does not seem to have been effective, since two years later they complained that the codes so drawn up and 'thrust . . . upon the employers' . . . 'generally go to such an alarming extent, both in the reduction of time and the advance of wages' that too many strikes resulted.[20]

Meanwhile the interest in the Saturday half-holiday continued, although the successful introduction of the system was confined to a number of towns around Lancashire and Cheshire and to Scotland.[21] On the other hand a great strike for it in Newcastle-upon-Tyne, which incidentally preceded even the Manchester reduction, ended in complete defeat for the men.[22]

The strength of the demand for shorter hours can be gauged by the repeated refusals of the men to be 'bought off' by wage increases. An employer in the Newcastle-under-Lyme area offered six and a quarter days' pay for six days' work in response to a demand for a half-hour reduction in daily hours. He was told curtly 'that it was shorter working time they had struck for, and if he offered 5s per week advance in money they would not accept it'.[23] In Huddersfield the masons struck for the nine-hour day in 1860. They reported that 'ultimately the masters actually offered 1s per day in advance. However, we had resolved to have nothing less than the nine hours'. Not always was the line held that firmly. In Wakefield (Yorkshire) an offer of a 2s advance in wages had split the men and in the end some had gone back to work at the higher wages while others had insisted on the shorter hours. Even here however the men were 'not without hope that ultimately the shorter hours of labour will yet be the rule'.

The very great importance attached to the issue of hours at this time emerges time and again out of the trade-union correspondence. In 1858 the Hamble (by Southampton) lodge of the masons applied for permission to strike for higher wages. The Altrincham lodge opposed this request, explaining that they 'would much rather support the brothers of Hamble in trying to reduce their hours of labour, as that would be a greater benefit to them and to the society'.[24]

In this atmosphere it was not surprising that the demand for a nine-hour day reappeared in London in 1857. This time it was led by the carpenters, whose several separate metropolitan unions sent a petition requesting the nine-hour day to their employers. These had refused the request since 'the question, although raised by the carpenters and joiners, is really a question involving all trades' and they could not accede to the request 'looking at the very large amount of the interests involved, not only as it regards the building trades, but obviously even beyond these bounds'.

Meanwhile the London building trades continued their agitation of the issue 'with the aid of that powerful engine, the "public press" ', and by the end of 1858 they 'have effected a pressure from without on the mind of the public, so much so that the question is becoming popular'. According to the masons' Central Committee this public sympathy was confined to the Saturday 'half-holiday, (which) has especial precedence, with the public, over the "Nine Hours Movement" ' so that 'wherever its claims are advocated it generally meets with success'.[25] Their judgment was in a sense borne out by the events of the next four years in London which have been amply described elsewhere.[26] We can sum them up by saying that the nine-hour demand was not met, but instead the Saturday half-holiday was granted in return for the acceptance of payment by the hour. This *quid pro quo* was demanded by the employers in an effort to shift the burden of reduced hours on to the employees. One might almost term this a traditional reaction.

The insistent pressure for reduced hours by the building trades had led to a reaction by the employers. They had formed Masters' Associations,

both in the provinces and in London, and had attempted through these to
defuse the issue of the hours of work by introducing payment by the hour.
While the London masters were able to achieve this in 1862, the first
attempt to introduce the system in the industrial north failed. There the
masters had formed an association soon after the Manchester hours
reduction of 1857 and had almost immediately announced that from May
1, 1858 they would pay all employees by the hour. On April 30, 1858
strikes had occurred in over ten large centres simultaneously and the
challenge had been completely defeated.[27]

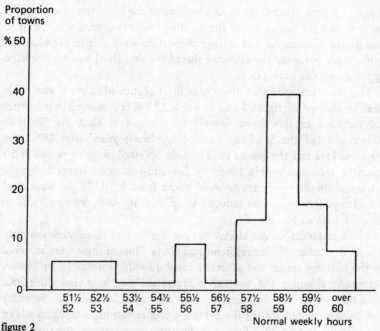

figure 2
England and Wales 1860: masons
Normal hours in certain towns
(unweighted per cent)
Source: *see* Notes to figures and tables

If this account of changes in normal hours should give the impression of a major movement it would be misleading. Figure 2 indicates for England and Wales the position of the masons in 70 towns and cities in 1860.[28] It is obvious that the great majority still worked ten- or ten-and-a-half-hour days, together with a four-o'clock Saturday and, in a few cases, a late start on Monday.[29] Even this overstates the proportion that had achieved shorter hours, because it is virtually certain that none of the towns not in this group had reduced their hours below the 58½-59 interval, although in Scotland a 57-hour week had been generally adopted among builders.

If this was the situation among the masons, who were the spearhead of the movement for shorter hours, what can be said about the other trades?

The other building trades shared some but not all of the reductions obtained by the masons, and although we know that they shared the reductions achieved in Scotland, Manchester and London (though this was actually not until 1862), there is no way of estimating their relative advance any more accurately. The part of figure 3, which gives the hours worked by general contractors in a number of major centres, does support the view that the experience of the building trades in general was similar to that of the masons, in that a large proportion were able to establish the four-o'clock Saturday though none shared the very short hours introduced by the masons in a few places.

That in other industries there was little change of hours is also made clear by the rest of figure 3 and by table 2.[30] A few changes in industries not included in this figure deserve brief mention. Thus the Sheffield cutlers adopted the Saturday half-holiday 'some years' after 1850; the brass workers and the smiths on Tyneside obtained working weeks of 59 hours by reducing weekly hours by five and two hours respectively; the Aberavon tin-plate workers reduced hours from 82 to 78 per week, and the Liverpool whitesmiths reduced their working week by two hours to obtain a week of 58 hours.[31]

These instances do not change the conclusion that this decade saw only a limited number of changes in normal hours. Most of these were achieved by the building trades and generally involved reductions of 1½ or 2 hours per week, although the Scottish builders achieved a general three-hour reduction. Only in Manchester was the adoption of the Saturday half-holiday shared by 'all the extensive and numerous establishments of workpeople' in that city. For their 'factory operatives and the operatives in the iron trades' it 'has long been enjoyed',[32] while the others obtained it during this decade.

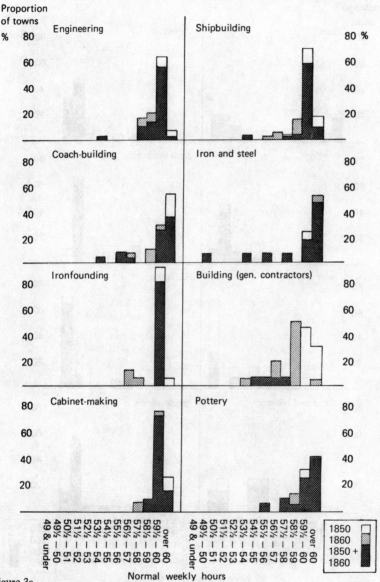

figure 3a
Great Britain 1850 and 1860: certain industries
Comparative frequency distributions of normal hours
(unweighted per cent of total sample of towns and areas)
Source: *see* Notes to figures and tables

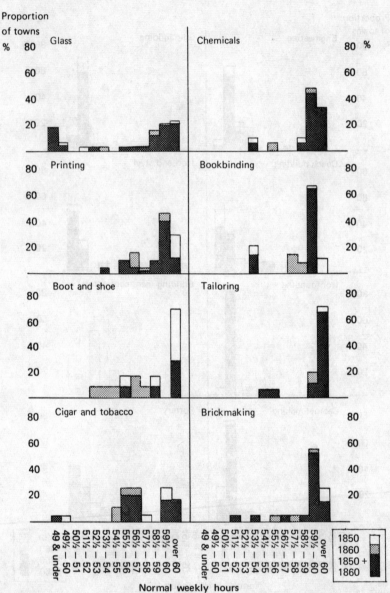

figure 3b
Great Britain 1850 and 1860: certain industries
Comparative frequency distributions of normal hours
(unweighted per cent of total sample of towns and areas)
Source: *see* Notes to figures and tables

table 2
Great Britain 1850 and 1860: average normal hours in certain towns and areas in
certain industries and percentage change in normal hours, 1850 as the base
(figures in parentheses refer to the number of towns and areas on which averages are
based)

industries	average normal hours		percentage change
	1850	1860	
engineering	59.5 (41)	59.4 (44)	−0.2
shipbuilding	59.9 (23)	59.4 (31)	−0.1
coach-building	60.4 (25)	59.9 (26)	−0.8
iron & steel	59.5 (15)	59.5 (15)	0
ironfounding	60.1 (14)	59.5 (16)	−0.1
building (general contractors)	60.1 (15)	58.1 (18)	−3.3
cabinet-makers	60.5 (11)	60.1 (12)	−0.7
brickmaking	59.3 (16)	59.0 (19)	−0.5
pottery	60.3 (17)	60.3 (19)	0
glass	56.5 (30)	56.9 (32)	+0.7
chemicals	59.9 (9)	60.2 (15)	+0.5
printing	59.8 (44)	58.9 (49)	−1.5
bookbinding	58.9 (9)	58.7 (14)	−0.3
boot & shoe	60.6 (6)	57.7 (11)	−4.8
tailoring	60.8 (14)	60.8 (15)	0
cigar & tobacco	57.6 (19)	57.4 (19)	−0.4

Source: see Notes to figures and tables

The reductions achieved by the coal-miners, on the other hand, were of
a different nature, since in most cases hours were reduced without a
compensating wage increase. Indeed any attempt to enforce the stint
where it was still nominally in existence became a matter of restricting
overtime − or to put it differently, of restricting each man to his stint. It
was therefore more in the nature of a share-the-work arrangement among
the men. Such restrictions were imposed successfully by the hewers of
South and West Yorkshire after a strike in which they had tried
unsuccessfully to gain a reduction of hours with a compensating wage
increase.[33] The same kind of adjustment was made to the hours of the
hewers of Northumberland and Durham, though their shift was shorter

than the eight-hour shift of Yorkshire, while in Staffordshire hours were reduced from 59 to 54 per week, or from roughly ten to nine per day, during this decade.[34] Meanwhile by 1856 the miners of the West of Scotland had once more induced most of their number to restrict themselves to one stint per day. Thus their masters complained in 1856 'that the men arbitrarily fix a day's work at what is termed a "day", an amount of labour which neither old nor young, weak nor strong, are permitted to exceed' so that 'the young man who can do his day's work in five hours is not permitted to earn more than the old man who takes nine or ten hours to perform the same amount of labour'. The practice was not universal, however, since in a 'few collieries . . . the men have had the courage to throw off these restrictions'. A strike in that year involved 40,000 men and lasted from March 8 until June 1, when it succeeded in reducing wages from 5s to 4s. This must have been a great inducement to more men 'to throw off the restriction "of the darg" '.[35]

In summary we can say that the pressure for reductions in normal hours came primarily from the building trades. The actual changes achieved were, however, of only moderate extent, consisting as they did mainly in the adoption of the four-o'clock Saturday; and they did not appreciably affect other trades or industries. In a few instances the introduction of the Saturday half-holiday was concentrated regionally rather than industrially and this reflected the existence of considerable public sympathy for this demand. In the most important case, that of Manchester, the heavy concentration of textile mills was significant since in these a Saturday half-holiday had been introduced by statute in 1850. The few reductions of hours in the coal-mines were 'share the work' arrangements rather than reductions of hours without loss of pay.

3 Hours of work: 1860 to 1870

This decade witnessed the beginning of a general readjustment of normal working hours. The actual reductions were more extensive, and affected a larger number of industries and a much larger proportion of the workers than the previous decade's changes had done. The concessions obtained by some individual trades, moreover, and most notably by the northern masons, were extensive.

The movement for shorter hours during this period was once more dominated by the building trades. The years 1860-1 saw the masons reap much of the harvest of their consistent pressure during the previous ten years, and among the advantages they gained were the first successes of the nine-hour movement. This pressure was interrupted by the slump of 1862, but was resumed with renewed vigour when that slump gave way to the boom of the middle sixties. It was during this boom that the demand for shorter hours was actively taken up by a number of other industries, whose activity led to the changes indicated in figure 4 and table 3. One noticeable result in most industries was an increased dispersion of normal hours, an indication that we have entered upon a period of transition.[36]

The activity of the masons in 1860-1 grew directly out of the events of 1859. Early in that year, while the London building trades were agitating for the nine-hour day, there came an extremely surprising report from the town of Todmorden, high up on the border between Lancashire and the West Riding, to the effect that a new lodge had been created there and that it was pleased to announce that 'the masons of Todmorden, together with their respective employers, are joined hand in hand, and are about to establish . . . a reduction in the hours of labour from ten to nine hours per day'. The Central Committee provided the only explanation: 'the success of this movement may be attributed to the co-operation of the employers', and indeed in this looking-glass world the employers had become members of the new union. The explanation must lie in the relative isolation of the Todmorden building market and an absence of competition between the master builders in this town. One of their motives may have been to forestall the rise of a militant union. The effects of their action spread like ripples on a pond, first to Oldham and then in early 1860, also without a strike, to Rochdale, Whitworth, Bacup, Heywood and other surrounding places. The rationale of the movement was made clear by a Rochdale mason who said that the nine-hour day was desirable to ease the physical suffering of the men, and in any event 'the pecuniary differences would not fall on the employers so much as on the capitalists'. The extent to which a reduction of the hours of work had come to be regarded as a panacea for all the ills of the workman is indicated by the fact that in these latter cases the workmen 'threw the question of wages aside and entirely left their case in the hands of the employers, whether they would maintain ten hours' wages for nine hours' work'. To the men in many other places it must have sounded like mockery to find out that in spite of this the wages had been maintained 'at the old rate'.[37]

By the end of 1860 the nine-hour day had been established in Huddersfield, in almost all of Bradford and in Halifax. What was surprising was that in these places the union was very weak − in Huddersfield, for example, only 58 out of 300 masons were members. The explanation was that on the issue of hours the union members could count on the support of the others. Indeed, after the Halifax lodge applied for support in

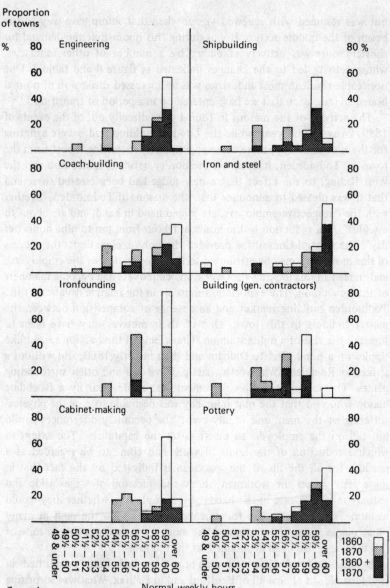

figure 4a
Great Britain 1860 and 1870: certain industries
Comparative frequency distributions of normal hours
(unweighted per cent of total sample of towns and areas)
Source: *see* Notes to figures and tables

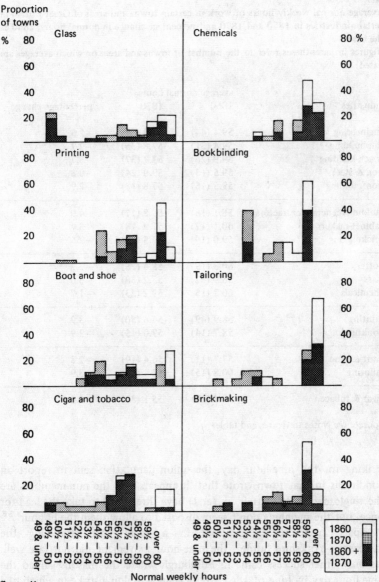

figure 4b
Great Britain 1860 and 1870: certain industries
Comparative frequency distributions of normal hours
(unweighted per cent of total sample of towns and areas)
Source: *see* Notes to figures and tables

table 3
Average normal weekly hours of work in certain towns and areas of Great Britain in certain industries in 1860 and 1870 and percentage change in normal hours, 1860 as the base
(figures in parentheses refer to the number of towns and areas on which averages are based)

industries	average normal hours 1860	1870	percentage change
engineering	59.4 (44)	57.9 (57)	−2.5
shipbuilding	59.4 (31)	57.8 (35)	−2.7
coach-building	59.9 (26)	57.7 (37)	−3.7
iron & steel	59.5 (15)	59.0 (24)	−0.8
ironfounding	59.5 (16)	57.8 (18)	−2.9
building (general contractors)	58.1 (18)	55.8 (17)	−4.0
cabinet-makers	60.1 (12)	57.9 (18)	−3.7
brickmaking	59.0 (19)	57.5 (27)	−2.5
pottery	60.3 (19)	58.4 (25)	−3.2
glass	56.9 (32)	55.2 (38)	−3.0
chemicals	60.2 (15)	59.2 (23)	−1.7
printing	58.9 (49)	56.6 (50)	−3.9
bookbinding	58.7 (14)	57.0 (15)	−2.9
boot & shoe	57.7 (11)	56.4 (19)	−2.3
tailoring	60.8 (15)	58.4 (18)	−3.9
cigar & tobacco	57.4 (19)	55.1 (30)	−4.0

Source: *see* Notes to figures and tables

striking for the nine-hour day, the union deputation sent to report on conditions in that town wrote that 'it appears that the non-members are the ringleaders in this affair ... (and) have threatened to take the lead for once, but the members don't seem disposed to allow them the honour'.[38]

Apart from these successes in a small area straddling the Lancashire-Yorkshire border, the nine-hour movement did not fare well. Its only other success came in Edinburgh where the masons gained the nine-hour day in June of 1861 after a general building strike in which 'the other trades all succumbed' and ended up 'still working the 10 hours'. The masons' success was possible, at least in part, because of 'a spectacular building boom and an extensive school building programme (which) made the trade position (in 1861) even more favourable than in the south'.[39] The only other major effort to obtain the nine-hour day was made in London and was entirely unsuccessful.

If this was the extent of the changes involving the nine-hour day, there were many other reductions of hours which involved the adoption of a Saturday half-holiday or of some other small advantage, like a Saturday four o'clock closing, an extra half hour for meals, a half hour less at the end of the day, or a late start on Monday morning. The introduction of the Saturday half-holiday was concentrated in Lancashire, where it was so extensive that by March 1862 the Southport lodge complained that 'we are almost the only town in Lancashire of any note that is not enjoying the benefit of either the half-holiday or the nine hours'.[40]

Outside the industrial areas of Lancashire and the West Riding the masons' hours were still 58½ or 60 per week, with a few instances of longer hours, of up to 63 per week. For the rest of the building trades the situation was similar, with the great majority still working a week of close to 60 hours. For them the exceptions were much less numerous and were confined to a few cities in Lancashire and the West Riding, which observed a Saturday half-holiday. Figure 12 gives the position of the carpenters in 1863, and may be deemed to indicate the state of the building trades generally.

There are few examples of reductions of hours being achieved in other industries during these two years. Only the tin-plate workers of Liverpool and Halifax were reported to have adopted the Saturday half-holiday in 1861.[41]

The year 1862 brought a severe recession, and this ended activity on the hours front, except that the London builders' strike and lock-out over the nine-hour day and payment by the hour, which had dragged on into 1862, was finally ended with the adoption of a 56½-hour week and payment by the hour.[42]

The unemployment experienced during the slump of 1862 only served to renew the pressure for reduced hours as a means of creating more jobs and of bringing about a permanent improvement in the condition of the workman. Frederick Harrison, the London labour lawyer, may have been overstating the case slightly but was not far off the mark when he said in 1862 that 'to shorten the period of labour is become almost the passion of the entire working class. By this means alone, they appear to think, can their position be permanently raised'.[43] Certainly this judgment would be corroborated by the frequent statements to this effect found in the Fortnightly Returns of the masons during the early 1860s. A typical contribution stated that a reduction of hours was 'the only remedy for the evils which prevail ... we view the advance of wages as a transient thing which flits away before a depression in trade. The shortening of the hours of labour, when permanently established, will equalise the winter with the summer, employ ten more men per hundred (thus employing our surplus hands), and will also give us more time to cultivate our mental faculties' which omits only one other widely held belief, namely that such a reduction will 'by creating a greater demand ... of itself bring an increase of wages'.[44]

When prosperity returned in the middle 1860s — and outside the textile trades it was a strong boom[45] — there was therefore a push for short hours which extended widely through the economy. Nevertheless, although most trades and areas were able to obtain some reductions, the numbers affected were a small minority of the whole labour force in each case. Yet the wide dispersion of the reductions achieved indicates the general nature of the demand for shorter hours, which by now seems to have extended throughout the economy. This same dispersion, however, makes a summary of the changes difficult, particularly since no obvious pattern emerges from the information that is available.

We shall simply attempt a summary of changes by industries. It both complements and confirms the general impression of the changes conveyed by figure 4 if we bear in mind that the figure's statistics overstate the extent of change in the aggregate because they over-represent the large centres in which hours were usually relatively short.

In the metal trades the major event was the failure of the engineering and shipbuilding strike in the north-east, to achieve the nine-hour day: the men had to return to work on the old week of 59 hours.[46] The changes that were effected in the metal-working sector all applied to specific trades or industries in specific areas and fell into three groups — the adoption of a Saturday half-holiday; the reduction of very long hours to 60 or something above that; and the winning of a nine-hour day. The first were all in Lancashire or the West of Scotland where the Saturday half-holiday was common, and affected the Clyde shipbuilders, the Liverpool whitesmiths and the coach-builders of Lancashire and Yorkshire. The second group affected the London boilermakers, the locksmiths of Willenhall and the tin-plate workers of Aberavon and Swansea, all of whom were able to reduce their very long hours though none could obtain a week below 60 hours. The third group affected only the smiths of Wednesbury, who obtained a 51-hour week, and some of the metal trades of Sheffield who obtained a 54-hour week.

The iron and steel trades of Staffordshire deserve some attention as the only example of a trade whose hours were increased during this period, going from 63 to 66 per week[47] although there is no information to indicate why.

In the coal-mines this decade saw the rise to prominence of the National Association of Miners and they concerned themselves from the beginning with the problem of restricting supply. Generally this was a matter of restricting output so that the 1863 conference resolved that since 'overtoil produces over-supply (and) low prices and low wages follow'[48] they would seek to gain an eight-hour day through legislation. This was to apply specifically only to boys, but the Northumberland and Durham miners who worked six-hour double shifts objected and suggested a ten-hour limit in an obvious attempt to protect their system. Apart from this 'special case' the demand seems to have been general among the miners. Nevertheless in this decade, in the coal-mines there were only a few actual reductions of hours, and where these applied to the hewers they were usually in the nature of share-the-work arrangements. Thus the Derbyshire hewers restricted themselves to eight hours per day, while the shifts of the other men in these pits were reduced to 10½ hours from twelve.[49] The men other than hewers in a number of Yorkshire pits, where the hewers had reduced or restricted their hours to eight in the 1850s, reduced their hours from ten to nine and in one case even from twelve to eight, while some reduction was also achieved in the pits of Lancashire and Cheshire.[50]

The printers and the bookbinders both began early in the decade to take an active interest in their hours. At the Manchester delegate meeting in 1861 the compositors had recommended that a reduction of hours should be sought, for 'other trades had not only raised their wages, but had shortened their hours of work, and the London Society of Compositors had often assisted them pecuniarily to do so': now 'it was high time that they should help themselves'.[51] By the end of the 1860s the bookbinders had achieved hours of between 54 and 57 in twelve provincial towns, while in London and all other towns the hours were still 60 or 63.[52] The printers were in a similar position. In 1865 the London Society of Compositors demanded a 58-hour week, but it settled in 1866 for a 60-hour week which represented a reduction of three hours, while the Lancashire printers were able to gain the Saturday half-holiday in common with many other trades in that area.[53]

In addition there were a number of small trades that obtained some reductions in hours. In every case it was a matter of obtaining the Saturday half-holiday — so it was, for instance, with the bleachers of Basford, the packing-case workers of London, and the silk weavers of Macclesfield, although these combined the half-holiday with an eleven-hour day.[54] The tailors began the slow process of organizing to improve the generally deplorable condition of their trade. In 1865 the newly formed Amalgamated Society of Journeymen Tailors could point to 16 of a total of 114 branches that enjoyed the Saturday half-holiday, but their subsequent efforts do not appear to have added greatly to this total, at least not south of the Border. North of it the tailors decided that the fact that their having had 'remained so long the longest worked and worst paid class of operatives, is entirely to be attributed to our want of union' and as a result they formed a union which adopted as its first resolution 'that 57 hours per week, 10 hours a day, and 7 hours on Saturday, be the recognized standard of working hours in the trade'. It appears that at this time the hours were twelve per day and sometimes more, and that an attempt to establish the ten-hour day had been made in Glasgow in the early 1850s but had failed. This time the tailors were more successful, and their second conference was called 'to inaugurate the shortening of your hours of labour' which had been achieved throughout the country. Their stated reasons for seeking shorter hours were identical to those put forward by the building trades. If anything there was an even greater faith in the working of supply and demand. Thus the Glasgow representative argued before the conference that for the reduction in hours to be achieved it had to be sought without a simultaneous increase in the wage rate. He stressed that this would be only a temporary difficulty, however, since 'supply and demand must regulate the price of our labour. And if our hours be shortened, the demand for our labour must necessarily be increased'.[55]

In spite of the extension of the hours movement to other trades the builders continued to be the most aggressive and the most successful exponents of it. Indeed their challenge became more powerful after the early 1860s because of the rise of strong trade unions to represent building trades other than the masons. The fact that the other trades could now provide substantial support to the masons in more and more areas greatly strengthened the movement as a whole as well as each trade within it. That this should be so is not surprising, but it is nevertheless interesting to note that previous changes in hours had been concentrated in areas where the masons had even earlier had such support from other building trades.

By the middle 1860s the only areas in England where the masons had achieved hours reductions, greater than those involved in the introduction of the short Saturday alone, were centred around Manchester and London, though the London area had lagged far behind in the establishment of these hours. Significantly, prior to 1860 Manchester was the base of the only strong building trades' unions that existed alongside the masons. Here the General Union of Carpenters and Joiners had been in existence since 1824. It extended through Lancashire, Cheshire and the West Riding of Yorkshire wielding a considerable influence. In time this was joined by the Manchester Order of Operative Bricklayers and the Manchester Alliance of Painters, in each case again the strongest organizations existing in these trades. This was at least part of the reason why the earliest successes of the nine-hour movement came in Lancashire and the border areas of Cheshire and the West Riding.

London lagged behind these areas partly because the other building trades could not give the masons any appreciable support until the end of the 1850s. Then in the early 1860s a number of new unions sprang up and in a couple of years the Saturday half-holiday was in existence. The most important of these new unions was the Amalgamated Society of Carpenters and Joiners (ASCJ) which was founded in 1860 and by 1864 had 3,279 members, an appreciable number at the time. These same years witnessed the formation of the National Association of Operative Plasterers and the United Operative Plumbers Association, which left only the painters without the beginnings of a viable trade society.[56]

If it is important to establish the connection between the rise of strong unions in the building trades and the success of the hours movement, it is equally important to point out the very important role played by the hours issue in making possible the establishment of these new unions. It has already been shown that it was recognized by the early unions that the hours issue was one in which they could confidently expect the support of the non-union men in their own trades. Therefore it is not surprising that as the non-union men repeatedly failed to achieve this desired end they saw the need for unionization. Hence the powerful new ASCJ sprang directly out of the protracted nine-hour strike of the London builders which had begun in 1859, and slightly more indirectly the same was true of the new bricklayers' and plasterers' societies. Such origins left their mark on the early statements and strategies of these unions. The First Annual Report of the ASCJ set out the aims of the society and in so doing pledged the society to the attainment of only one specific advance, namely 'to secure (the) reduction of the hours of labour, argued in the Preface to be our right'.[57]

With the rise of these new unions the hours movement scored numerous successes in the middle 1860s. Although the masons continued to be the most successful, the reductions now tended to be shared more completely by the other building trades and the entire movement managed to spread into entirely new areas of the country. By 1867, when prosperity came to an end, the building trades generally had achieved a significant reduction in normal hours. This had involved the introduction of the Saturday half-holiday into the large centres of the north and the north-east, the Potteries and parts of the midlands, as well as its extension in London. In many of the smaller places within these areas, and in most places of any significance outside them, the Saturday four-o'clock closing was introduced where it did not already exist. At the same time the carpenters obtained the nine-hour day in those areas of the West Riding and of Lancashire where the masons had introduced it at the beginning of the decade. The masons, on the other hand, were able to introduce the nine-hour day throughout Lancashire, the greater part of the West Riding (excluding only the south-eastern part including Sheffield, Rotherham and Doncaster), and Scotland;[58] they also managed to introduce the system into an entirely new area, namely Newcastle-on-Tyne.

In May of 1866 a general strike of builders had broken out in Newcastle, with the object of establishing a 50½-hour week. This had led to the formation of an employers' association which determined to introduce payment by the hour. After almost a year only the masons remained on strike, and the masters determined to settle the matter by a vote. The two alternatives they posed were a 55½-hour week with 30s or a 50½-hour week with 27s. The vote was held on condition that non-union men were to be allowed to participate, but in spite of this and in spite also of the fact that the 55½-hour week carried a slightly higher hourly rate, the vote was 401 to 21 for the 50½-hour week. Clearly the demand for shorter hours was very strong and not confined to the union members.[59]

The move to a Saturday half-holiday and the adoption of other forms of hours reductions are clearly visible in the part of figure 4 referring to building. Once more these figures exaggerate the actual changes because they refer to only a few large centres. The extent of this exaggeration can be gauged by comparing them with those given in figures 10, 11 and 12, which give the hours of masons and carpenters in a much larger sample. The comparison confirms the conclusion that figure 4, while not useful for indicating the actual magnitude of changes, does indicate the presence or absence of significant trends.

In 1867 the prosperity of the building trades came to an abrupt end, and with it for the time being most of the activity on the hours front. Early in the year the London masons had taken up the nine-hours issue once more, but after obtaining the Central Committee's permission to strike for this and for the abolition of payment by *the hour,* they confined themselves to a resolution at a meeting in October 'that all masons working for employers who are willing to give the nine hours accept it' while issuing a veiled threat to the rest of the employers. In December they resolved 'to leave the hours question in abeyance this winter' in spite of the fact that by then there were 870 masons working a nine-hour day with 740 still working ten hours.[60] The reason for this abrupt change of heart was the sudden decline in the prosperity of the trade. This was reflected in the drastic increase in the unemployment benefit paid by the ASCJ to its members. In the years 1864 to 1866 this had been between 1s 3d and 3s 5d *per capita* per annum. In 1867 and 1868 the comparable figures were 13s 2d and 13s 5½d.[61]

With the slump in trade the pressure for shorter hours ceased and the employers went over to the offensive. In 29 towns in the industrial north they presented their own 'code of working rules' which were to supplant those then in existence. One of these stated that 'all rules relating to reckoning of time and a quarter time etc, to be rescinded and in lieu thereof wages will be paid at the rate of 7½d per hour to efficient workmen'. This obvious attempt to nullify the effects of the reductions in normal hours was defeated by the unions everywhere except in Manchester, Liverpool and Birmingham. Here the employers were strongly organized, and these places lost their codes of rules. Though they retained their nominal working day it lost much of its significance.[62]

The slump which came over the building trades lasted to the end of the decade and into the 1870s, and doomed any attempt that might have been made to reduce hours. Thus the movement for shorter hours disappeared while the bricklayers complained of the loss of membership 'caused by the lengthened depression of trade generally throughout the whole country',[63] and a small London carpenters' union began its own little business to put its unemployed members to work.[64]

A list of the hours worked by various trades in London in 1870 confirms the picture we have outlined, with the majority of trades working 58½ hours or a ten-hour day with a four-o'clock Saturday, while some are still working sixty hours, and a few, mostly in building, have established a Saturday half-holiday. The list includes the following:

60 hours	Bookbinders (some), Printers (some), Locksmiths, metal flatters
57½-58½ hours	Bookbinders (some), Brassfounders, Coppersmiths, Engineers, pattern makers (iron), shipbuilders, smiths and fitters
56-56½ hours	Bricklayers, Carpenters, Painters, Engineers, Boot and Shoe, Printers, Tailors (women)
50 hours and less	Glass blowers, Plate-glass workers.[65]

In conclusion it should be noted that it was during this decade that the Factory Acts were extended to apply to factories and workshops outside the textile industry. Though they only restricted hours to 60 per week and applied only to women and children, they did establish for these employees a Saturday half-holiday, and this certainly had its influence on subsequent events.

4 Hours of work: 1870 to 1880

In 1870 the economy began to pick up and this upswing continued until it culminated in one of the greatest booms on record. With this boom came a general readjustment of the hours of work on a scale that had no counterpart in earlier years, and was to have none later until the end of the First World War.

The movement spread throughout the economy and brought substantial reductions to virtually all of the organized trades. Even the unorganized and the unorganizable were swept up by the events, so that in June 1872 there were 'strikes for more pay and fewer hours of work . . . spreading through all industrial occupations: miners, carpenters and joiners, flax-spinners, agricultural labourers, bricklayers, railway porters, gardeners and washerwomen are out on strike for this twofold object', while in May of that year at Leamington 'a crowded meeting of butlers, coachmen, footmen, gardeners and stablemen demanded shorter hours and more pay'.[66] While any reductions the domestic servants may have gained have gone unrecorded, the success of the organized industrial classes in drastically altering the map of the normal hours of work is not in doubt. By 1875 the normal week of from 54 to 56½ hours predominated, and in the industries where regular work had been introduced the nine-hour day[67] had replaced the ten-hour day in the majority of cases.

Almost all of the changes recorded in this decade were obtained in the three years 1872-4, and more of them in 1872 than in the two years following. Although the first reductions came immediately with the upswing in the business cycle in 1870 when the Glasgow carpenters obtained the nine-hour day already being worked by the masons,[68] the major move came from the Sunderland engineers, who announced at a meeting in March of 1871 that they were giving one week's notice before they would strike for a nine-hour day.[69] The strike duly took place and ended only in October of that year with an agreement which reduced hours to 57 per week immediately and to 54 per week from January 1 1872. This was less of a victory for the men than it seemed because during the course of the strike they had had to agree to a number of conditions which made their gains nominal, at least in the short run. On the one hand they had had to accept the new hours *at the old hourly rate of wages,* and indeed had turned down an offer of a 57-hour week with an advance in wages on the grounds that 'the "higgling of the market" would soon restore any reduction suffered in wages'. On the other hand the agreement stated that 'the men . . . agree to work overtime when and to the extent required by the employers' at the old overtime rates.[70] Whatever the men had hoped to achieve, they would not now achieve it in the short run, but they must have felt that the settlement would give them a stronger base from which to negotiate in future. Their preference for this agreement, even over the 57 hours with a wage increase, provides one key to their purposes. Their action makes sense if their dominant motive was fear of the future unemployment of their present membership, a point that will be elaborated later. Suffice it to say that under these conditions an immediate demand for leisure is not likely to have been the major motive of the men.

Even while the Sunderland strike was still in progress, and before it was clear that it would be successful, other trades had entered the arena. By August 1871 the Central Committee of the masons complained that 'premature striking has become the order of the day' and asked for restraint from the lodges,[71] while by the end of 1871 the carpenters had already established the nine-hour day in at least seven major towns.[72] By the end of 1871 the flood of agreements to reduce hours had begun, although almost all of the actual reductions came in 1872. By the New Year 'not one important firm in England withheld the promise' of the 54-hour week from its engineers, and this movement included 'all kinds of engineers . . . not only millwrights and turners, but all other kinds of engineering work as well, locomotive engineers, shipbuilding engineers, the mechanics about the mines, those who attended the textile machinery, and minor groups too numerous to mention'.[73]

By 1874 virtually the whole of the metal trades had followed suit. Thus the coach-builders announced that they were working 54 hours in 78 of their towns.[74] The same hours were obtained by the Sheffield metal-working trades, where 'in most branches hours had been reduced to 54 per week in 1866-7 and 1871-3',[75] and by the founders and moulders, for 'in 1873 English moulders had won a 54, and Scottish a 51-hour week'.[76] All the rest of the evidence relating to the metal trades is entirely consistent with these statements: in all but a very few instances they adopted a 54-hour working week at this time. The trend is clearly visible in the parts of figure 5 and table 4 that apply to these trades, namely those for engineering, shipbuilding, ironfounding, coach-building and iron and steel. It should be pointed out that henceforth these figures can be regarded as more representative of the trades in question, since most industries now provide information for at least twenty, and often as many as 50 centres; though with trades like building and tailoring, which are scattered over the whole of the country, even this number represents a small sample in terms of the number of towns, but since it includes the major centres the proportion of operatives represented is generally much larger.

The information relating to the smaller metal trades suggests that they also adopted the 54-hour week at this time. It was so with the boilermakers, the brass workers, the smiths, the whitesmiths and the tin-plate workers.[77] Two other trades achieved reductions of hours without establishing a 54-hour week: the locksmiths of Willenhall changed their weekly hours from 65 to 58; and the chain and nail workers reduced hours in three areas from 64, 63 and 48, to 60, 56 and 40 respectively.[78]

The only exception to this trend is once more to be found in the iron furnaces. As figure 5 illustrates there was a move towards 54 hours in this industry, but it was of a lesser magnitude and a good proportion of the trade continued to work over sixty hours per week. Indeed the hours of iron and steel workers in Staffordshire actually increased during this decade from 66 to 72 per week,[79] while the Ironworkers' Union proclaimed in 1872 that their success in curtailing Sunday 'fettling' in some areas 'was the first success in time policy in this trade'.[80] Clearly those working shifts on the furnaces did not come near attaining the 54-hour week; they appear to have been the only significant group of workers in the metal trades not to have shared in the general movement.

While the reductions achieved in the building trades were not quite as uniform and extensive as those obtained in the metal trades, they were still larger than any obtained in any comparable period before. While figure 5 suggests that in this industry the changes were largely a matter of towns

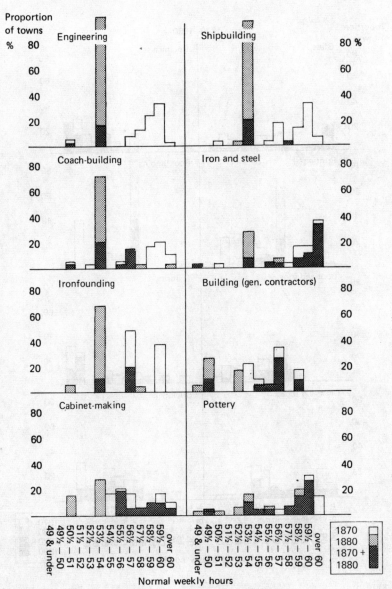

figure 5a
Great Britain 1870 and 1880: certain industries
Comparative frequency distributions of normal hours
(unweighted per cent of total sample of towns and areas)
Source: *see* Notes to figures and tables

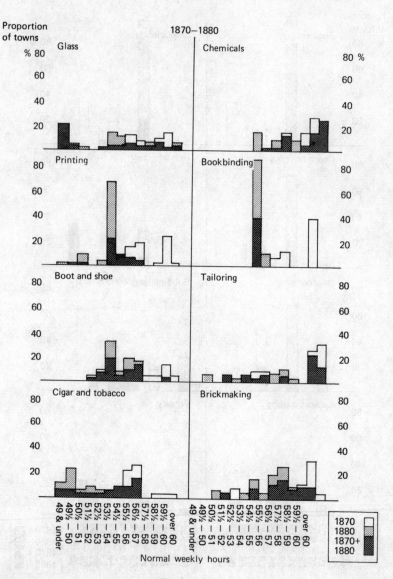

figure 5b
Great Britain 1870 and 1880: certain industries
Comparative frequency distributions of normal hours
(unweighted per cent of total sample of towns and areas)
Source: *see* Notes to figures and tables

table 4
Average normal weekly hours of work in certain towns and areas of Great Britain in certain industries in 1870 and 1880 and percentage change in normal hours, 1870 as the base
(figures in parentheses refer to the number of towns and areas on which averages are based)

industries	average normal hours 1870	1880	percentage change
engineering	57.9 (57)	53.9 (65)	−6.9
shipbuilding	57.8 (35)	54.1 (39)	−6.4
coach-building	57.7 (37)	54.8 (38)	−5.0
iron & steel	59.0 (24)	58.1 (26)	−1.5
ironfounding	57.8 (18)	54.5 (24)	−5.7
building (general contractors)	55.8 (17)	54.1 (18)	−3.0
cabinet-makers	57.9 (18)	55.8 (20)	−3.6
brickmaking	57.5 (27)	56.5 (35)	−1.7
pottery	58.4 (25)	56.8 (29)	−2.7
glass	55.2 (38)	54.0 (41)	−2.2
chemicals	59.2 (23)	58.4 (35)	−1.4
printing	56.6 (50)	53.9 (57)	−4.8
bookbinding	57.0 (15)	54.1 (19)	−5.1
boot & shoe	56.4 (19)	55.1 (32)	−2.3
tailoring	58.4 (18)	56.6 (29)	−3.1
cigar & tobacco	55.1 (30)	52.6 (32)	−4.5

Source: *see* Notes to figures and tables

that had been working a week of 54 to 55 hours now establishing a normal week of 50 or 53 hours, it is apt to be misleading in this respect because it is based on only 18 towns. The much larger sample of towns in figures 10, 11 and 12 in part 6 of this chapter show that the change in the masons' hours is very similar to that shown for building in figure 5, while that of the carpenters and joiners is from a bi-modal distribution with peaks at 56 and 59 hours, to a tri-modal with peaks at 50, 54 and 57 hours. For reasons which we shall discuss in part 6, the experience of the carpenters is more typical of the building trades as a whole. It should be noted that the figures of part 6 refer to England and Wales only. In Scotland the masons had established the nine-hour day and a 51-hour week by 1866, while the rest of the building trades obtained 51, and in a very few cases 54, hour weeks between 1870 and 1874.[81]

In general the building trades achieved large and widespread reductions of hours between 1871 and 1876,[82] though the great majority of them came in 1872-4. The movement was general throughout most of the country, and was known to be so by those taking part in it. Thus the ASCJ Annual Report for 1872 stated that 'the Carpenters followed the Tyne 9 hours movement all over the country', while in the same year the Builders' Trade Circular stated 'that the 9 hour agitation is spreading throughout the country and masters must make an attempt to meet it with uniform action'.[83]

These two sectors of the economy, the metal trades and building, contained most of the men who worked regulated hours, and could be said to have established these hours in some sort of bargain between themselves and their employers, although this 'bargain' did not always take the explicit form of the 'codes of rules' of the stronger building trades. But there were other smaller trades that worked on a regular basis and could exert some influence on the hours of work through negotiation with their employers. Naturally this was possible only where the hours to be worked were part of the contract of hire and where they had to be synchronized for groups of workmen. In many of these trades also, the nine-hour day was adopted at this time.

Chief among them were the printers and the bookbinders, both of whom were strongly organized, had agreements with their employers in many towns, and had shown an interest in the reduction of hours in the 1860s. Figure 5 illustrates the strong shift to the 54-hour week by these trades, and this is fully confirmed by other evidence. While in the middle of 1871 the bookbinders had hours between 54 and 57 per week in 12 provincial towns, by 1877 they worked between 54 and 55 in 39 towns including London, with four towns working less and only two more than this. Furthermore virtually all of these reductions came in 1872, so that by the end of that year 'the adult males were able to secure about 54 hours in most of the chief centres in the kingdom' and by March 1873 they worked between 54 and 55 hours in 17 out of twenty towns. While the progress of the printers was less spectacular, they also introduced the 54-hour week in the vast majority of their centres, and in London they, like the bookbinders, introduced the 54-hour week in 1872.[84]

There were few other trades in a similar position. The cabinet-makers, who approached it, secured reductions in a number of towns, and the coopers obtained the nine-hour day in most places.[85] The tailors who might have been included in this group did not have a strong union and their advances were few. In Scotland, where their new union had begun so hopefully in 1866 by enforcing the 57-hour week in its first year of existence, their efforts to maintain it had run into serious difficulties. In 1870 they had reported that 'a departure from the same (the ten-hour day) has taken place in many of the branches', and when in 1873 there was a motion to press for a 51-hour week, 'fifty-one hours being now the recognized period of a week's labour by most of the principal trades', the motion was defeated by 14 votes to 5 and it was decided instead to try to enforce the 57-hour week properly.[86]

In the textile industries, although regular hours were certainly worked, there were special conditions, including in particular the high proportion of women and children in the labour force — 75% in 1875[87] — that made organization of the trade particularly difficult. Industrial action in any case came up against the great economic power wielded by the employers. Nevertheless there were some relatively strong, though small, unions. They consisted of the adult males who performed certain kinds of work which women and children were not able to do. With these as its nucleus a movement for shorter hours had begun early in this industry. Indeed it had preceded the successful move by the engineers, reflecting the fact that prosperity had returned to the textiles industry by 1870. Thus numerous memorials for shorter hours were submitted to employers throughout Lancashire in 1870, and in April 1871 there had been a short strike in Oldham, which had however been quickly crushed.[88]

By 1871 the movement had turned its attention to Parliament which was an obvious alternative for this industry since the same high proportion of females and young people that made industrial action so difficult had proved legislation to be a feasible alternative. The widespread reductions achieved in other trades, the strength of feeling of the operatives, and the extent of public sympathy with the issue had made some concession virtually inevitable. Thus the suggestion of Mr Mundella, ever a champion of conciliation, that the search for shorter hours should be carried on through Parliament, 'rather than (that) the trade should be disturbed by a series of strikes'[89] must have been as welcome to the employers as to the operatives, especially since the former always preferred, if reductions of hours had to be granted, that all of them should be affected alike.

In any event the operatives kept up their agitation. Thus in 1872 there was 'a mass meeting of the Leeds flax operatives ... at which it was unanimously resolved to remain firm to the nine-hours demand and to accept no compromise'[90] and such meetings abounded and increased as 1873 wore on without action.[91] Then in 1874 an Act was passed to reduce hours in the textile mills to 56½ hours per week by extending meal breaks to two hours each day and shortening the Saturday by one hour. Although the operatives continued to demand a nine-hour day — i.e. a 54-hour week — the peak of prosperity had passed, and with it their opportunity of success.

The rest of the trades fell into two groups, those in which shifts were used, and those in which working was still mostly irregular.

In the first group we find such industries as the iron furnaces, the glass houses, the paper mills, the gas works and the chemical plants. On the whole there were no reductions in these trades, although there are a few examples of the introduction of an eight-hour shift. The most important of these was in the chemical industry of Newcastle-on-Tyne, where it was confirmed by an arbitration decision in 1875,[92] and in the tin-plate works of South Wales, which we have already considered. In addition, in some of the industries in which only a portion of the labour force worked shifts, such as that of glass, and the iron furnaces, those that did not work shifts were able to obtain the nine-hour day in many cases.[93] This accounts for the nature of the changes indicated for the glass industry in figure 5, where neither the very short nor the very long hours underwent any change, since these were for shift workers, while there was a readjustment over the central range, indicative of a shift from 58½ and 60 hours to 54 and 55 hours for the non-shift workers.

This leaves only the irregular trades, and most important among these were the domestic clothing trades, the pottery trades and the mines. A very few of the clothing trades were in fact able to obtain a 54-hour week. This was true of the lace dressers, as well as the bleachers and calico-printers around Nottingham and of a good number of the boot and shoe workers in the East Midlands and East Anglia, though this trade was still largely domestic. Otherwise the hours of the domestic workers still fluctuated with the state of trade, and when things were prosperous they were like the Worcestershire glovers in the first half of the 1870s who worked 'very much at their own discretion, but usually short hours'.[94]

The potteries did have nominal working hours and the changes in them are shown in figure 5, but the work was still extremely irregular. Thus a government commission in 1876 spoke of the potters rabbit racing Monday and Tuesday and then working the whole of Friday night, while a Board of Arbitration in that same year was told that 'we make it a rule amongst ourselves to work only four days (as) it is impossible to do six days' work (as) either one or another of the men would be off'. In view of these working habits it is not surprising to find the hours of these men varying with the state of trade in the typical manner of the hours of domestic workers. Thus in 1880 it was said that the potters 'by their manly determination to seek compensation for reduction in rates by increased diligence, have been enabled to earn the same, and in many cases higher wages than before'.[95]

The irregularity of hours in the coal industry led Bowley to the conclusion that 'there is no such thing as a normal week in the coal trade in the sense that there is a 56½ hours week in the textile or a 54 hours week in the engineering trades'.[96] It has been shown that this situation was due in part to the early introduction of the stint in this industry. This meant that the contract stipulated the amount of work done, rather than the amount of time spent at work, and this necessarily led to irregular hours. Although the stint had been largely defunct by the 1840s, it has already been pointed out that subsequent periods of prosperity had enabled the men in many instances to reimpose restrictions on their own hours. This meant that by 1870 there were many places where the hewers were once more working the stint, while there were others where they now worked regular shifts of varying lengths. The great diversity of practice in this industry was possible in part because of the intense competition between the large numbers of producers and also between the many different coal producing regions. As a result there was not the same pressure from employers to limit competition by standardizing the hours of work, nor were the men able to impose such uniformity, because their own unions were very much regional in nature.

In addition to the hewers the mines employed the so-called surface workers, whose labour did not lend itself to the stint and who had always worked standard day shifts of varying lengths, but often extending over twelve hours. The prosperity of the early 1870s created favourable conditions for the reduction of hours of all of the men, whether they were hewers working the stint, or hewers or surface workers on a regular day shift. Thus one finds that in the coal-mines too substantial reductions of hours took place at this time.

The hewers were able to establish the eight-hour shift, which had long been regarded as 'proper' for this job, in large parts of Staffordshire, Derbyshire, Nottinghamshire and Yorkshire, while an 8½-hour day was obtained in Leicester and a nine-hour shift in both South and North Wales. In the north-east many places adopted a 6½-hour shift and as a result 'questions of hours ceased to attract the men, who worked the shortest hours of any trade in the kingdom'. Gains for surface and other day workers were less spectacular, but a good number of them had their daily hours reduced to ten per day and in a few cases a nine-hour day was established.[97]

By 1875 the nation-wide recession was deepening and the movement for shorter hours was ended. The situation it left behind was entirely different from that existing at the beginning of the decade. Whereas then the overwhelming majority of trades had worked a normal week of 58½ to 60 hours with the few working a 56½-hour week, concentrated in the building trades and a few Lancashire trades, now the great majority of the trades working regular days had established the 54-hour week, with the exception of the textile trades which were working a 56½-hour week. The miners had reduced the hours for hewers to something between 48 and 54 in most cases.

This situation was described in some detail by a government commission of 1876.[98] It found the Saturday half-holiday to be all but universal. The textile trades worked the 56½ hours prescribed by statute. The nine- and the nine-and-a-half-hour day was common in the metal trades. Indeed in the commission's own words, in 'some of the most important, and notably in the iron and brass founding, machine making and other heavy metal trades, the so-called nine hours movement has been carried to a successful issue' although they add 'that it only recently took place, at a time of exceptional commercial prosperity' so that they are 'unable to form any opinion as to the probability of the nine hours movement being permanently maintained'.

The subsequent reports of the factory inspectors showed that the metal trades worked 54 hours in virtually all districts. Only the blast furnaces worked twelve-hour shifts — often seven days a week — while the tin-plate industry worked shifts of twelve or of eight hours. The 54-hour week was also dominant among the printers and bookbinders, though occasionally these were said to work slightly more than this. Hours in the potteries were less regular and of those in the West of England (29 potteries) we are told only that they 'scarcely ever exceed' ten hours a day, while hours in the glass trades varied from 45 to 60, the latter being rather rare. The paper mills without exception were reported to work two twelve-hour shifts. The workshops in the smaller industries worked overall days of 6 am to 6 pm or the same span beginning from 7 or even 8 am; it is not clear how much time was usually allowed for meals, whether 1½ or 2 hours, but a Saturday half-holiday was observed in almost every instance.

When the movement for shorter hours came to an end in 1875, the employers launched an attempt to regain some of the lost ground. As early as April 1875 the engineers in Staffordshire and at Barrow had to strike in order to retain the nine-hour day. At the end of 1876 the engineering employers gave notice of a general return to ten hours, but a resolute stand by the union, which announced that the principle was one 'for which the Society is prepared to fight any battle or make any sacrifice', prevented it.[99] In many other trades the experience was similar, with attempts to restore the longer hours that had ruled before 1872 foundering on the strong opposition of the workmen, who were invariably willing to sustain wage cuts in order to protect their working hours.[100] Nevertheless in a few trades hours were increased,[101] and this must be kept in mind in interpreting figure 5, which in showing the net change between 1870 and 1880 understates somewhat the actual extent of the reductions achieved during the first half of the 1870s.

Although only a few trades and places actually suffered an extension of their normal hours, these few instances, together with the general reversal of fortunes of the unions, gave rise to a general alarm. A speech to the Trades Union Congress in 1879 lamented that 'men disbanded from their Trade Unions in thousands. . . . They even suffered and made no protest against further reductions, and many, which made matters worse, worked a longer day for the reduced wage'.[102] Indeed, if one read only the reports of some of the building unions in the midst of the employers' offensive one would suppose that the losses suffered with respect to hours were extensive.

Actually, as we have seen, the building industry sustained its activity longer than the rest of the economy. As late as 1877 the London building trades went on strike for a fifty-hour week and an increase in wages, though some of the smaller unions warned that the movement was inopportune 'on the ground of the depression of trade'.[103] The advice should have been heeded, for by March 1878 the strike had been 'utterly lost' and the unions seriously weakened. As a result they were in no position to meet the employers' challenge when these gave notice in many towns in November 1878 that there would be wage reductions and increases in hours early the next year. Indeed by January the masons' society, traditionally one of the strongest, had to declare all strikes closed as its funds were exhausted and the men had to 'submit to reductions of wages and increases of hours all over the country'. The plumbers too reported that between 1878 and 1882 'every advantage was taken by employers to increase the hours of labour and reduce the wages'.[104]

In spite of these drastic reports it appears that the actual extensions of normal hours which occurred during these years was of no great consequence. Figure 8 shows that of more than 300 lodges of the ASCJ only sixteen suffered increases of normal hours between 1878 and 1881. Other evidence shows that for the masons, for example, few towns were affected by increases of hours – only 29 among more than 200 – and that in most cases the increase was a matter of ½ to 1½ hours per week.

On balance in all those reported cases of 'reductions of wages and increases of hours' there tended to be much of the former and little of the latter. Thus we are told that the attempts of the National Association of Master Builders, formed in 1878, 'to lengthen hours were largely forestalled by agreements to reduce wages'. It is likely that many of these trades had experiences similar to those of the slaters, whose union, based in Manchester, broke up in the last half of the 1870s and who as a result suffered wage cuts and lost many privileges, including their right to 'walking time'. Yet 'the time was fairly maintained at 54 hours (with) only a few infringements, (although) working hours were entirely abolished and men were often put on short time'.[105]

5 Hours of work: 1880 to 1890
From our point of view the dominant feature of this decade was the absence of any significant reductions in normal hours. For most of the period including the boom of 1881-2 the old craft unions were still suffering from the setbacks of the end of the 1870s, while the unskilled had not yet been able to organize effectively. It was only with the return of prosperity at the end of the decade that any reductions were achieved, and even these were extremely few.

If there were few actual reductions of normal hours at this time it was not because of a lack of interest in the issue by the working-men. The decade saw the rise of a 'new unionism' of many of those who had not been able to establish themselves among the labour aristocracy of the previous twenty-five years and including many of the unskilled. Since it is clear that the relative position of that 'aristocracy' depended on its exclusion of outsiders and its ability to restrict supply within a protected labour market, it is significant that the 'new unionism' sprang up among the 'excluded' after the success of the organized trades in reducing their hours and that 'the demand for a legal eight hours' day' became 'the test issue between the parties' at the Trades Union Congresses.[106]

From the beginning of the decade socialist thought had been on the rise and with it had come a greater familiarity with the eight-hour day, which had been advocated by both the First and the Second Internationals. By

1890 the issue had become dominant among the trade unions and a number of great public meetings were held in London in support of this issue.[107] In spite of the intense agitation and in spite of 'the rising and organisation for labour purposes of classes of the working population never previously organised', which commenced 'during the latter part of 1888' and which 'spread with a force and quickness never before equalled',[108] the eight-hour movement achieved its only significant success in the gas works where 'from 20,000 to 30,000, in different parts of the country, had obtained the eight hours day'.[109] At least in London this was combined with a 54-hour week for non-shift workers.[110] While these reductions had caused little friction, there was a great deal of dispute in this industry at this time over the question of non-union labour, indicating that the 'new unionism' had learned from their predecessors in the craft unions that a reduction of hours must be combined with the erection of barriers around the trade, if it was to improve the economic position of those in it.

The key to the understanding of the conflict between the new and old unionists lies here. What the new unionists were ultimately trying to prevent was precisely this reaction by the gas workers — though they would and could not have opposed it openly in any particular instance. It was not their aim simply to elevate a few small groups of workers into the 'aristocracy' by enabling them through organization to differentiate their market sufficiently to make the effective restriction of supply feasible. This, coupled with their recognition that unionism in the unskilled sectors would always be in a weak bargaining position, in spite of the impressive numbers that had been organized, led them to demand the restriction of hours by legislation. Their position was summed up in a resolution of the London International Labour Congress of 1888, which stated that 'owing to the concentration of capital, and the relative weakness of trade unions in proportion to the number of workers, it is impossible to further reduce the hours of labour without the aid of the State, and that in every case eight hours should be the maximum number of hours worked'.[111] Their preoccupation with the issue of hours, finally, reflected the fact that while competition could and did allow the unorganized to share to some extent in the growth of the economy through rises in their real wages, it did not take a similar effect by way of shortening their hours. This could be achieved only through the exertion of institutional pressures either in the industrial or in the political arena. Once again the issue of reduced working hours appears as an important stimulant to trade-union growth.

On the whole it is possible to state with some certainty that the normal

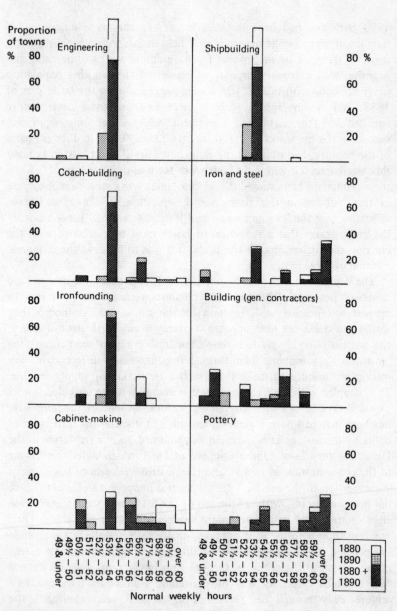

figure 6a
Great Britain 1880 and 1890: certain industries
Comparative frequency distributions of normal hours
(unweighted per cent of total sample of towns and areas)
Source: *see* Notes to figures and tables

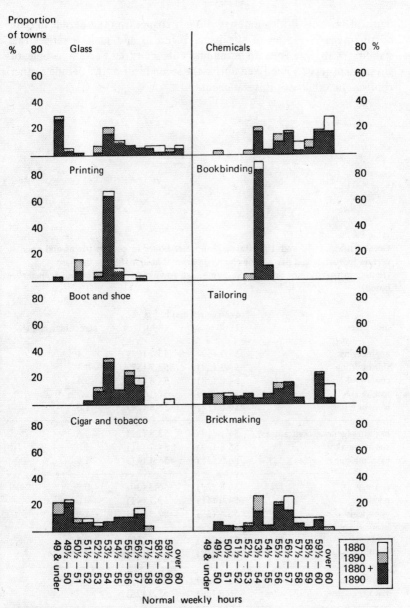

figure 6b
Great Britain 1880 and 1890: certain industries
Comparative frequency distributions of normal hours
(unweighted per cent of total sample of towns and areas)
Source: *see* Notes to figures and tables

hours of work of British industry did not change over this decade in spite of an intense agitation of the issue. Figure 6 and table 5 reflect this stability with reference to a number of industries, and a couple of government reports published during the second half of this decade further confirm the validity of this statement.

table 5
Great Britain 1880 and 1890: average normal hours in certain towns and areas in certain industries and percentage change in normal hours, 1880 as the base
(figures in parentheses refer to the number of towns and areas on which averages are based)

industries	average normal hours 1880	1890	percentage change
engineering	53.9 (65)	53.7 (67)	−0.4
shipbuilding	54.1 (39)	53.7 (57)	−0.7
coach-building	54.8 (38)	54.6 (42)	−0.4
iron & steel	58.1 (26)	57.1 (30)	−1.7
ironfounding	54.5 (24)	53.6 (24)	−1.6
building (general contractors)	54.1 (18)	53.8 (22)	−0.6
cabinet-makers	55.8 (20)	54.7 (21)	−2.0
brickmaking	56.5 (35)	55.4 (41)	−1.9
pottery	56.8 (29)	56.3 (30)	−0.9
glass	54.0 (41)	53.7 (41)	−0.6
chemicals	58.4 (35)	57.3 (39)	−1.9
printing	53.9 (57)	53.6 (59)	−0.6
bookbinding	54.1 (19)	54.1 (19)	0
boot & shoe	55.1 (32)	54.9 (35)	0.4
tailoring	56.6 (29)	55.9 (28)	1.2
cigar & tobacco	52.6 (32)	52.4 (35)	0.4

Source: *see* Notes to figures and tables

Thus in 1886 the engineers and the machine makers worked a 54-hour week, although a 'very few' were still working 56½ and even 58½ hours, reflecting undoubtedly the slight losses sustained during the 1879 depression. In iron and steel shipbuilding the hours were 54, while in brass and metal ware they ranged from 51 to 55½ with '54 being most general'. Other trades which worked 54 hours throughout were the railway carriage builders, the boot and shoe trades, the printers and compositors, and the coopers. Those in chemical manure worked 54 to 60 hours, while the hours for those in brickmaking are reported as from 50 to 60, and for those in the tin-plate industry from 52 to 60. The only industry not working a normal week of around 54 hours was pig iron. Here the men on the furnaces worked twelve-hour shifts for seven days of the week in almost all cases, while the others not on the furnaces or working shifts, worked between 51 and 62 hours per week.[112]

As this summary indicates, normal hours in these manufacturing industries had not changed since 1875. The same was true of the textile industries which, of course, had their normal hours prescribed by statute. There is no doubt about the adherence of the cotton and woollen industries to the 56½-hour week, and a survey of hours in the minor textile trades in 1886 shows that this sector, which was estimated to employ about 220,000 people, also worked a normal week of 56½, or in some cases 56, hours. The only exceptions were for the Leek silk workers, with 54 hours, and the Nottingham hosiery and lace workers, who had between 50 and 54 hours.[113]

Figures 10, 11 and 12 show that in the building trades normal hours remained stationary from the end of the 1870s to the end of the 1880s. The slight increases in hours which these figures show were those suffered during the 1879 depression.

The position in the coal-mines is more difficult to summarize because of the great disparity in hours and the varying length of the working day depending on whether it is 'bank to bank' or not. A report of 1886 shows the hours for various groups and areas. The hours given here for men working underground were those worked at the face. For hewers, hours were shown as between eight and nine per day in all areas, except for Northumberland and Durham where they were but 36 to 40 per week. Most other areas in fact worked between 46 and 51 hours, but the whole of Wales and most of the Midlands worked about 54 hours.[114] Underground workers other than hewers worked 54 hours in all areas except Cumberland, Yorkshire, North Staffordshire, Somerset and the Forest of Dean, and the East of Scotland; here they worked about 48 hours, while in Northumberland and Durham their hours were from 55 to 60. For surface workers there were only two areas which did not work a 54-hour week in general, namely Northumberland and Durham where hours were 55 to 60, and North Staffordshire, where they were 48.

This picture is confirmed by figure 7, which is based on the returns from more than 700 pits in Great Britain but excludes Northumberland and Durham. The dominance of the eight- and nine-hour days is apparent.

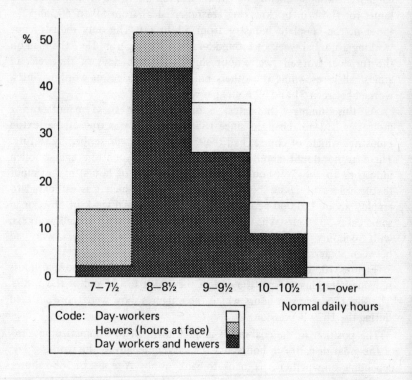

figure 7
Great Britain (except Northumberland and Durham) 1890: coal-mining
Frequency distribution of normal hours
(number of pits as per cent of total sample)
Source: *see* Notes to figures and tables

table 6
Great Britain 1890: coal-mining (daymen)
Regional distribution of normal hours
(figures in parentheses refer to the number of pits in the region for which data was available)

region	number of pits with normal hours of										average normal hours
	7	7.5	8	8.5	9	9.5	10	10.5	11	11.5 or more	
Lancashire & Cheshire (167)	1	1	20	12	63	16	42	9	–	3	9.3
Yorkshire (121)	–	2	63	9	38	2	5	2	–	–	8.5
Derbyshire (68)	–	–	17	18	20	9	4	–	–	–	8.7
North Stafford-shire (36)	–	–	18	13	3	1	–	–	–	1	8.4
South Stafford-shire (50)	–	–	46	–	2	1	1	–	–	–	8.1
Somerset & The Forest of Dean (36)	3	5	21	1	–	1	4	–	–	1	8.2
Bristol (10)	–	–	2	–	–	–	1	1	3	3	10.6
Leicestershire (33)	–	–	4	13	13	1	2	–	–	–	8.8
Cumberland (16)	–	–	8	2	4	–	2	–	–	–	8.6
North Wales (20)	–	–	3	4	9	1	3	–	–	–	8.9
South Wales (91)	–	–	1	7	46	15	17	5	–	–	9.3
Shropshire (5)	–	–	3	1	1	–	–	–	–	–	8.3
Warwickshire (17)	–	–	17	–	–	–	–	–	–	–	8.0
Scotland (30)	–	1	4	1	7	12	–	–	–	–	9.3

Source: *see* Notes to figures and tables

An indication that these hours 'at the face' varied considerably from those from 'bank to bank' comes in 1890 from the Mine Owners' Federation, which answered a demand for an eight-hour shift from bank to bank by saying among other things that such a system would reduce output, because 'the usual practice in the Midland Counties, Lancashire and Cheshire, and North and South Wales is to work a single shift' and 'to wind coals from 8 to 10 hours. If every person employed underground is to be drawn out within eight hours of the time he goes down, it is manifest that coal winding cannot be carried on for more than 6½ to 7 hours'.[115]

It is clear from this that the men are wound down and up before and after coal has been wound for 8 to 10 hours so that usually winding times must be added on to the hours worked at the face to get an estimate of hours from bank to bank.[116] The total time taken to wind a man up and down varied from five to 120 minutes and the average for over 700 pits in 1890 was 37 minutes.

It is interesting to note that the differences in hours worked in various pits were not offset by the differences in winding times. Thus the 76 pits whose winding times were fifteen minutes or less did not on average work longer hours at the face (8.41 hours) than the 150 pits that had winding times of 60 minutes or more (8.46 hours).

Table 6 shows the regional differences in normal hours of day-workers in 700 pits. It appears that the longest hours were worked in Lancashire, Wales and Scotland, though for Scotland there are relatively few figures. Bristol appears to have the longest hours but this is based on only ten pits. On the whole the differences between areas continue to be considerable.

In so far as we have comparable data for the hours in the mines at the end of the 1870s, it appears that no great changes in hours took place during the 1880s, and this indeed must be our conclusion for the labour force as a whole during this decade.

6 Hours of work in the building trades: 1860 to 1895

The preceding general description of the changes in the normal hours of work has brought out the extreme discontinuity of such changes on a macro-economic level. As it is at this level of aggregation that this pattern of change is most unexpected and most in need of explanation, it was deemed useful to complement this picture with a detailed analysis of the changes which took place during this same period in the building trades.

The choice of the building trades was based on a number of considerations, not the least of which was the availability of a surprisingly complete set of statistics. But apart from this the industry suggested itself on account of the leading role which it played throughout this period in the movement for shorter hours. Since it had achieved by far the most significant reductions of hours before 1872, its changes in hours would almost certainly be least discontinuous. Any discontinuity found in this industry, therefore, would serve to emphasize the extent of this phenomenon in the economy in general.

Once the general pattern of hours reductions in this industry has been established, the significance of any regional or occupational differences which may have persisted in its normal working hours will be investigated.

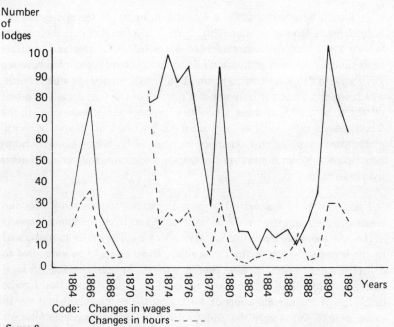

figure 8
England and Wales 1864-1892: number of lodges of Amalgamated Society of
Carpenters and Joiners obtaining changes in basic weekly wages and in normal hours
of work
Source: *see* Notes to figures and tables

In order to determine the frequency of changes in normal hours among
carpenters, figure 8 gives the number of lodges in England and Wales that
changed their weekly hours in every year from 1864 to 1892, as a
percentage of the total number of lodges in the Society. In order to
determine whether the apparent wide fluctuations in this measure have
any significance apart from reflecting the state of trade and the mechanics
of the bargain, they have been compared with a similar series showing the
proportion of the Society that was affected by changes in the weekly wage
rate in any one year. The result shows clearly that changes in normal hours
are included in only a minority of agreements, implying that most
agreements concerned themselves only with changes in the wage rate. The
changes in hours can also be seen to be more discontinuous than those in
wages in the sense that the one year with the greatest number of changes
in hours, 1872, accounted for 22 per cent of the total number of such
changes between 1864 and 1889, while for wages the corresponding figure
is only 10 per cent.

It should be noted that the actual discontinuity of the changes in the normal hours is even greater than figure 8 suggests, because the changes around 1872, and those around 1865-6, tended to be large and to affect both summer and winter hours, while of the 75 changes recorded between 1879 and 1889 more than 50 involved only small changes in winter hours, which were in force for only about a quarter of the year. In addition half of these latter 75 changes involved a proportionate reduction of the weekly wage rate, so that they must be regarded as 'share the work' arrangements, while the changes around 1872 were almost always accompanied by an increase in the weekly wage rate, and certainly never by a reduction.

Figures 9 to 12 elaborate this general pattern, with statistics for the masons and the carpenters. These were collected from the annual reports of the ASCJ and the Operative Society of Masons. They refer in most cases to the hours set down in the union rules. These came to be embodied in collective agreements in due course, though in the absence of legal sanctions the collective agreement afforded no greater protection for the definition of the normal hours of work than the union rules had done. In either case it was simply the ability of the union to protect its interests that prevented any change.[117]

Since detailed figures as to the number of masons or carpenters in each town are not readily available, and would in any event fluctuate considerably, weights have been attached to the statistics on normal hours, on the basis of the population of each town in 1871.

Figure 9 shows the movements in the first and third quartiles, and the median and mode, of the normal hours of the masons. The substantial movement in all three of these measures over the years 1872-4 indicates that the changes in this period affected all parts of the trade and reduced hours in general by about four per week. The fact that in 1867 the quartiles already lay between the relatively low figures of 55 to 57 hours reflects the previous success of the masons in obtaining reductions of hours. An extension of this series back over time would show a shift of the inter-quartile range to about 57-60 in 1865-6, and about 59-60 in 1860, but firm data for large numbers of towns are not available for this earlier period. The extension of the inter-quartile range to four hours, after 1874, indicates a good deal of dispersion in hours in this trade, which in itself must be expected to provide an incentive to reduce hours for those lagging behind.

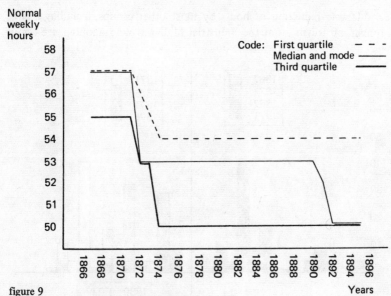

figure 9
England and Wales 1867-1895: masons
Quartiles of frequency distribution of normal hours
(weighted by population at 1871 census)
Source: *see* Notes to figures and tables

Figure 10 breaks this situation down further and shows the frequency distribution of normal hours for masons at several points in time just before and after periods of some change. It emerges from these figures that 1867-71 was a period of no change, 1876-89 a period of some slight extension of hours, while 1871-7 and 1890-5 were periods of hours reductions. The shape of the distributions reflects the considerable regional differences that existed. The group of values around 50 hours in 1867 is made up entirely of the few places in Lancashire, Cheshire and the West Riding where the masons had introduced the nine-hour day with a short Saturday in 1860-1 and 1864-6. The growth of this group in 1877 was due to the extension of the nine-hour movement in the above areas, as well as its extension into the north-eastern industrial district, while its dominant position after the early 1890s was due entirely to the adoption of this system by the London builders in 1890-1. The other groups in the distribution are dominated by the experience of the London masons, who reduced their hours to 52½ in 1872-3 and then to 50 in the 1890s. While the London reduction accounts for virtually the whole of the change recorded in the first half of the 1890s, the period from 1871-7 saw a considerable reduction of hours by most other groups, including a large number of towns from the industrial Midlands who adopted a 54-hour week.

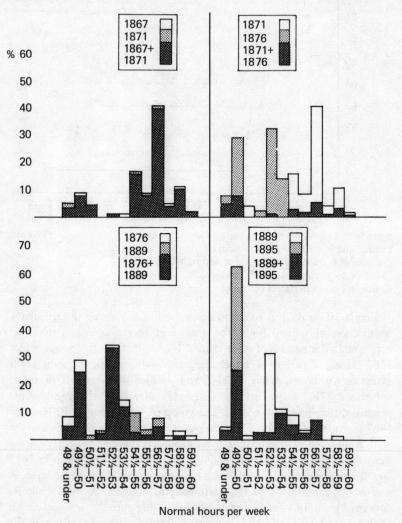

figure 10
England and Wales 1867-1895: masons
Comparative frequency distributions of normal hours
(per cent of sample weighted by population at 1871 census)
Source: *see* Notes to figures and tables

Because of the extent to which the experience of the London masons obscures other trends in figure 10, and in order to determine whether there were noticeable differences between hours in very large cities and other places, the hours of cities of a population of over 100,000 and of all others have been presented in separate frequency distributions in figure 11. The result shows that the changes in the towns with a population of under 100,000 came almost exclusively during the period 1871-7, but that on the whole the changes experienced by the two groups were very similar.

This finding raises a difficulty, since it is possible that the similarity of these results is determined to a considerable extent by the fact that the large cities tend to dominate the country around them, and that the lodges of the unions tended to concentrate in these same areas. To the extent that the members of the trade were also concentrated in these same areas the significance of the results is not impaired, but it is also true that these figures tell us little about the hours in totally unrepresented rural areas.

Figure 12 presents the hours of carpenters and these show that the experience of the building trades in general was similar to that of the masons, except that at every stage the masons were somewhat in advance of the others in terms of short hours. The hours of work of the carpenters are the most representative of the building trades as a whole because, as will be shown later, they always occupied a middle position between the short hours of the masons and the longer hours of the bricklayers, and also because their figures are drawn from as many as 300 different towns distributed over the whole of England and Wales.

Some interesting points emerge from a comparison of the hours of masons and carpenters. Both series exhibit the same basic patterns, with some changes occurring in the middle 1860s and the early 1890s while by far the biggest reductions took place in the early 1870s. This pattern was general to the industry and reflected the experience of the economy as a whole. An interesting difference that emerges is the complete absence by 1867 of any towns where carpenters worked a week of 50 hours or less. The fact that the masons had already achieved these hours in a number of towns emphasizes the extent to which that trade was the spearhead of the hours movement within the building trades, although in subsequent years the carpenters made good much of this early difference.

This continued difference between the hours of the masons and carpenters was, however, smaller than it appears and may indeed be entirely a statistical illusion. While there is no doubt about the early differences, the later ones are due in part to the fact that different weighting systems were used for the figures of the two trades, with the

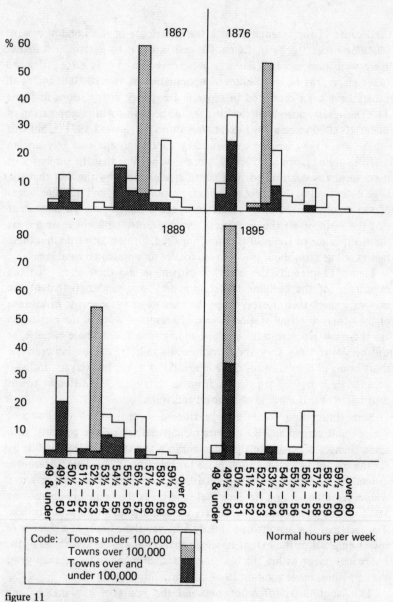

figure 11

England and Wales 1867-1895: masons

Comparative frequency distributions of normal hours in towns of over and under
100,000 population

(per cent of total in each group weighted by population at 1871 census)

Source: *see* Notes to figures and tables

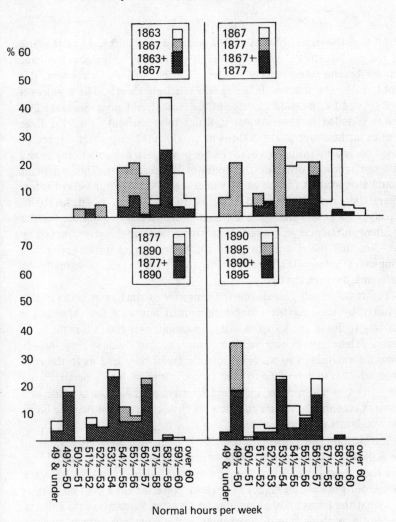

figure 12
England and Wales 1863-1895: carpenters
Comparative frequency distributions of normal hours
(per cent of sample weighted by population at 1871 census)
Source: *see* Notes to figures and tables

result that the largest centres exert a greater weight in the aggregate figure of the masons than they do for the carpenters. Since hours in the large centres became progressively shorter compared to hours elsewhere, this would make the masons' hours appear relatively shorter. The problem is exacerbated by the wide coverage of the carpenters' figures. Since the 200 towns included in the masons' statistics took account of all the large centres in the country, the 300 towns on which the carpenters' figures are based necessarily included a much higher proportion of smaller centres and this too tends to overstate the hours of the carpenters. This last point would also account for the continued existence of large numbers of towns where the carpenters worked from 54 to 56½ hours as late as 1890. Finally, the belief that these difficulties are largely responsible for the apparent differences in hours between these two trades is strengthened by the fact that when one compares the hours worked in towns with a population below 100,000 by these two trades there is virtually no difference between the two.

Figure 13 merely rounds out the summary of changes in hours in this industry by showing the changes in normal hours of the three major building trades in the six cities with populations over 200,000 at the 1871 census. These figures require little comment, but because they include some information as to the hours of bricklayers they lead us to the next issue, which is to determine to what extent it is possible to generalize from the figures of the masons and the carpenters to the building trade as a whole. Certainly the figures for these six large cities suggest that the hours for bricklayers were comparable.

The masons and carpenters together comprised a large proportion of the skilled labour force in building — probably close to 50 per cent[118] so that their hours alone would be an important element in any aggregate average for the building trades as a whole. Nevertheless it is of interest to find what the hours in other building trades were. Since complete series of figures are available only for carpenters and masons our estimates of the others' hours are based on references as to the length of their hours relative to those two series. All such incidental evidence for the hours of the other building trades suggests that while these were not always the same as those of the masons or the carpenters they were usually very similar. This is not surprising since the different trades work together, and with the extension of the general contracting system their conditions became more similar.

It is possible to check these rather vague assertions more accurately at three points in time. In 1872 we have a list of the rules and customs of the

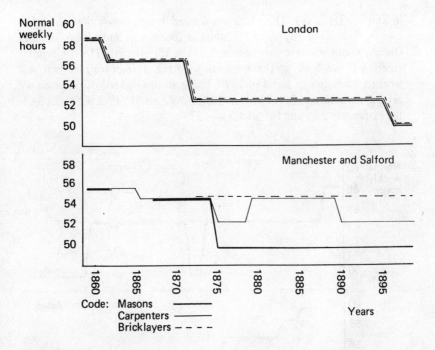

figure 13a
Major cities 1860-1895: masons, carpenters, bricklayers (where available)
Normal hours of work
Source: *see* Notes to figures and tables

bricklayers in some 90 towns, and figure 14 compares the hours of a number of these with the hours of carpenters and of masons in identical samples of towns. The result shows that while the hours of the bricklayers were slightly longer than those of the other trades, the difference was small. The second check is possible in 1886, for which we have a list of hours in all the building trades in various areas of the country. These figures, given in table 7, show quite decisively that the hours in all of the building trades were very similar, though again it appears that it is the bricklayers whose hours are slightly longer than those of other trades in the industry. Finally in 1890 we have information about the hours of plasterers, plumbers and carpenters in sixteen major cities.[119] In all but two of these the hours of carpenters and plasterers were identical — carpenters worked slightly longer in one town (Oldham), and slightly less in another (Halifax). The plumbers worked longer hours than the other two in five towns (by ½ to 2½ hours in four towns and by 6½ hours in Oldham), but considerably less in London (5½ hours). The same point emerges if we look at the proportion of the different trades that still worked 56 hours or more in 1890. Using an unweighted distribution we get for plasterers 21%; for masons 24%; for slaters 28%; for plumbers 34%; for carpenters 36% and for bricklayers 57%.

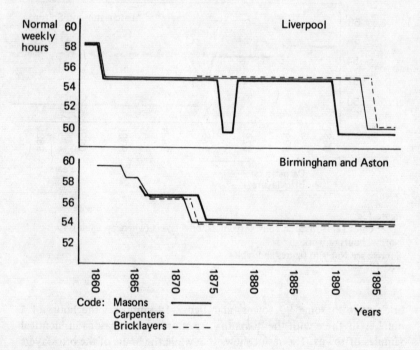

figure 13b
Major cities 1860–1895: masons, carpenters, bricklayers (where available)
Normal hours of work
Source: *see* Notes to figures and tables

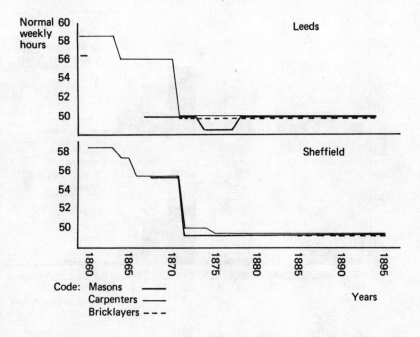

figure 13c
Major cities 1860-1895: masons, carpenters, bricklayers (where available)
Normal hours of work
Source: *see* Notes to figures and tables

A complete picture of the building trades in 1890 emerges from figure 15, which shows frequency distributions for the hours of all seven building trades and confirms the general point that though their hours were not identical they were very similar. Those of the masons continue to be the shortest. Table 8 shows the unweighted mean averages of normal hours for each trade in figure 15 and brings out once more the short hours of the masons and the middle position of the carpenters which makes their figures the most representative of those of the building trades as a whole.

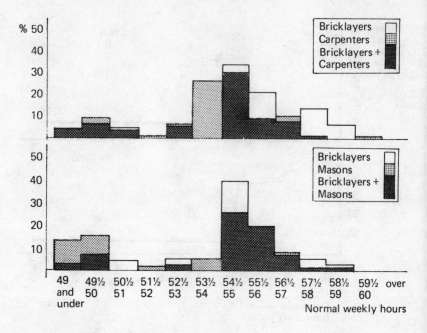

figure 14
England and Wales 1872: frequency distribution of normal hours of bricklayers
compared to that of carpenters and masons from an identical sample in each case
(unweighted per cent of total sample)
Source: *see* Notes to figures and tables

table 7
Great Britain 1886: building trades
Normal summer hours by region

trades	London	South West	Midlands & Cheshire	Lancashire	Yorkshire	The North
masons	52.5-55	54	54	48.5-54.5	49.5-54	50
bricklayers	52.5-56.5	56.5	54-59	54.5-55	50-54	50-53
carpenters	52.5-56.5	54-57	54-59	49-55	49.5-54	50-53
plumbers	47-51	54-56.5	54-59	49.5-55.5	50-54	–
painters	52.5-56.5	54-57.5	54-59	49.5-55	52-54	–
plasterers	52.5-55	54-56.5	54	49-55	50	50-53
slaters	–	–	54-59	49-55	49.5-50	53

Source: *see* Notes to figures and tables

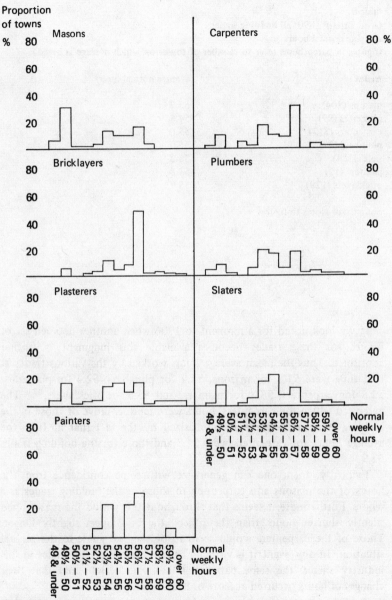

figure 15
England and Wales 1890: seven building trades
Frequency distributions of normal hours
(unweighted per cent of separate samples of towns)
Source: *see* Notes to figures and tables

table 8
Great Britain 1890: all building trades
Average normal hours
(figures in parentheses refer to number of towns on which average is based)

trades	average normal hours
masons (204)	53.2
plasterers (99)	54.5
carpenters (317)	55.0
plumbers (97)	55.0
slaters (84)	55.0
painters (12)	55.8
bricklayers (129)	55.9

Source: *see* Notes to figures

If we look ahead for a moment to 1906 when another detailed set of figures for these trades becomes available this judgment is further confirmed. Thus the mean average hours worked by the various trades at that time were 51.8 for masons, 52.2 for plumbers, 52.4 for plasterers, 52.8 for carpenters, 53.3 for painters, and 53.6 for bricklayers.[120] The extent to which the carpenters' hours were representative of those in the building trade as a whole is emphasized by the fact that in 1906 the average hours for carpenters were 52.8 and those for the building trades 52.9.

Evidently, then, one can generalize with some confidence from the hours of the masons and carpenters to those of the building trades as a whole. Furthermore it seems that throughout this period the masons had slightly shorter hours than the others, the bricklayers slightly longer. Those of the carpenters would seem to be the best guide to the general situation. In any event it is virtually certain that all of the trades in this industry shared the same patterns in hours reductions and that their changes of hours occurred at more or less the same times.

A further issue which arises out of parts of the above discussion is that of regional differences. There is no doubt that there were such differences, but it is of interest to inquire whether they remained unchanged over time.

The evidence presented in the preceding sections of this chapter, and
borne out by the figures of table 7, indicates that in fact they changed, but
that at the same time certain areas remained in the groups with short or
long hours for the whole of this period. Keeping in mind that the masons'
experience was slightly different from that of the rest of the building
trades, we can conclude that Lancashire and the West Riding tended to
lead in the matter of shorter hours, while the industrial north-east made
good in the early 1870s the ground it had lost earlier. London narrowed
the gap between itself and the leaders in the early 70s, but did not draw
abreast of them until 1890-1, while the midlands and the rest of the
country lagged consistently behind these areas. Hours in large towns were
generally found to be shorter than elsewhere. These differences between
various areas and between large towns and others remained unchanged.
Table 9 shows that in 1906 hours in London, in the north, and in large
cities generally were substantially shorter than elsewhere. The fifty-hour
week was most common in London, in the north and in the great towns of
Lancashire and Yorkshire. Hours in the midlands were 53 in the great
towns while in most other places a 56½-hour week was still common.[121]
In short this survey entirely confirms the pattern of regional differences
which was established early in the second half of the nineteenth century.

table 9
Great Britain 1906: all building trades
Average normal hours by region and by size of towns

region	towns over 100,000	towns under 100,000	average
London	–	–	50.7
The North	50.3	50.8	50.6
Lancashire, Yorkshire & Cheshire	50.8	52.6	51.9
North & West Midlands	54.6	55.3	55.1
Rest	55.5	56.4	56.3

Source: *see* Notes to figures and tables

Finally it should be pointed out that these hours are all summer hours. It is justifiable to ignore winter hours when one is identifying the pattern of changes in normal hours: because winter hours were worked for only about 16 weeks of the year, so that changes in them have a much smaller effect on working time as a whole; because the scope for change in winter hours was relatively small, since for the 'outside' trades these hours were in any case limited by those of daylight and were no more than 48 per week;[122] and because where winter hours were not shorter than summer hours, as was the case with the carpenters during this period,[123] most changes in winter hours came at the same time as those in the summer hours. The only exception to this came during 1879-89. It has been noted that in those years there were a number of reductions of winter hours only. The significance of these was much less than might at first appear, because half of them involved reductions in wage rates as well. While the net effect of these reductions was negligible, the tendency to reduce winter hours when the unions were in a weak position, is worth noting. It represented in almost every case an effort to alleviate the serious unemployment of the winter months through work-sharing arrangements.

7 Summary

A summary of the findings of this chapter must begin with the great discontinuity in the recorded changes in working hours. Whereas much of this forty-year period passed without recording any changes in working hours, the years from 1871 to 1874 brought changes that were so widespread and extensive that they can be said to have radically altered the country's conception of what constituted a day's work. Although there had been some changes in the 1860s, virtually the whole of this readjustment took place in this one four-year period, and it is this fact above all others that requires explanation. The observation was the more significant because the discontinuity was shown not to be merely a reflection of a similar discontinuity in the bargaining strength of the unions, because wage changes were achieved in a very much less discontinuous manner.

While it would be merely repetitious to summarize all the changes in hours that were achieved during this period, there were a number of interesting issues raised in the course of the discussion which might benefit from a short summary. Some of these issues will come to the fore again when the attempt is made to find explanations at a macro-economic level for the events recorded so far.

There was found to be a distinct connection between the strength of trade unions and the success of the movement for reduced hours. Hence reductions were found to have been achieved first in areas and by trades having strong trade unions. The timing of such changes was also found to be associated with the rise of strong trade unions. Hence also the fact that the reductions that were achieved were always achieved at times of great prosperity and low unemployment. Since these are times when the bargaining position of the unions is strongest this points again to a connection between union strength and the reduction of hours.

This is not an unexpected relationship. Thus it was argued that while wages could be raised under the normal competitive pressures of the market, this was not true of the reduction of hours. It was because of this difference that institutional pressure was deemed essential if reductions in hours were to be achieved.

This leads to the next important observation, which was that the demand for shorter hours was a very important rallying point around which many new unions were established. This was particularly true of the craft unions that were begun during the early part of this period, many of whom arose directly out of the struggle for the nine-hour day. Again, this was not surprising. The men realized soon enough that whereas the market would push wages up (and down) they would have to organize to achieve a reduction in hours. Hence the repeated comments by the unions during the 1850s that it was on this issue more than on any other that they could count on the support of the non-union members of the trade. When this issue became the dominant concern of the workmen it induced the non-union men to join the union. But why did this issue become dominant? It became dominant because it was the logical outcome of the craft-union approach to the labour market. This approach had been adopted by many trades from the 1830s and 1840s onwards and it depended for its success on the ability of the men to erect barriers to entry around their trade which would protect them from the competition of those outside. Once they had achieved this, they naturally turned their attention to the restriction of supply, which meant reducing their hours.

The success of the organized trades and in particular the craft unions in achieving a substantial reduction in hours in the 1870s was in part responsible for the rise of the 'new unionism' in the 1880s. The success of the craft unions had been at least in part at the expense of the 'excluded' mass of the unskilled and this was their reaction. But the same strategy was not open to them since they were not in a position to build barriers to entry and in any event, as the more enlightened of their leaders realized, they had no one to exclude except some of their own number. It was for this reason that this movement adopted as its battle cry the eight-hour day *by legislation.* Only thus could they hope to achieve such a reduction and only thus could they hope to draw abreast of the craftsmen. It is equally significant to note that the craft unions in most cases refused to support this demand and asked that it be left to the men to achieve it for themselves. Thus they could use it to strengthen further their position and to widen further the gap between themselves and the unskilled mass.

Apart from these major observations there were some minor points that may have contributed to the successful reduction of hours. Thus there was a distinct increase in the demand for holidays on the part of the workmen in the 1850s and this was associated with the prosperity reigning at that time, with the increasing enthusiasm for holidays and also possibly with the rising popularity of the cheap day railway excursions. On the employers' side there was an increasing desire for the regulation of competition as firms came to be more solidly established and this led often to a desire to standardize hours throughout the industry. In addition their success in introducing payment by the hour, reduced their opposition to reductions of normal hours, since it made them more confident that men could be induced to work past this nominal limit, because the men themselves would bear the economic burden of the shorter hours. In this respect it is interesting to note that the overtime rate came to be their ally in undermining the efforts of the men to restrict supply. This is ironic since the overtime premium had once been introduced in order to dissuade the employer from using overtime. Now it became the means by which he was better able to introduce it.

On the whole this period saw the efforts of the first craft unions come to fruition, and witnessed the rise of a new form of unionism to represent those who had been left out of the restrictive craft-union world. It was the first period during which a large proportion of workmen settled their hours through a bargain with their employers and though they did achieve a significant reduction in their hours it proved to be a painful process which depended for its success on a variety of factors. How soon would it be before they could repeat their success?

Chapter five
Changes in normal hours: 1890 to 1965

1 Introduction

The pattern of change in normal hours retained as its dominant feature the extreme discontinuity of the recorded changes. This discontinuity is remarkable since in most industries there is no reason why frequent small changes in hours could not be arranged, and the traditional indifference curve analysis, in which leisure is traded off against income, would lead us to expect a gradual reduction of hours over time while the workman's position was improving. But this is not what we find: the changes in hours are much more discontinuous than those in wages. This chapter will show the extent of the discontinuity, and subsequent chapters will deal with the reasons for it.

We shall confine ourselves here almost entirely to a presentation of the available statistics, to establish the nature and extent of the changes at a macro-economic level. The discussion will remain at this level, with only a few excursions to a lower level of aggregation in order to point out the 'special' nature of some of the changes recorded in the macro-economic statistics. This treatment evidently differs from the more detailed investigation of previous changes. It was in the nature of those changes and our existing knowledge of them, that the pattern of change in the aggregate could be discerned only after particular changes had been established in their regional and industrial diversity. But from 1890 onwards, not only are aggregate statistics already available, but the component changes are much more uniform between regions and industries, and much more concentrated in time.

2 Aggregate changes in normal weekly hours: 1890 to 1965

A complete summary of the aggregate net changes in normal weekly hours of work is provided by figure 16. It shows at a glance that the entire total of the reductions achieved in this 76-year span was brought about within four short periods of one to three years each.

The figure shows the aggregate net reduction of weekly hours (average number of hours reduced times the number of people affected) achieved annually. Since the labour force grew considerably over this period the complete absence of any upward trend indicates how insignificant were the changes during the years between the outstanding adjustments of hours.

Two aspects of this picture deserve some further attention. Apart from the four major changes, there are five points in time at which some slight reductions were achieved, amounting to at least one million net weekly hours. Of these five, three were entirely due to legislation restricting hours in certain industries. The 1902 reduction was the result of an Act reducing hours in the textile industry by one hour a week; that of 1909 was due to an Act restricting work underground in the coal-mines to eight hours bank to bank; while that of 1939-40 resulted from an Act restricting the hours of young persons under 16 in factories generally.[1] The other two small reductions were achieved by collective bargaining, but they were inflated by special circumstances in each case. The 1937 reductions were accounted for to a large extent by reductions in the coal industry, where

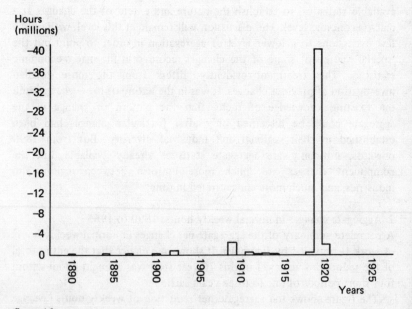

figure 16a
U.K. 1890-1925: all industries
Aggregate annual net changes in normal weekly hours
Source: *see* Notes to figures and tables

the miners were still making good the losses they suffered in 1926. That reversal is, of course, clearly visible in figure 16 as the only substantial increase in hours to occur within this whole period, and its introduction was the occasion for the general strike of 1926. The 1957 reduction was less unusual, but here too a large proportion of the change was accounted for by a reduction in the hours of Post-Office employees, whose collective agreements might be expected to be influenced by considerations other than those typical of the economy in general.

The other feature of figure 16 that calls for present notice is the virtual absence of any changes during the 1890s, a period long regarded as one of great activity on the hours front. In a subsequent section of this chapter we shall return briefly to a lower level of aggregation in order to look at the changes that did take place in that decade.

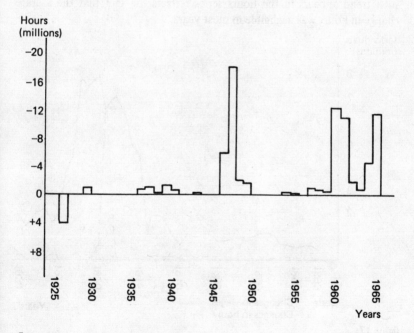

figure 16b
U.K. 1925-1965: all industries
Aggregate annual net changes in normal weekly hours
Source: *see* Notes to figures and tables

In the light of the traditional labour-leisure indifference curve analysis the pronounced nature of the discontinuities found in the changes in normal hours demands explanation. In what direction this should be sought depends on whether the pattern of changes of hours is matched by that of changes of wages. If it is, then an explanation could be provided simply by an extended application of the factors that enable unions to press wage demands successfully at certain times. If it is not, then some explanation must be found for the difference in the pattern of change of the two variables, as well as for the particular pattern of change in normal hours.

Figure 17 shows that the two patterns are wholly different. Changes in wages affect a large number of workers in almost every year, but the changes in normal hours are highly discontinuous. The series show the total number of individuals affected by either a change in the wage rate or in the normal hours of work. Since the size of the labour force was rising continually, this accounts for the rising trend of the wage series. That no such trend appears in the hours series reflects the fact that the average change in hours was negligible in most years.

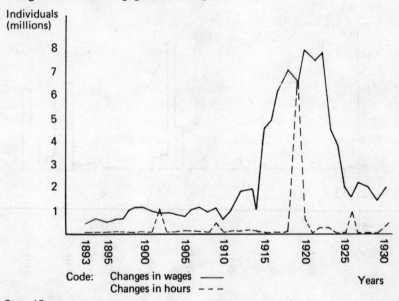

figure 17a
U.K. 1893-1930: all industries
Annual aggregate number of individuals affected by changes in basic weekly wages or normal hours
Source: *see* Notes to figures and tables

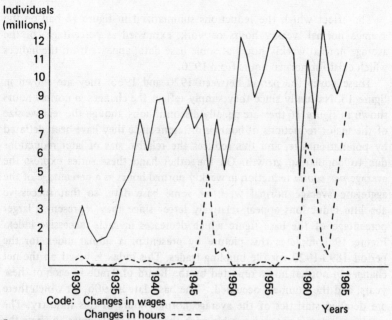

figure 17b
U.K. 1930-1965
Annual aggregate number of individuals affected by changes in basic weekly wages or normal hours
Source: *see* Notes to figures and tables

We may also ask at this point whether figure 17 suggests that the increase of the wage rate and the decrease of hours were alternatives. The three major peaks of hours reductions (ignoring 1965 for the moment) were associated with troughs in the number affected by wage changes. In the changes around 1959-60, the one-year lag between trough and peak can be explained by the fact that a very large proportion of the changes in hours which took place in 1960 were negotiated in 1959. In any event this association between peaks in the changes of hours and troughs in the changes of wages indicates the extent to which hours are reduced 'without loss of pay'. The increase in the size of the associated troughs, from 1919 to 1947 and 1959, probably indicates the increased popularity of such agreements. The changes in 1919 were almost all made in conjunction with an increase in the wage rate, as had been the case with the builders in 1872-4; the subsequent changes were more often in the form of hours reductions with no change in the basic weekly wage, though this of course involved an increase in the hourly wage.

The effect which the reductions summarized in figure 16 had on the average normal weekly hours of work, expressed as percentages of the average normal weekly hours at some base date, appears from the indices which exist for normal hours from 1920.

These cover the period between 1920 and 1966: they are shown in figure 18. Naturally since they simply reflect the changes in normal hours shown in figure 16 they are equally discontinuous, though the relative size of the major reductions of hours is different since they have been deflated by population size, and this reduces the relative size of later reductions due to population growth. On the other hand these series express the average *per capita* reduction in weekly normal hours as a percentage of the aggregate average normal week at some base date, so that successive absolute reductions appear relatively larger since they represent a larger percentage of the base figure which decreases in each successive index. Figure 19 completes this picture by presenting a similar index for the period 1893-1920 for the building trades. This index is based on the net changes in normal hours reported by the Board of Trade in each of these years, and the numbers occupied.[2] The base date is 1906, for which there are detailed statistics of the average normal hours in this industry. The resulting index is not comparable with the others, but serves to show the approximate magnitude of the changes in average normal hours in building in these earlier years. Once again the building trades show something of the same discontinuity as other industries, but its extent was markedly less than it was in the other major industrial sectors. Though there is no index for these others, it is known that of the reductions achieved between 1893 and 1920 in the building trades, less than 80 per cent came in 1919-20, whereas slightly more than 90 per cent of those in metals came in 1919 alone. In mining and textiles, if we remove the effects of the legislative reductions in 1909 and 1902 respectively, the proportion of the reductions achieved in 1919 would also be well above 90 per cent.

3 Hours of work: 1890 to 1906

Because the 1890s saw the temporary victory of the 'new unionism' at the Trades Union Congress and the subsequent advocacy by the Congress of the legal enforcement of an eight-hour day; because of the achievement of the eight-hour day by the gas stokers and the fifty-hour week by the London builders; and finally because of the great eight-hour strike by the engineers in 1897, this decade has generally been regarded as one marked by a substantial shortening of the normal hours of labour. Yet our figures show that the aggregate changes achieved were in fact small, and indeed

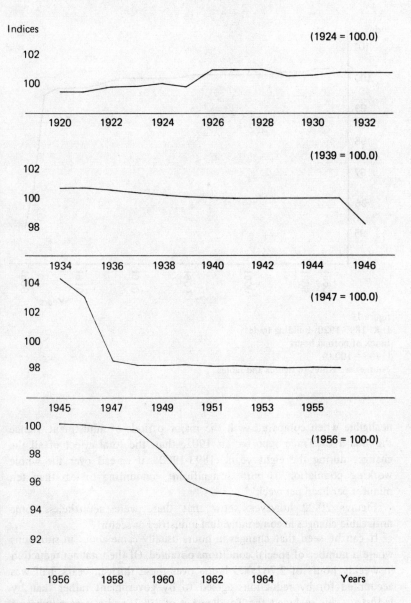

figure 18
U.K. 1920-1965: all industries
Indices of normal hours
Source: *see* Notes to figures and tables

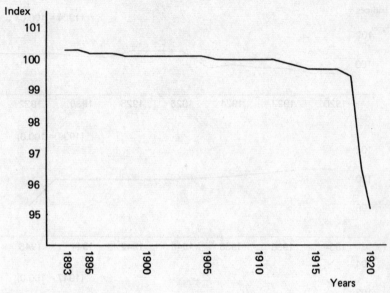

figure 19
U.K. 1893-1920: building trades
Index of normal hours
(1906 = 100.0)
Source: *see* Notes to figures and tables

negligible when compared with the major periods of adjustment. Hence
the Board of Trade reported in 1901, that 'the total effect of all the
changes during the eight years (1893-1900), if spread over the whole
working population, is quite insignificant, amounting to less than ten
minutes per head per week'.[3]

Figures 20-22 however, show that there were nevertheless some
noticeable changes in some individual industries or sectors.[4]

It can be seen that changes in hours usually came about in situations
where a number of special conditions obtained. Of the total net reduction
in weekly hours of 2,762,000 hours over these thirteen years, half was
accounted for by reductions agreed to by government rather than by
industry. This included the Textiles Act of 1902, and a large number of
reductions agreed to by authorities determining the hours of various
groups of government employees, including 43,000 who were granted the
eight-hour day in 1894.[5]

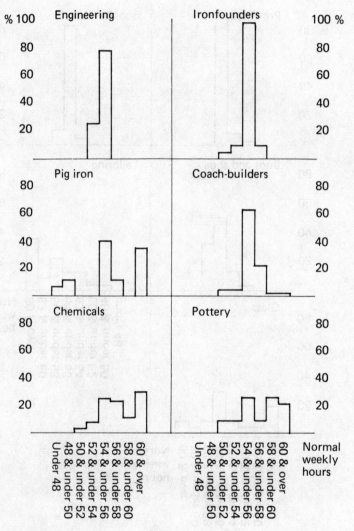

figure 20a
Great Britain 1890: certain industries
Frequency distributions of normal hours
(unweighted per cent of total sample of towns and areas)
Source: *see* Notes to figures and tables

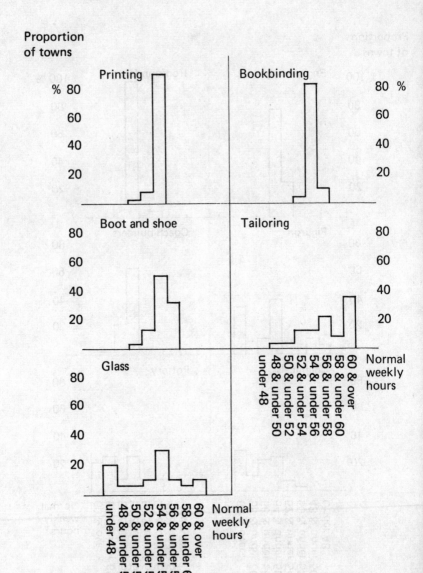

figure 20b
Great Britain 1890: certain industries
Frequency distributions of normal hours
(unweighted per cent of total sample of towns and areas)
Source: *see* Notes to figures and tables

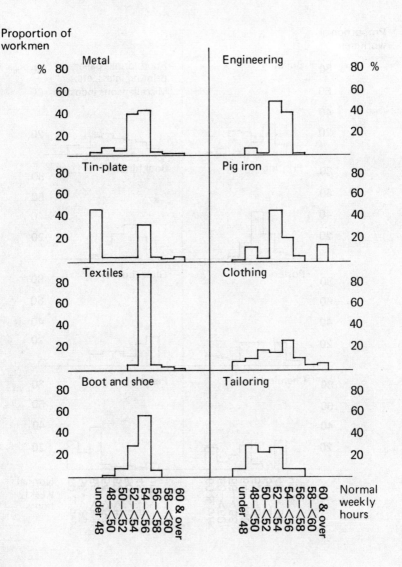

Proportion of workmen

Metal   Engineering

Tin-plate   Pig iron

Textiles   Clothing

Boot and shoe   Tailoring

under 48
48—<50
50—<52
52—<54
54—<56
56—<58
58—<60
60 & over

Normal weekly hours

figure 21a
U.K. 1906: selected industrial sectors and industries
Frequency distributions of normal hours
(per cent of total sample of individuals)
Source: *see* Notes to figures and tables

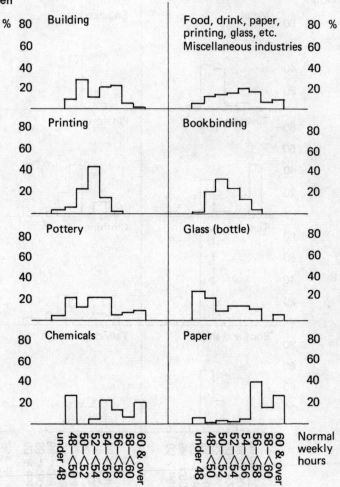

figure 21b
U.K. 1906: selected industrial sectors and industries
Frequency distributions of normal hours
(per cent of total sample of individuals)
Source: *see* Notes to figures and tables

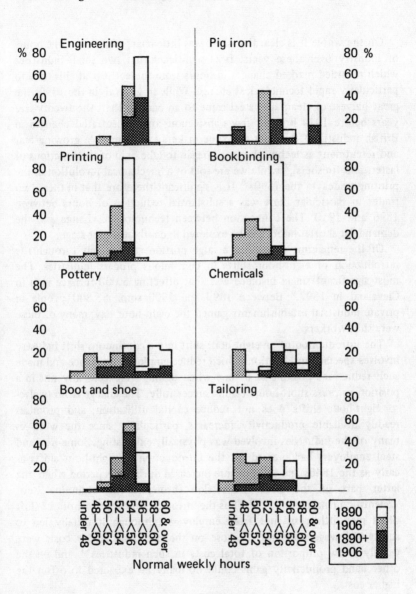

figure 22
figures 20 and 21 superimposed for eight industries
(it should be noted that they are not strictly comparable because the coverage
differs)
Source: *see* Notes to figures and tables

On the whole it is clear that there was little change in the normal hours of industry over these years. It is significant that two small industries which recorded marked changes in hours were subject just at this time to particularly rapid technological change. While in general 'in the 1890s the great harvest of steam and steel came to an end' so that 'the twenty-five years before 1914 brought few conspicuous or concentrated changes in British industry',[6] the boot and shoe makers experienced 'a growing fear and resentment as technical change began to take hold of the functions of lasters and finishers',[7] while we are told of a 'mechanical revolution in the printing trades' in the 1890s.[8] It is significant therefore that in these two trades in particular there was a substantial reduction of hours between 1890 and 1910. The connection between technological change and the demand for shorter hours will be explored in depth at a later stage.

Of the remaining reductions a large portion came about through the introduction of eight-hour shifts in continuous process industries. The most significant single instance was that affecting 5,000 furnace men in Cleveland in 1897.[9] Between 1893 and 1900 some 53,800 people in private industrial establishments gained the eight-hour day; many of these were shift workers.

The introduction of an eight-hour shift into a continuous shift industry involves special considerations which reduce employer resistance and made such reductions possible at a time when unions were generally not in a position to press short-hours claims successfully. The change from twelve- to eight-hour shifts does not reduce capital utilization, and promises readily available productivity increases, particularly since the work in many of the industries involved was physically exhausting. Some iron and steel employers had pressed for the introduction of eight-hour shifts as early as the 1840s and this pressure increased during this period when 'the latter part of the Great Depression (brought) the beginning . . . of "scientific management" '.[10] Thus the introduction of the eight-hour shift often met little resistance from employers (although it usually led to substantial wage increases) because on the one hand labour costs were usually a low proportion of total costs in such industries[11] and on the other hand productivity gains could normally be expected to offset the higher costs.

A contemporary pointed out this mechanism when he wrote that not only technological changes led to increased productivity. 'Not less effective are improvements . . . (in) the general organization of . . . industry. Thus all employers who have already introduced the eight hours day dwell upon the great advantage (of) . . . the fact the breaks for rest and meals can now be dispensed with. In other cases the eight hours day led to the introduction of double, even of treble shifts'.[12]

To the working man most such changes in organization would be felt to be just another case of 'speeding up'. In the Leeds gas-works the workmen complained that the employers, after conceding the eight-hour shift in 1850 'tried to put such a frightful amount of work upon them (the workmen) as would make them beg for the twelve hours day again'.[13] The possibility of increasing productivity through technological change was a major influence in the shift-working trades also. It is significant that in the gas-works the sudden upsurge of a number of separate unions and their unanimous demand for an eight-hour day in 1889 coincided with the beginnings of a technological revolution in that industry, which was heralded by the arrival of the inclined retort, 'undoubtedly the most important method of saving labour in gas works'. Though labour productivity had risen steadily since the early 1870s, and this may mark some intensification of labour, this is unlikely to account for the strong and unanimous movement for shorter hours in 1889. The threat of technology which was cited by the union's pioneers as the cause of their movement was almost certainly a more powerful stimulant to this movement.[14]

The coal-miners continued to occupy a special position in the movement for shorter hours. From the end of the 1880s they were in the forefront of the movement for the legislative enactment of the eight-hour day — bank to bank. There is no doubt that a major motive for this demand was the desire to counteract the low price of coal by restricting its supply, and the miners made many statements to this effect.[15] Their decision to seek a reduction of hours through legislation was based on: the proven effectiveness of legislation in restricting actual hours in an industry where payment by the piece and irregular work had often induced the men to defy union attempts to impose restraints on hours; the need to restrict supply nationally in the face of national markets; and the relatively weak position of the unions by reason of the falling productivity — the fall had begun in the early 1880s, and by 'the early 1900s productivity had fallen off by an eighth'[16] from its 1880 peak.

This fall in productivity more generally had the effect of making it imperative for the men to do away with the stint, or indeed any piece-work system, since these meant that the miner bore a large part of the added costs imposed by the need to exploit less accessible seams. The establishment of a fixed time at a fixed time-rate, instead of a fixed quantity at a fixed piece-rate, would relieve him of this burden.

If these factors help to explain the active part played by the miners in the pressure for the eight-hour day during 1890-1910, the reasons for their success in 1908-9 are still not obvious. Naturally the rising political power of labour was very much involved, but it is not clear whether any economic factors such as the prospect of increased productivity disposed employers more favourably to such a change.

Apart from these exceptions the efforts to achieve reductions in hours were largely abortive. The great engineering strike of 1897 reflected all the pressures that bore on this issue. It has been argued that the strike concerned primarily 'the prerogatives of management in the workshop',[17] but these 'prerogatives of management' were with one minor exception all concerned with the union's traditional attempts to establish barriers around the trade and to restrict supply within the protected market.[18] It was thus not merely accidental that the immediate cause of the strike was a demand for an eight-hour day.

This demand drew a counter-attack from the employers, who were induced to form strong associations. Like the builder's masters in the years 1858-72, they not only opposed the demand for shorter hours, but sought to remove the conditions under which such a demand made economic sense. This they succeeded in doing by denying the union the ability to protect its labour market, both by insisting on the right to employ non-unionists and on the right to put unskilled men on to work requiring little skill even if it was traditionally craftsmen's work. Their success in this endeavour had far-reaching repercussions for British industrial relations. The engineers, denied the essential conditions under which to pursue the policies of the old craftsman became militant. Indeed 'the history of (militant labour) movements since the British lock-out of 1897 can be largely written in terms of the metal workers'.[19]

4 Summary

From 1890 to 1965 reductions in normal hours were heavily concentrated in three short periods: 1919-20; 1946-9; and 1960-2/64-6. Of the total aggregate net reduction of normal weekly hours over this period, 90 per cent came about during these eleven years. Wages did not share this pattern of change.

Of the remaining 10 per cent of the changes in hours, almost half were accounted for by three reductions brought about by specific pieces of legislation, so that only five or six per cent of the total remains as having been established through collective bargaining in the course of the remaining 62 years.

One of the more surprising findings is the lack of change in hours during the 1890s, a period whose labour problems were dominated by the eight-hour movement. What reductions in hours did take place through collective bargaining were confined to certain industries in which either rapid technological change was threatening the labour force or certain factors mitigated employer resistance.

The previous chapter had shown that during the first extensive period when the hours of work had been established through collective bargaining they had been adjusted only in a very discontinuous manner. This chapter has shown that this discontinuity not only continued but became more extreme over the course of the next seventy years. Subsequent chapters will concern themselves with the explanation of this phenomenon.

Chapter six

The normal week under collective bargaining

1 Introduction

Under collective bargaining, reductions in the number of hours which constitute a normal work week have been achieved in a way for which economic theory does not prepare us; they have come about in waves of settlements occurring at intervals, while between these waves the great majority of collective bargains have dealt exclusively with other terms of employment. In Great Britain, for instance, there have been three such periods of change in this century — namely in 1919, 1948, and in 1960-2/64-6. (The last may be largely regarded as the same shift in two stages since 'many of the changes in rates of wages and hours of work which came into operation during 1964 were the consequence of agreements made at earlier dates'.[1]) Economic theory does not lead us to expect this. It has usually regarded earnings and leisure[2] as two goods which the employee regards as desirable, and between which he will choose in accordance with the normal two-good utility maximizing apparatus.[3] Since in many industries there is no reason why small changes in weekly hours should not be made at the same time as small changes in other terms of employment, the traditional approach does not prepare us for the fact that change has rarely occurred in this manner.

The deficiency of the theory is due to the inapplicability of the normal utility or revealed preference analysis to collective bargaining about hours. But an appropriate modification of the theory does lead us to expect the outcome found in practice. Such a modification would not have been needed to analyse the behaviour of the eighteenth-century hand-loom weaver, who as an individual had complete discretion over his working time since he worked in his own home. The modified model set out below to describe the behaviour of the later industrial worker is necessary because he works in a factory, where working time is standardized and this standardization is effected through collective bargaining.

2 The model

Figure 23 represents a situation in a labour market which will serve as an example. Along the y axis weekly income is measured in pounds (£/wk), at constant prices, while leisure is measured in hours along the *x* axis. Since the number of hours in a week is finite there are two points of reference on the *x* axis – namely the origin, *0*, from which we measure leisure to the right, and *X*, which represents the total number of hours in a week and from which we measure hours of work to the left. We assume that *E* represents the initial agreement between two hypothetical bargainers. At this point the employee has *OH* hours of leisure, works *XH* hours and has a weekly income of £ *OW*. The hourly wage rate is represented by the slope of the line *XY* (i.e. $\frac{OY}{OX}$ or $\frac{OW}{HX}$).

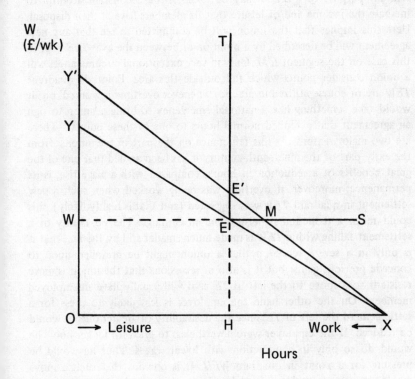

figure 23

An improvement in the employee's situation will involve a clockwise rotation of XY, about X. Let us assume that a new settlement is reached which involves the wage rate represented by XY'. Which point on this line would be the new contract point? Much more often than not in the real world it will be E'. But according to the theory as it stands, any point is possible, depending on the relative strengths of the substitution and income effects. E' is clearly compatible with the theory, but there is nothing in the theory, on the other hand, that would lead us to expect E' to the exclusion of other possibilities.

This apparatus requires modification if it is to be a meaningful representation of a collective bargaining situation. The fact that the employee is represented by a union introduces an initial constraint on the area within which we might expect to find a new point of agreement. The relevant purpose of a union may be taken to be a constant attempt to increase the income and/or leisure that its members have at their disposal. Here this implies that the union will be committed to see that any new agreement will be described by a point on or between the axes TES — or in this case on the segment $E'M$. Only in very exceptional circumstances will a union consider points which fall outside this area. Points in quadrant TEW are of course utilized in practice whenever overtime is worked, but it would take something like a national emergency to bring a union to sign an agreement that extended normal hours to one of these points.[4] There are two major reasons for this reluctance on the part of the unions: from the early part of the nineteenth century it has been argued that one of the great benefits of a reduction in hours, compared with a wage rise, is its permanence; moreover, if overtime was being worked when such a new settlement in quadrant TEW was suggested (and that is highly likely), this could mean a reduction in leisure *and* in earnings. The possibility of a settlement falling within TEW is made much smaller still by the fact that it is only in a severe recession that a union might be prevailed upon to concede previous gains: but it is also in recessions that the union is more resistant to a move to the left of TE as it will usually have unemployed members. On the other hand the employer is less likely to press for a settlement to the left of TE since the desirability of greater output would be reduced. If the employer were nevertheless to press for longer hours he would do so only in conjunction with lower wages. Thus he would be pressing for a point in quadrant WEH. It is obvious that such a move would be very strongly resisted by the union, as indeed it was by the British miners in 1926. Points within quadrant HES will again be strongly resisted at any bargain. While such points are not unusual as temporary measures, e.g. work-sharing arrangements which are represented by points on *EX*, it is rare that they would be agreed upon as a normal week. If the union were forced, by a depression, to accept a point outside *TES* it would prefer points within this quadrant (*HES*) to those discussed previously. Very occasionally, as we have shown, a union is willing to accept such a point, but such cases are rare and will be discussed later in connection with the special circumstances that give rise to them. The relative weakness in union resistance caused by a depression is more than offset by the fact that not only will the employer not press for a settlement in quadrant *HES*, but he will himself oppose such a move because of the future difficulty of reversing a reduction in the normal week. This reservation by the employers would apply throughout *HES* except for movement along *EH*. It is for this reason that if there was sufficient pressure to compel a union to move out of quadrant *TES*, such a move would most probably take place along *EH* since here union resistance will be relatively weak while employer pressure may be strong. Except under the special conditions of a severe recession, we can however concentrate on the area between the *TES* axes in our search for a new contract point. This is done in figure 24, which should be seen as the *TES* axes lifted out of figure 23 and magnified.

We must now depart further from the traditional analysis, by recognizing that the lines *XY* and *XY'* can in no sense be treated as budget lines. The employee is at no time presented with such a range of alternatives among which he is free to choose. The collective bargain does not merely specify the hourly wage rate, but establishes that rate on condition that a certain number of hours constitute a normal week. This is made necessary by the conditions of factory employment. For the old hand-loom weaver lines such as *XY* and *XY'* would have represented approximations of budget lines.[5] For the factory employee, however, the effective budget line is represented by the locus of points to which the employer is indifferent.

To derive this locus we assume initially that the employer is a profit maximizer and therefore his relative valuation of hours and wages depends entirely on their respective additions to unit costs, i.e. he will be indifferent between any two points which make the same total contribution to unit costs. In figure 24 any point between the axes represents a certain increase in weekly income and a certain reduction in the hours constituting a normal full week. Each of these makes some contribution to unit costs, but their combined effect will clearly be indicated by the total difference between the new and the old unit costs.

Thus if y is the change in income per man-week; W is the initial income per man-week; F represents all overheads — i.e. all non-wage costs that do not vary directly with output; F' represents overheads per man-week or $\frac{F}{N}$, where N represents the number of employees; H is the number of hours in the initial normal week; x represents changes in the hours of leisure; and P is a measure of hourly productivity, the new unit cost is $\dfrac{N(W+y+F')}{PN(H-x)}$,

while the original unit cost was $\dfrac{N(W+F')}{PNH}$. Since the employer's indifference curve is the locus of equal increases in total unit costs, its equation is

$$\frac{N(W+y+F')}{PN(H-x)} - \frac{N(W+F')}{PNH} = K \qquad (1)$$

where K is a constant.

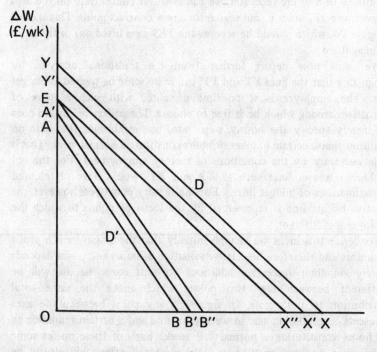

figure 24

$\triangle$ Leisure (Hours)

If we ignore the possibility of adjusting the level of employment for the moment, and also treat P as a constant, this becomes

$$y = PHK - \frac{(PHK + W + F')}{H} x \qquad (2)$$

We are justified in treating P as a constant only so long as there is no change in productivity *as a result* of the reduction in hours or the change in wages. Such related changes in productivity have often occurred in practice and we shall examine their effects on the function later. For the moment we ignore them and are thus left with the simplest form of the employer's indifference curve, which also represents the employee's budget line, because all the points between which he is free to choose, given any particular level of concessions, lie on it. Its slope is

$$- \frac{PHK + W + F'}{H}$$

This means that the employer's indifference curve is a straight line with a slope that depends on wage costs and fixed costs as well as the absolute size of the increase under consideration. As this latter factor, i.e. *PHK*, increases, the slope of the function increases numerically. This may at first be puzzling but the mystery disappears upon closer examination. Since a change in hours, without reduction in the weekly wage, affects unit costs through the denominator, it is the proportion of that change which is important, rather than its absolute size. Thus suppose that a change in hours of α % without reduction in the weekly wage adds as much to unit costs as a change in wages of β % without reduction of hours: then as hours of work decrease, α % of hours comes to represent an ever smaller absolute amount of time, while wages are increasing and β % of wages represents an ever larger absolute amount of money. Hence the change in the slope — an ever smaller absolute reduction in hours is offset by an ever larger absolute increase in wages per man-week.

We now turn to the employee's indifference curve. Unfortunately there is no one straightforward assumption that will allow us to specify it; but two separate assumptions will allow us to do so, for any single point in time. The changes to which it is subject over time will be discussed subsequently. We assume first, that at any one time the relative values placed on income and leisure are not subject to significant diminishing returns within the range of variation with which we are concerned; and secondly, that initially the employee values his leisure time at the margin at the rate at which he is being paid for his labour at the margin.

The implication of the first assumption is that the indifference curve of the single employee, or group of employees, is a straight line, within the relevant range, at any one point in time. The relevant range is that range which is likely to be discussed at any one bargain. This assumption is made initially in spite of the fact that it is highly likely that the employees' function is to some extent convex to the origin. However, in the relatively small segment of this curve considered here, the non-linearity would be correspondingly small. While we are developing this model we shall therefore treat this function as a straight line for the sake of simplicity, but subsequently we shall briefly examine the effect of allowing for some non-linearity.

The second assumption is useful only in providing a starting point from which to pursue our inquiry. The slope of our linear indifference curve could conceivably lie anywhere in the range from infinity to zero. In practice, however, the union's relative valuation of income and leisure is unlikely to have diverged greatly from the equilibrium implicit in the last settlement. We shall begin by assuming that, at the level of total benefit (i.e. income and leisure together) then attained, the union is in an equilibrium position – i.e. a position where the desired and actual relative levels of leisure and income coincide. In such a situation the most plausible assumption is that the employee values his time, particularly his time at work and thus his potential leisure time, at the rate at which he is being paid for it. The last hour of work each day is in effect being traded for a certain amount of money – i.e. the going rate, and we may assume that it is transformed into money value at that rate in the employee's indifference function. We begin then with a situation where the employee values his leisure at the margin, or (what amounts to the same thing) his last hour at work, at the going rate. The question then is, in what form will the union want to realize further increments in the total benefit.

These two assumptions enable us to construct an indifference curve for the employee: it will be a straight line with a slope determined by the hourly wage rate. Using the same symbols as in the employer's function, it may be written as

$$y = K - \frac{W}{H} x \qquad (3)$$

We are now ready to examine the interaction of these two functions. Let us begin by looking at their respective slopes. We saw that the employer's function has a slope of $-\dfrac{PHK + W + F'}{H}$, while that of the employees has a slope of $-\dfrac{W}{H}$ Therefore, so long as $PK + \dfrac{F'}{H} > 0$, the employer's curve is steeper than that of the employees. This implies that the larger are the fixed costs per man-week, the greater the concessions considered and the higher the productivity, the greater is the discrepancy between the relative values placed on hours and wages by employers and employees. Let us look at the implications of this fact for a bargaining situation.

In figure 24 we look at what we would expect to happen in a bargaining situation given the indifference functions which we have established. We begin with the union making large demands, represented by the points on XY. It will of course state its demands in terms of one point on this line, let us say D, but we have established that it is in fact indifferent as between D and the other points on XY. The employer in turn makes a token offer of, let us say, D', but again we know that he is indifferent as between D' and the other points on AB. A settlement will be reached when three conditions have been fulfilled. The two parties must agree on a common point. Given in each case the concession made by the other party, the union must at this point have maximized its gains and the employer minimized his losses. Or in other words we assume that movement in the bargaining positions will not stop until a situation of Pareto optimality obtains, so that no point can be a contract point if by moving from it one party can improve its position without harming the other party. The bargaining concerns itself with trying to move the original offer curves. The employer tries to get the union to make some concession and thus to shift XY towards the origin — let us say to $X'Y'$. The union on the other hand tries to make the employer move away from the origin, let us say to $A'B'$. It must be stressed that we are saying nothing here about the way in which this bargaining will proceed. Why, how or by whom the concessions will be made lies outside our scope at this point. But if agreement is to be reached at all, the curves must get shifted in this way. If they are, it is clear that because of their relative slopes the first common point they will reach will lie on the y axis — i.e. let us say at E. It can easily be shown that if any point not on the y axis was chosen it would be possible for one party to improve its position while leaving the other indifferent to the change.

Thus this modified labour-leisure analysis leads us to expect that collective bargaining, should 'normally' be expected to result in increases in income only. It remains to be seen how the functions developed may be expected to change over time, and how such changes can account for the occasional occurrence of waves of settlements in which increases in leisure predominate.

3 Effect of changes in certain parameters on the employer's indifference curve

The result we have postulated is necessitated by the relative shapes and slopes of the two indifference functions developed. Any change in this result must be due to changes in the relative positions of these functions.

In this section we shall discuss the changes in the employer's function which result from relaxation of some of the previously postulated assumptions. We shall examine in turn the effects of changes in employment, productivity and short-term fixed costs per man-week.

The effect of reduced hours on unit costs clearly depends on their effect on output. In many cases it is possible for the employer to offset this effect by changing the size of his labour force. In order to determine what effect such a policy would have on the employer's indifference curve we shall also consider the possibility that short-term fixed costs vary with the level of employment in the long run. Therefore if N_0 represents the original labour force; N_1 the new labour force; F_0 the original total fixed cost; and F_1 the new total fixed cost, while P is still assumed constant, then the employer's indifference curve becomes

$$\frac{N_1(W+y+F_1/N_1)}{N_1(H-x)} - \frac{N_0(W+F_0/N_0)}{N_0 H} = PK \qquad (4)$$

which can be rearranged to

$$y = PHK + \left(\frac{F_0}{N_0} - \frac{F_1}{N_1}\right) - \left[\frac{PHK + W + F_0/N_0}{H}\right] x \qquad (5)$$

The slope of this function is $-\dfrac{PHK + W + F_0/N_0}{H}$ which is the same as

the slope of the original employer's curve (Eq. 1), where we disregarded the possibility of changing employment. It is the y intercept which has changed in this case — the extent or direction of its shift depending on the relative values of $\dfrac{F_0}{N_0}$ and $\dfrac{F_1}{N_1}$

Two specific instances illustrate the meaning of this result. If the proportionate increase in fixed costs is the same as the proportionate increase in employment, then $\dfrac{F_0}{N_0} - \dfrac{F_1}{N_1} = 0,$ and the employer's indifference function remains the same in all respects as it was before N was considered as a variable. Such a situation becomes plausible in as far as an industry or firm is labour intensive; has very short continuous processes and as a result low worker inter-dependence which occasions individually oriented facilities and equipment; and is operating at optimal output prior to the change in hours and employment.

On the other hand if we assume that $F_0 = F_1$, or in other words that employment can be increased without changing the absolute level of fixed costs, the employer's function becomes

$$y = PHK + F_0 \left(\frac{1}{N_0} - \frac{1}{N_1} \right) - \frac{PHK + W + F'}{H} \, x \, . \tag{6}$$

If we now assume that employment is increased by the same proportion as hours are decreased, then $\frac{N_1}{N_0} = \frac{H}{H-x}$ .and substituting for N_1 in Equation 6, we get

$$y = PHK - \frac{PHK + W}{H} \, x \, . \tag{7}$$

Thus, on these assumptions, the employer's curve becomes flatter, making a settlement concerning hours more likely. The change in the slope of the function in this case is due to the arbitrary assumption that $N = f(x)$. The other assumptions made in this instance are not very plausible, unless the firm in question has idle capacity at the outset.

In general it may be said that the effect of changing N when P is constant, depends on its effect on fixed costs. If fixed costs rise proportionately more than N, then $\frac{F_0}{N_0} - \frac{F_1}{N_1} < 0,$ and the y intercept of the indifference curve in question falls, which implies that the curves in general become steeper. This is due to the fact that the curves as originally postulated increase in slope as they move away from the origin. (See p. 167). This effect can more easily be seen with the aid of figure 25. AB is an employer's indifference curve before there is any change in N. Its y intercept is PHK (see Eq. 7), or in this case, OA. If we now allow for a change in N and this changes F, so that $\left[\dfrac{F_0}{N_0} - \dfrac{F_1}{N_1} \right] = \alpha,$ then the new indifference curve, having the same slope but a different y intercept, would be CD. Since the curves get steeper as we move up the axis, the indifference curve after the change in N, that has the y intercept A, i.e. AB', must be steeper than CD, and therefore it must be steeper than AB.

Thus the whole set of indifference curves becomes steeper. Similarly it can be shown that if $\left[\dfrac{F_0}{N_0} - \dfrac{F_1}{N_1}\right] > 0,$ the set of indifference curves would become flatter; but if we begin with a firm of optimal size operating at its optimal output, the only possibilities are that $\dfrac{F_0}{N_0} - \dfrac{F_1}{N_1} \leqslant 0.$

The effect of changing employment, therefore, will be to steepen the indifference curves or to leave them unchanged, thus making a reduction in hours less likely under optimal conditions.

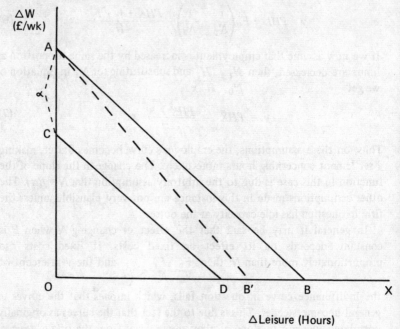

figure 25

One might wonder therefore why such a change in employment would be considered in the face of a reduction in hours. It would be, in so far as the employer was not a profit maximizer, at least in the short run, but was more interested in keeping his share of the market. It would indeed also be considered by a profit maximizer who had a view to the long run and either wished to retain customer loyalty or expected the demand curve in his market to be shifting steadily outward in future. Alternatively, the

possibility that $\dfrac{F_0}{N_0} - \dfrac{F_1}{N_1} > 0$, might be considered if we conceded that in
reality firms often operate below their optimal output, not to mention the
likelihood of the existence of firms of non-optimal size. In this case
employment could profitably be expanded to offset some of the cost of
reducing hours. But the employment could profitably have been expanded
even if hours had not been reduced, so that the extent to which the saving
thus incurred can be correctly used to offset the cost of reduced hours is
questionable. Finally there is the case where shift work is possible. This is
clearly an instance where the fixed costs will not increase by the same
proportion as employment and therefore the employer's curve will become
flatter. This however is a reasonable conclusion only if the reduction in
hours is in some way causally related to the employment of shift work —
i.e. a reduction in hours may be necessary if shifts are to be used. In any
event it is clear that shift work is not always a possible alternative, either
because of technological considerations or because of the state of the
labour market.

We now examine a slightly different but related alternative. Instead of
increasing the number of men employed, the employer may simply
compensate for the negotiated reduction by inducing the employees to
work overtime. In other words there may not be a reduction in actual
hours worked. This case can be seen in figure 26. The bargain begins at E.
But now the employer bargains in the knowledge or belief that he can and
will work his plant XH hours after the bargain as he has done before it.
When he now considers the cost of striking a bargain at E', he does not use
the previously suggested 'unit cost' equation. The bargain at E' will quite
simply represent the same cost as raising the weekly rate of pay to C. The
slope of the line $E'C$, is simply the new overtime wage rate, which if
overtime were paid at double the standard rate, would be $-\dfrac{2W}{H-x}$. Whether

this would be more or less steep than the slope of the equation originally
developed for the employer, would depend on the relative importance of
fixed costs.

When we first derived the employer's function we eliminated
productivity as a variable by assuming that it would not change as a result
of a reduction in hours. Let us now forego that assumption and see what
the effects of a causally related change in productivity would be. Let P
represent a level of hourly productivity existing before the change in
hours. The change in hours causes this to change to a new level, P'. Let r
represent the ratio between these two levels of productivity — i.e. $r \dfrac{P'}{P} f(x)$.

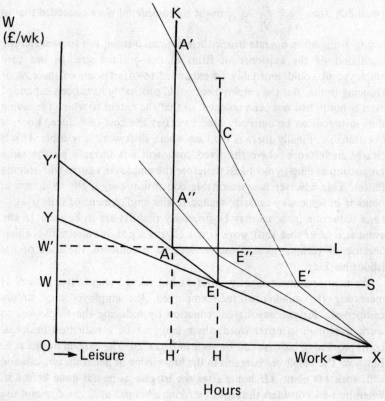

figure 26

Now the employer's function becomes

$$\frac{W+y+F'}{P'(H-x)} - \frac{W+F'}{PH} = K \tag{8}$$

which becomes

$$\frac{W+y+F'}{r(H-x)} - \frac{W+F'}{H} = PK \tag{9}$$

or alternatively

$$y = rPHK - rx\frac{PHK+W+F'}{H} + (W+F')(r-1) \tag{10}$$

Thus if productivity did not in fact change, then $r = 1$, and Equation 10 becomes the same as Equation 2.

We cannot determine from Equation 10 what effect any change in P will have on its slope, since $r = f(x)$. If we now assume for the sake of simplicity that r is a linear function of x – i.e. $r = a + bx$, and since we know that when $x = 0, r = 1$ then

$$r = 1 + bx \qquad (11)$$

and if we substitute into Equation 10, we get

$$y = PHK(1 + bx) - (1 + bx)x \left[\frac{PHK + W + F'}{H} \right] + (W + F')(1 + bx - 1) \quad (12)$$

which can be written

$$y = PHK - \left(\frac{PHK + W + F'}{H} \right)(x + bx^2 - Hbx) \qquad (13)$$

This function has a slope

$$\frac{dy}{dx} = -\left(\frac{PHK + W + F'}{H} \right)(1 + 2bx - Hb)$$

This means that if productivity decreases as weekly hours are reduced, i.e. if $b < 0$, we have $(1 + 2bx - Hb) > 1$ so long as $H > 2x$, i.e. so long as hours are not reduced by more than half; and within this range the slope of the function would be numerically greater than if productivity were invariant. Conversely, in the more likely case of productivity rising with a reduction in weekly hours, i.e. $b > 0$, the slope of the function would be numerically smaller within the same range – that is, employers would be more willing to concede reductions in weekly hours. A productivity agreement would thus seem to be an instance where employers and employees make joint efforts to flatten out the former's indifference curve.

Finally it is interesting to consider the case where productivity increases always so as to offset the effect of a change in hours – i.e. $r = 1 + \frac{x}{H-x}$. In this case the employer's indifference curve would become $y = PHK$, or in other words a horizontal straight line at any height PHK. So long as this was true the employer would freely grant reductions in hours. It may seem unreasonable that as each hour becomes more productive the employer should value it less, relative to a given wage increase. The answer to this dilemma is a reminder that we are dealing only with increases in productivity which result from reduced hours. The only way in which the employer could have his cake and eat it, in this case, would be through the introduction of shift work.

The increase in hourly productivity resulting from a reduction in hours is a very familiar result of the early documented instances of such reductions.[6] There is some doubt however whether this would still manifest itself in reductions below a working day of approximately eight hours. The answer to this question undoubtedly depends on the specific task under consideration. It is interesting to note in this connection that as hours are reduced, any absolute reduction represents a greater proportionate reduction in the total working time and would therefore require a greater increase in productivity to offset it. This is indicated by the fact that the slope of the employer's indifference curve increases numerically as x becomes a larger proportion of H. This would suggest that reductions in hours will be progressively more difficult to achieve — or at any rate, will be more costly to the employer.

There is also a possibility that productivity would increase as a result of an increase in wages, through an improvement in worker morale. This would simply mean that the employer's indifference curve would become steeper or, put another way, that the employer would regard a bigger wage increase as the equivalent of a given reduction in hours. This would only serve to strengthen the expectation that any agreement would deal with increases in wage rates to the exclusion of reductions in hours.

Finally, a brief look at the effect on the employer's function of a change in productivity which is not causally related to a change in hours or wages, tells us that such a change in productivity does not affect the shape of this function. This may seem surprising since the parameter P appears in the expression determining the slope of the function — i.e. $-\dfrac{PHK + W + F'}{H}$

If P changes then surely that slope changes as well. It does indeed, but so does the y intercept — i.e. PHK — and the significant thing is, that the curve which intersects the y axis at any particular point still has the same slope. Thus the indifference map is unchanged. An autonomous change in productivity may in fact affect the final result of the bargain inasmuch as it may make the employer more or less willing or able to make concessions. This will, however, affect only the size of the settlement and we have pointed out that this is outside the scope of this discussion. The composition of the settlement depends on the slopes of the two curves, and in this case they have not changed.

4 Summary

It can be seen that the relative rarity of adjustments in the normal hours of work, when these are fixed under collective bargaining, is not surprising once the various interests in the bargain have been properly identified. Indeed one should expect the great majority of settlements to deal with wages and other fringe benefits, excluding the hours of work. This is so mainly because hours of work are valued differently by employers and employed: the employer usually values their maintenance more highly than the employee values their reduction. This was demonstrated on certain not very restrictive assumptions about both sides; but it will also appear that the inclusion of some initially excluded factors would only tend to reinforce this result.

On the employer's side it was assumed that he values the hours in question strictly according to the effect of variations in them on his unit costs. The most important of other considerations increase his reluctance to reduce hours. Thus, if he were an output maximizer, his resistance to a reduction in hours, under normal circumstances,[7] would certainly increase. It would do this also if, more reasonably, the employer were an output maximizer with some profit constraint — i.e. a need to secure some minimum profit.[8] The employer may also experience a non-financial reluctance to reduce hours on the grounds that this interferes excessively with the 'prerogatives of management' and necessitates adjustments in production schedules.

On the employee's side it was initially assumed that marginal working time was valued at the 'going rate' of wages: an equilibrium was hypothesized in which the marginal unit of time was traded off 'willingly' against the marginal unit of income. The difficulty with this assumption is that it deals necessarily with the average preference of a group: but individuals within this group have different preferences, so that if the group may be posited in equilibrium there will always be individuals within it who are not in equilibrium, some with a greater, some with a smaller income preference than the group as a whole. This has been shown to induce the union to concentrate on increases in wages rather than reductions in hours, primarily because the opposition of leisure preferrers to an increase in income is likely to be much less strong than that of income preferrers to an increase in leisure.[9] Here again the major influence outside the stated assumptions has the effect of making reductions of hours less likely.

It is interesting to note that the same considerations which have operated to make reductions in hours relatively rare, have had the opposite effect on some other benefits, because here the relative value of the concession to the employee was higher than the relative cost to the employer. Many benefits such as pension funds, insurance schemes, even staff canteens come into this category. In each case it is a matter of the employer providing a good or a service to the employee at a price below the market price, so that the employee's net gain is greater than the employer's net loss. Indeed there is no need for the employer to make a loss at all. Such possibilities are of course much more readily available to large employers because only they can avail themselves of the economies of scale in the provision of these benefits.

All of this argues that at the level of the individual bargain – whether for a firm, an industry, or a nation – reductions in hours must be expected to occur only rarely. We have, however, found just such a pattern of rare and intermittent change not only in the bargains struck in individual firms or industries but in the economy as a whole and this poses the question why the reductions in different industries should be synchronous. The next chapter will deal with the observed discontinuities in the changes of normal hours on a macro-economic level.

Chapter seven
The causes of changes in normal hours

1 Reasons for discontinuity at the macro-economic level

Although it has been shown that reductions in normal hours should be expected to occur only at infrequent intervals, in any particular collective bargain, some explanation must still be found for the fact that all the bargaining units in the economy tended to achieve these reductions at about the same time. Three possible explanations present themselves: the synchronization may merely be the reflection of the mechanics of the bargain; it may depend on the phenomenon known elsewhere as 'price leadership'; or it may be due to the fact that certain economic and/or other factors change the relative preferences of employers and employed and that these influences are general to the whole economy.

Discontinuity on a macro-economic level might be accounted for by the mechanics of bargaining in a number of ways. Most important is the size of the bargaining unit. Clearly if the conditions for all workmen were settled at one bargain then the arguments of the previous chapter would suffice to explain the discontinuity in changes of normal hours at the macro level. Thus 'the displacement of district by national or industry-wide negotiations, a trend already existing but greatly accelerated by the First World War and taken further by the Second',[1] would be expected to have increased the likelihood of discontinuous change in the national aggregates. Nevertheless, the number of individual bargains is still so large that changes in the various industries, if they were spread over time, would produce a gradual shift, and in any event the discontinuity of these changes was their most marked feature even during the nineteenth century, before the major extension of the bargaining area. Finally the influence of this factor can be discounted once it is apparent that changes in the basic wage which are subject to the same institutional arrangements are very much less discontinuous.

One recent development in the nature of the collective bargain in Britain may, however, prove conducive to less concentrated changes of hours in future. The widespread adoption of 'long-term' agreements, lasting for periods up to three years, may have such an effect. Certainly this played a part in reducing the size of the reduction obtained in 1960-1 and spreading some of these reductions to 1964-6. Hence the *Ministry of*

Labour Gazette pointed out in 1965, that 'many of the changes in rates of wages and hours of work which came into operation during 1964 were the consequence of agreements made at earlier dates. In general they were the second instalments of long-term agreements, usually for periods of three years'.[2] The result of this may be either to split the infrequent substantial reductions in normal hours which do take place into two or more parts – it is this that seems to have happened in the 1960s – or to bring about more frequent adjustments in the hours of work. This latter result would occur if the employees' preference for increments in income was subject to diminishing returns, so that because a three-year agreement deals with a larger settlement it is more likely that increases in leisure would come to be considered. To put the same point another way, such agreements eliminate the effect of the worker's becoming accustomed to his new income and adjusting his relative preferences accordingly.

The second explanation of the observed pattern of change in hours on a macro-economic level is similar to the 'price leader' argument; it suggests that once a certain strategic sector of the economy has achieved such a change, the rest will follow. This suggestion is supported by the fact that each of the four major reductions in hours was led by the engineering and shipbuilding trades. The role of these trades in the 1871-3 changes has been discussed at length. The 1919 reductions began 'with the engineering and shipbuilding trades who agreed shortly after the armistice'.[3] In the post-war years these trades negotiated their reduction in 1946. In the late 1950s there is evidence of the same potential leadership. Although the printing unions opened this campaign with their prolonged strike in 1959, *The Times* commented that although 'the fight for the 40 hour week is of course being carried on intensively at the moment by the printing unions . . . a break through by them would not necessarily spread throughout industry as would a break through by the confederation (of shipbuilding and engineering unions)'.[4] Here is the price leader argument in undiluted form.

If one were to accept this argument, an explanation of the discontinuity of hours changes in engineering would suffice to explain it in the whole economy, and to explain the actual timings one need then look only at the factors affecting the preferences and the bargaining positions of engineering employers and workers. But unfortunately, this argument is too facile. It is true that a reduction of hours in any important industry, and especially one so big and pervasive as engineering, if it comes at a time when there is a general demand for reduced hours, may act as a catalyst, convincing others that the time is ripe. It is thus a 'cause' of the reductions in other industries only in the most superficial sense. Whether the initial move remains isolated or forms the first step in a general move depends on the demands being made by the other unions at that time. The engineers' reduction of their hours in 1890, from 54 to 53 per week in the north-east, did not induce others to follow − not even the rest of the same industry. Again, when the engineers struck for the eight-hour day in 1897, no other trades moved for it, even though a large number of London engineering shops actually worked these hours for some time during the strike. By contrast in 1871 a good number of trades were striking for the nine hours even before the engineering strike had concluded. In the end it is this, namely the speed with which the other reductions follow those of the engineers, which makes it clear that what we are witnessing is a general movement in which for strategic reasons the engineers are pushed into the forefront; but the other trades do not demand the reduction in hours merely because the engineers got it.

The failure of extensive reductions in hours sponsored by the government to precipitate wide-spread reductions makes the same point: neither the Textile Acts, nor the Coal Mines Acts, nor the adoption of the eight-hour day in many government establishments in 1894,[5] led to any subsequent general reductions, even though such expressions of government attitudes might be thought to augur well for attempts at reduction elsewhere. In fact these changes did not lead to general reductions because they came at times when in many of the large unions the demand for reduced hours was not strong, or when their bargaining position was weak. The possible exception here is the 1874 Textiles Act, but it quite clearly was part of the general movement of hours in 1872-4 and came too late in the day to be considered a possible cause of that movement.

All this suggests that the cause of the periods of reduction must be sought in the general economic circumstances which influenced the preferences of employers and employees alike. According to this view the preferences of both parties to any bargain are determined by a number of circumstances, including the state of trade in the particular industry and in the market in general. If these are to explain the great concentration of changes in hours then the general market conditions must predominate, and the following sections will discuss their bearing on changes in hours. Here one can point to the regional pattern of hours reductions in building in the nineteenth century, when the market conditions of the industry were general only to particular regions. The industrial areas, again, tended to reduce hours in various local industries at much the same time, presumably because they were subject to similar market conditions. We may note also the similarity of hours in many of the large cities.

Let us now turn to examine those general market conditions that may have influenced the preferences of the parties to collective bargains in Britain.

2 Factors likely to affect bargainers' preferences: real wages

On the very simplest level of economic analysis the real-wage rate is the most important determinant of the number of hours which people are willing to work. Thus in the traditional labour-leisure analysis, 'on the supply side there is a stable, negatively inclined long-run schedule relating average hours of work per head to the average real wage rate'.[6] Furthermore, in order to arrive at such a relationship between real wages and leisure preference (supply schedule of hours of work) it must be assumed 'that the tastes for leisure are very stable in the long run'.[7] Neither of these assumptions is acceptable as it stands.

The smooth negatively inclined supply schedule of hours of work, it is true, has much evidence to support it. Indeed on a global scale our findings corroborate it entirely. We found pressure to reduce the number of hours spent at work during periods of high real wages, such as the fifteenth century, the first half of the eighteenth century, and the entire period from 1850 to 1965. We found the same relationship for the domestic workers throughout though with a few complications. This consistency is particularly surprising since it is generally agreed that there has been a fundamental change in the working man's attitude to work. Thus Coleman tells us that the backward sloping supply curve of labour was a reality in the seventeenth century because this was 'a normal part of the backward economy in which the volume and variety of cheap consumer goods is small, in which economic horizons are strictly limited both on the demand side and on the supply side'.[8] In 1894 Brentano argued that this was amply proven to be true of backward economies but that it no longer held true of the industrialized countries because 'the working class has changed'.[9] This change was observed by Siemens while he was trying to establish a copper foundry in the Caucasus in the 1880s. 'The wants of the people of that country being extremely few, they have no inducements to work much. As soon as they have earned enough money to live on for a few weeks they stop working and take their ease'. Anticipating by some years the precepts of Madison Avenue, Siemens concluded that 'the only remedy for such a state of things was to habituate them to wants which could only be satisfied by continuous labour', and this he proceeded to do with the desired results.[10]

From this it is tempting to conclude that once the necessary wants have been created the workman will work more if given a higher real-wage rate, but this conclusion would be erroneous. Indeed, Brentano does not in fact challenge the view that the working man works fewer hours when real wages rise: he agrees that he will work fewer hours, but argues that he will raise his weekly output none the less because his output per hour will rise more than his weekly hours fall. Modern studies of this problem have confirmed the view that the number of hours worked decreases when the real-wage rate increases, even though these studies are subject to some criticisms which we shall consider when we discuss leisure preference separately. What is in question in these studies is normally not the fact of the relationship, but the imputed causal relation.

On balance it appears justifiable to assume some inverse relationship between the real-wage rate and the number of hours people are willing to spend at work, and in very broad terms our evidence supports this view. But it does not appear on closer examination that variations in the rate of rise of real wages have been associated with corresponding variations in the reductions achieved in hours since the 1850s. Figure 27 shows that there is nothing in the pattern of change of real wages to provide any clue to the discontinuous pattern of change in normal hours. The much greater regularity in money-wage changes has already been observed, and the changes in real wages are even steadier. True, figure 27 shows that the periods of hours reduction have all been associated with rising real wages, but then the great majority of years showed some rise in real wages, and the rises accompanying or immediately preceding the reductions in hours were not particularly large.

This being so the reductions in hours can be explained by the changes in the real-wage rate only if we assume that the worker's relative income and leisure preference was constant over time, or in other words, that pressure for leisure was cumulative. This is neither likely nor borne out by the evidence. It is not likely, in view of the tendency of people to accommodate themselves to a higher income and to regard it as normal after only a short time, a process which is speeded up to the extent that advertising creates a 'keeping up with the Joneses' atmosphere. In recent times the expectation of a steady rise in income has further strengthened this process. The hypothesis is also not borne out by the evidence: the decade from 1861 to 1871 which led up to one of the periods of hours reductions saw a rise in real wages of 21 points but the rise was 24 points from 1867 to 1877, and 34 points from 1880 to 1890, and neither of those decades led up to any appreciable reduction in hours.

Our analysis so far suggests that what actually took place was that in the short run each real-wage rise created a demand for leisure, but it was in the nature of the opposing interests being resolved under the collective bargain that this demand for leisure was repeatedly 'bought off' by the employers. This was possible because of the workman's continually shifting conception of his 'normal' or 'expected' income, which in a sense constantly made him revise the base line from which he measured the income increase to be compared to an increase in leisure. Thus, the fact that the thwarted desire for leisure cannot be treated as cumulative means that it may perpetually lose its unequal battle against the worker's own income preferences, and the employer's willingness to 'buy him off'.

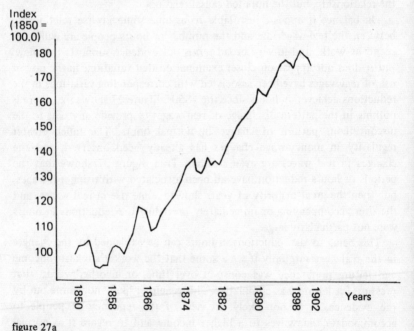

figure 27a
U.K. 1850-1902: index of real wages
Source: *see* Notes to figures and tables

The next variable that may affect the relative preferences of the bargainers is suggested by the observation that all the reductions in normal hours have been accompanied not only by rising real wages, but by real wages that rose in spite of rising prices.

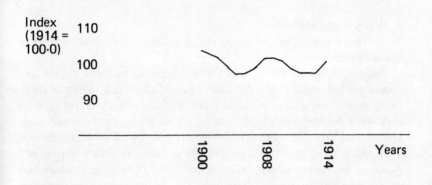

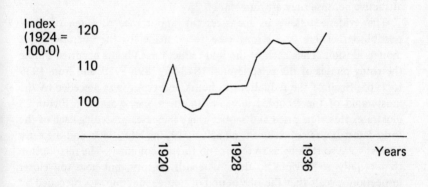

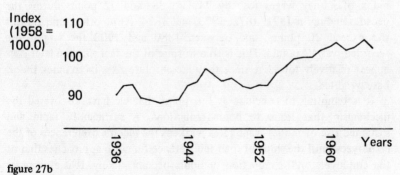

figure 27b
U.K. 1900–1965: index of real wages
Source: *see* Notes to figures and tables

3 Money wages and prices

These two variables will be considered together as they tend to move in the same direction.

Rising prices and money wages may affect the worker's income and leisure preferences in four different ways: if there is a money illusion, rising money wages have the same effect as rising real wages; rising prices may force the union to concentrate its efforts on raising the money-wage rate in order to avoid losses in real wages; repeated wage rises accompanied by steadily rising prices may increasingly destroy the money illusion and point up the futility of wage rises; major fluctuations in prices which lead to fluctuations in wages strengthen the feeling that wage rises are temporary and illusory gains, and make reductions in hours relatively attractive because they are durable.

The evidence allows us to assess the importance of some of these possibilities. There is a strong case to be made for the operation of a money illusion. Thus each of the four reductions in hours occurred during the rising phases of the price level – 1848-75; 1896-1920; and from 1935 to 1965. Each of the reductions in hours, moreover, was preceded by the most rapid of the recorded increases in the money-wage rate. Figure 28 illustrates this. The price and money-wage increases preceding each of the three latest hours reductions – namely 1919, the late 1940s, and the early 1960s – are so striking as to require no further comment. The relationship is not quite so obvious in the nineteenth century, but here too closer inspection reveals that the one period of hours reduction was preceded by the most rapid money-wage increases recorded. Table 10 shows that if one looks at the net change in the money-wage index over moving ten-year periods, from 1850 to 1902, by far the largest net increases in this index occurred in the decades coming to an end in the early 1870s. Thus the index of money wages rose by 24, 30, 38, and 32 points during the decades ending in 1871, 1872, 1873, and 1874. At no other time did this rise exceed 20 points, and between 1880 and 1902 the largest rise recorded was 17 points. This is true in spite of the fact that the later rises appear relatively too large since they are absolute rises in an index that is base weighted.

It is tempting to conclude at this point that we have discovered the mechanism that leads to hours reductions. A sufficiently rapid and sustained rise of money-wage rates weakens the income preferences of the employees until the slope of their indifference function approaches that of the employers and a reduction of hours becomes likely. It is even more likely if there is an economic boom in the offing thus making large concessions by the employers a greater possibility. But this would leave two observations unexplained: why when the reduction of hours is achieved is it as large as it is, and why do reductions not continue so long as the rapid rise in money wages continues?

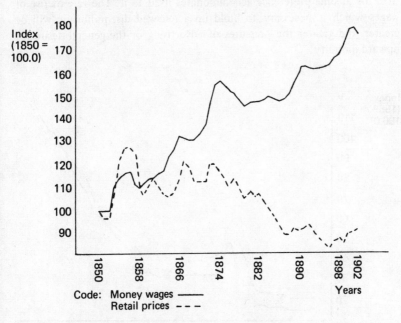

figure 28a
U.K. 1850-1902: average money wage rates and retail prices
Source: *see* Notes to figures and tables

The first question might be answered by supposing that people deem leisure valuable only when it comes in substantial quantities – i.e. that the marginal utility of leisure increases as a certain increase becomes sufficiently large to make certain identifiable activities possible; but this supposition is not verifiable, and appears merely to say that people choose leisure in this way 'because that is how they want it'. An alternative supposition, namely that the unions' dominant motive for the change is not leisure preference but insurance against potential unemployment raises the possibility that the changes must be appreciable if they are to have any impact on job security. An answer to the second question may be found in the difficulties of the bargaining mechanism discussed in chapter six. A rapid rise in the money wage builds up a disequilibrium between the worker's actual and desired leisure: once he is able to adjust this he returns to equilibrium in the sense of bringing his marginal valuation of leisure and his marginal rate of pay into balance, and from there on his relative leisure preference can only build up again slowly as his income rises more rapidly than his income preference accommodates itself to it. The rate of rise of wages which is necessary to build up a renewed disequilibrium will be greater, the greater the pressures of advertising or the general desire for upward mobility.

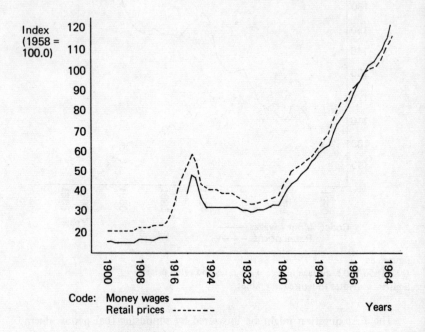

figure 28b
U.K. 1900-1965: average money wage rates and retail prices
Source: *see* Notes to figures and tables

table 10
Net change in the index of money wages over the ten-year period preceding any given date, 1860 to 1902

year	net change	year	net change
1860	+14	1881	+ 9
1861	+14	1882	+ 1
1862	+16	1883	− 6
1863	+ 7	1884	− 6
1864	+10	1885	− 5
1865	+10	1886	− 4
1866	+16	1887	− 2
1867	+19	1888	+ 3
1868	+20	1889	+10
1869	+18	1890	+16
1870	+19	1891	+16
1871	+24	1892	+15
1872	+30	1893	+13
1873	+38	1894	+12
1874	+32	1895	+13
1875	+28	1896	+15
1876	+20	1897	+17
1877	+20	1898	+16
1878	+18	1899	+16
1879	+16	1900	+16
1880	+14	1901	+16
		1902	+15

Source: *see* Notes to figures and tables

This brings us to the second effect that rising prices and money wages might have on hours reductions, namely that rapidly rising prices force the unions to concentrate on raising wages in order to keep real wages from falling. In a sense this possibility has already been disposed of by the observation that periods of rapid price and money-wage rises have in fact been associated with reductions in hours, so that each of the years 1872, 1919, 1947 and 1961 saw both a large reduction in hours and an increase in retail prices larger than the average over the preceding ten years.

The evidence thus casts doubt on this proposition as one of the fundamental causes of hours reductions. At the same time it leaves open the possibility that in a very immediate sense this factor may have been an effective catalyst. This could be true if the hours reductions, although they occurred at times when the price trend was basically upward, were themselves accompanied or immediately preceded by a temporary break in this rising trend. This hypothesis is received much more favourably by the evidence. Hence two of the four major reductions were clearly associated with a break in the upward price trend, while in the remaining two cases other 'special' circumstances brought about by the preceding wars may have served a similar purpose. There is thus some support for the view that a respite from the need to 'chase prices' played a part in allowing the unions to turn their attention to other issues, though there remains the need to explain why they should wish to turn to 'other issues', and under what circumstances the issue they turn to is the reduction of the hours of work.

The hours reductions of the early 1870s were preceded by a period of price stability that interrupted the otherwise steep ascent of prices. This much can be said with some confidence, even though nineteenth-century price data must be treated with caution and are ill-equipped to deal with the establishment of a sequence of events separated by relatively short periods of time. Nevertheless there is a broad consensus on this issue. Rostow after his painstaking analysis of this period concluded as did a contemporary volume of the *Economist Review*, that the price rises that were experienced between 1868 and 1871 were 'confined to the last quarter of 1871'.[11] Although this would mean that by the time the engineers reached their agreement on the nine-hour day prices had already begun to rise again, there is no doubt that the final onslaught on hours had been launched during the period of temporary price stability and this is irrespective of the exact date at which prices resumed their upward drive.

The 1960-1 hours reductions were also achieved just at the end of a lengthy and substantial interruption in a steep upward price trend. The Consumer Price Index marks this 'stutter' in the price level clearly. Thus in the period from 1956 to 1958 the Index rose by 7.0 points. In the following period it levelled off markedly, increasing by a modest 1.7 points in total between 1958 and 1960. Then in 1960-1 it resumed its upward trend and in this one year alone it rose by 3.8 points. Again one can say that although the movement for shorter hours came to fruition largely after the resumption in price increases it was effectively launched during the preceding lull in prices.

These events support the contention that a slowing down of price increases plays a role in allowing unions to turn their attention to issues other than wages. In this case there were some additional circumstances that help to explain why the unions would wish to turn their attention to 'other issues'. The diversion of the unions' attention from wage issues in the 1950s was not only made possible by the behaviour of wages, but was also imposed on them by government policy. Thus in July 1957 it was announced that 'the . . . Government . . . has called a halt, for a temporary period, to wage demands', and unionists at the time rightly pointed out that 'this has focused attention upon other Trade Union demands which have tended to recede into the background in the post war period. These demands concern the 40 hour week, better holidays with pay and general improvements in other working conditions'.[1,2]

The hours reductions of 1919, and of the late 1940s, were not similarly preceded or accompanied by a significant break in the upward price trend. Nevertheless the same effect may have been achieved by the forced saving which was a feature of both World Wars. It can be argued, therefore, that in the former two cases the levelling off of prices reduced the need for wage rises to maintain the material position of the workmen unchanged, and that the same effect was achieved by the substantial savings which people had accumulated over the war years.

On balance it appears that a reduction in the urgency with which wage increases have been required to maintain the *status quo,* has been an important contributory cause of the major reductions in hours.

The third potential effect of rising prices and money wages on the employee's leisure-income preference is a slackening interest in wage increases as these are continually eroded by price rises. Naturally this becomes a possibility only when there has been a sustained period of continuing price rise, such as the one that has occurred over the last twenty years.

The period from 1848 to 1873, as we have seen, was also marked by a sustained rapid upward trend in prices even though great fluctuations about the trend tended to obscure it. A letter to *The Penny Bee Hive* in 1870 stated that 'it does appear ... that working-men have *erred in judgment* (emphasis in original) ... in one particular. They have greatly over-rated the value of increased wages. The only true way of estimating wages is by considering the "commodities" they will obtain' and since 'the cost of commodities is almost wholly composed of wages ... double wages are no advantage if the cost of all a workman wants is doubled by the process'.[13] The writer evidently considered that 'money illusion' was rife among the trade unionists of the time.

In modern times partly because of the greater diffusion of information and partly because of the much steadier rise in prices the erosion of wages through rising prices is more generally recognized. 'Nearly all unions in the post-war period have been able to show a steady advance on the wages front, although most of the concessions gained have been subsequently wiped out by increases in the cost of living'. Nevertheless when this was written it was in connection with an article stating that most of the union conferences to be held that year 'will be giving priority to the current wages struggle'.[14] Clearly the recognition that prices erode wage rises may simply lead to increased pressure on wages in an effort to push them ahead faster.

The fourth way in which price and money-wage changes may affect the demand for hours reductions is that fluctuating prices which bring with them fluctuating money wages may engender a feeling that the raising of wages is a futile business, and a higher wage is a 'transient thing which flits away before a depression in trade'. Thus in the years from 1850 to 1874, when there was a sharp upward trend in prices accompanied by considerable fluctuations, there is an abundance of union statements to this effect. Such sentiments were noted among the masons in the late 1830s and early 1840s, and they returned to prominence just after the 1856-8 fall in money wages. A masons' lodge summed up this feeling in 1859 when they explained that 'the shortening of the hours of labour is the only thing that will permanently benefit the working classes. (Even) if at the commencement they suffer a reduction of wages' they should 'go for eight hours per day (for) had the members of the society taken this view of the case twenty-six years ago, eight hours a day would have been the rule in all the large towns of England, with the wages the same as at present'. It appeared then that wages took care of themselves, and in this belief the Bacup Lodge of the masons asked in 1861 for a code of rules to be ratified which did not lay down a wage rate 'as supply and demand to a certain extent regulate wages'.[15] On this assumption it was clearly reasonable to press for reductions of hours instead, both because any gain would be durable and because the consequent restriction of the supply of labour would help to keep its price up.

The 'permanence' of the reduction of hours, as against the 'transitory' nature of wage-rate changes, is a tenet that has survived until the modern day. Bevin expressed this view in 1922 when he said that 'to get the 48 hour week established it took thirty years of effort' and 'while you can recover wages . . . conditions take years to recover . . . and you must fight to keep them'.[16] The long persistence and the generality of this belief in the permanence of hours reductions requires some explanation. Is there a reason why in a period of bad trade the employer could not reverse changes in hours as well as changes in wages? Indeed such extensions of hours were shown to have taken place in the past, but in every case they were achieved with great difficulty, and often they were observed only in the course of some major social upheaval which introduced fundamental changes in working relationships. Extensions of hours due merely to a downward swing in the trade cycle were rare, and of little consequence when they did occur. This fact formed the basis for the belief in the permanence of hours reductions. The explanation of this phenomenon is that in times of bad trade when the employer is in the strongest position *vis-à-vis* the union he is least likely to want longer hours. The employers recognized this from an early date, and it reinforced their opposition to reductions. This strand in the employers' thinking was revealed clearly at the time of the nine-hour strike by the engineers. At that time *The Bee Hive* reported that Sir William Armstrong, the spokesman of the employers' federation, 'lets the secret of the masters' resistance out with a simple unconsciousness quite pleasant to notice. "Wages fluctuate", he says, "with demand, but shortened hours of work do not alter; and, therefore, there is less objection to increase wages than to decrease time". Can anything be more frank than this?' The paper then proceeds to explain that 'the masters know if they have the long day, they can shorten it when trade is slack, and when trade is brisk they have the profit of it without being called on inconveniently to invest capital in new machinery. They know, too, that the only time in which they want it (the long day) is when trade is active, and that at such a time they dare not attack the men to obtain it'.[17]

In short, in an insecure world the permanence of an hours reduction was recognized as one of its most important assets. It strengthened union demands for it, and also increased employer opposition to it, and meant that clashes on this issue often turned into major conflicts. In the end, in a nice tautological manner, the belief in the permanence of hours reductions was justified, at least in part, because the belief itself induced the unionist to accept enormous sacrifices to defend what he had once gained.

This raises the entire problem of the employers' resistance to reductions of hours, and how this was affected by rapidly rising prices and money wages. Sustained and rapid price increases indicate the existence of 'soft markets' in which large concessions can be achieved by the unions, but there is no reason why the employers should be more than usually willing to make these concessions in the form of reductions of hours. The difference seems rather to arise on the workers' side: the possibility of large concessions being gained makes a reduction in hours more attractive to them, to the extent that their demand for additional income is subject to diminishing returns. In addition, the fact that the reductions under discussion are usually large, for reasons discussed elsewhere, means that they become attainable only at points in time when markets are very soft.

That markets during each of the periods of reduction were 'soft' is indicated by the large price rises they witnessed. This is most evident in the hyper-inflation that followed the First World War, but even current post-war markets have been consistently able to absorb higher prices. The situation in the early 1870s was summarized by Rostow when he spoke of the 'breezy atmosphere of 1871-2 when . . . wages were raised freely, and prices rose without loss of new orders'.[18]

The size of the concessions made in such periods depends also on the great bargaining strength of the unions then. But such periods are also usually associated with low unemployment — as in the Phillips curve — and this is the next factor that will concern us.

4 Unemployment

The most cursory examination of any union's discussion of shorter hours reveals that in virtually all cases the reduction of unemployment is a major motivation. The idea appears at all times, from the early agitation in the textile mills to the present day. A modern analyst has written that 'the most common argument advanced in recent years in support of shorter hours has been the unemployment argument',[19] and although the argument has not always been predominant, being overshadowed in earlier days by the health and welfare arguments, it has been prominent from the earliest days.

It has been argued elsewhere that the foundation of this demand is to be found in some version of the 'fixed work-fund' theory,[20] which asserts that there is a certain amount of work to be done, so that if each man does less there will be employment for more men. As such it had a particular attraction for and relevance to certain industries in which demand was deemed unresponsive to changes in price, and took the form of large units of output each of which provided employment for a considerable period of time. Building was such an industry, and there is no doubt that these factors were partly responsible for its prominent position in the early movement for shorter hours. Occasionally the men referred to these special conditions in their discussions, as when the London masons sent a memorial requesting the twelve-o'clock Saturday and assured the employers that they 'fully believe the public will bear you harmless, as regards pecuniary loss', or when the Manchester masons blandly accompanied a similar request with the reminder that any losses that might be incurred could be recouped by higher prices. It is clear that there was a feeling that the number of buildings that would be erected would not be appreciably affected by a rise in labour costs. In the larger towns where there were more projects funded on very long-term bases this may not have been unreasonable. Also the fact that in this industry demand comes in the form of large indivisible units naturally led immediately to the idea that a certain job represents work for so many masons for so many months, and here it is true that less work by some would mean work for others, especially in smaller communities where there was often but one big site and the end of it would send men tramping. In one such place the men refused to work overtime as they 'had a better idea in view by shortening the hours of labour, which would cause the works to be longer in hand, or give employment to some unemployed masons'.[21] The alternative of adding more labour did usually exist in this industry as capital/labour ratios were low and presumably diminishing marginal productivity set in only slowly.

If these conditions made the builders particularly susceptible to the appeal of shorter hours to combat unemployment, this belief soon passed to other trades, as these came to terms with the transformation of what had been local and regional markets into national markets. The dynamics by which this change led the unions to take a greater interest in the issue of hours are highly interesting and deserve attention.

One of the first and most striking indications that the working man had of the changing nature of the markets in which he worked, was the dramatic change in the nature of the unemployment problem that periodically confronted him. While markets had been essentially local the workman's defence against a slump in demand for his labour had been the 'tramping system' which allowed the unemployed to escape such local depressions, but this system had clearly outlived its usefulness when the economy took on a national character and the periodic fluctuations in trade became general. Hobsbawm has shown that it was the 'cataclysmic, cyclical unemployment of 1820-50', and in particular the extraordinary slump of 1842, which brought the unions face to face with the need for new institutions to confront new problems and 'led to a major change: the spread of ordinary unemployment relief'.[22] It now appears that this same readjustment brought the issue of hours to a position of prominence, if not of predominance.

The essence of the problem confronting the unions was that unemployed members could no longer always be expected to move on in search of work, and so provision had to be made to look after them while they waited for trade to revive. This led naturally to the establishment of unemployment relief as a means of alleviating their suffering, but it also focused attention on the reduction of hours of work as a means of preventing or reducing the evil of unemployment itself. Thus the earliest instances of 'static out-of-work pay' were recorded in the late 1830s, at the same time as the craft unions were developing an active interest in the reduction of hours, and in the 1850s the great amalgamated unions sprang up with their major aim of combating unemployment through hours reductions and the provision of relief.

The Amalgamated Society of Engineers was founded in 1851 in the midst of a struggle to curtail overtime and to regulate hours and from its inception it boasted a strong out-of-work fund as one of its major attractions. Similarly the great Amalgamated Carpenters' Union (ASCJ) was begun in 1860 as a direct result of the great London builders' strike for the nine-hour day. It too placed great emphasis on unemployment relief but was ultimately founded to help to do away with the root causes of the problem that made such relief necessary. Thus it pledged itself to policies 'that may lead to correction of the defective working of our political system, which . . . presents the degrading anomaly of tens of thousands at the same moment seeking employment, but in vain', and to this end and 'consistently with the safety of the Society, all proper means will be employed to secure a reduction of the hours of labour'.[23]

The acute concern over unemployment which was growing in the labour movement reflected not only the emergence of the national trade cycle and the resulting collapse of the tramping system. The fact that unemployment was now experienced in very concentrated and massive doses intensified its impact and increased the suffering it caused.

Furthermore, and almost paradoxically, the increasing regularity of work and the general decline of casual labour intensified the distinction between 'work' and 'unemployment' and raised the disutility of the latter. In addition the rising wages and the consequent rise in the status of the artisan, and in particular the 'aristocracy of labour', raised the psychological cost of unemployment and intensified the workman's demands for action. Hence it was no accident that the engineers took a leading part in the movement for shorter hours, since their wages were relatively high while at the same time 'from 1860 onwards the figure (for the recurrent unemployment in the metals sector) developed a lead (over the average rate) which increased in size as time went by, (so that) by 1860-70 the margin was 16 per cent'.[24]

The decision to combat unemployment, by reducing hours, involved a paradox for the unions, exactly analogous to the problem of the employer who feared that at the only times when he would be in a position to extend hours he would not wish to do so: the unions had to fear that at the only time when the union was in a position to reduce the hours of work the members would not wish to do so. Figure 29 illustrates the extent of this problem. Leaving aside the 1960s, we find that the three reductions in hours are associated with the three periods of the fullest employment on record: the two wars need no comment here, while the years 1871-3 have been described elsewhere as 'an almost classic case of full employment'.[25] The question then is, why did the demand for a remedy against unemployment take its greatest effect at times when unemployment was not a problem?

The answer to this question is that union pressure for reductions in normal hours is occasioned more by the threat of unemployment than by its existence. Occasionally and under special circumstances the direct connection between unemployment and shorter hours is revealed by the evidence, whereas normally the unions' bargaining strength is so reduced by the existence of unemployment that its demands cannot be realized.

When the pressure for reductions was not channelled through the collective bargain its major successes did come during periods of particularly high unemployment. This has already been noted of the two major Textile Factory Acts, those of 1833 and 1847. The Act of 1902 also came at a time of rapidly rising unemployment, and the Coal Mines Act of 1908 was passed in the year of the worst unemployment since 1879. Clearly, in the political arena, bad trade did not weaken the workman's influence, and there is distinct evidence that it was labour pressure that induced the passage of these laws. Thus the government in 1833 deplored the 'injurious effect on the manufacturing interests' but had decided to act because 'the general feeling and excitement throughout the country had made it necessary that Parliament should interfere'.[26] Hence, when the hours issue is removed out of the framework of the collective bargain the importance of the unemployment issue asserts itself in that reductions are achieved when unemployment is at its height.

Even when the problem found expression in the collective bargain one direct connection between short hours and unemployment did remain. The actual existence of unemployment often found unionists willing to implement various forms of 'share-the-work' arrangements, and to accept a reduction in income through temporary short-time working or by curtailing or outlawing overtime. Such expedients had found favour as direct remedies for unemployment from an early date. Thus in 1811-12 'many of the factories at Manchester did not work above half-time', while before 1816 the potters 'in many cases . . . (were) limited to three or four days a week',[27] and mention has been made of the many cases of self-imposed short-time working by the miners. But if it is true that such arrangements were very common at times of bad trade, it is also true that the men often refused to accept such restrictions.

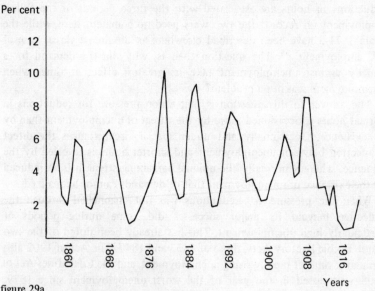

figure 29a
U.K. 1857-1919: unemployment (per cent)
(estimated national rate)
Source: *see* Notes to figures and tables

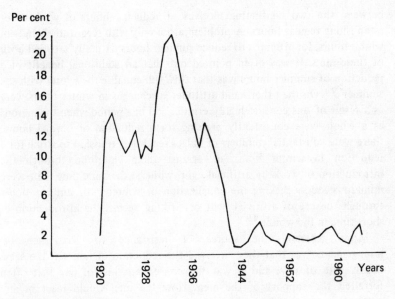

figure 29b
U.K. 1920-1965: unemployment (per cent)
(estimated national rate)
Source: *see* Notes to figures and tables

In some cases refusals to accept short-time arrangements reflected a basic conflict in union aims usually arising out of the seasonal nature of the work in question. It is this that explains the fact that the builders were often reluctant to accept such arrangements even though they were always in the vanguard of the movement for the permanent reduction of normal hours. Thus one of the major functions of a union is to regulate the rate at which a certain amount of work is exchanged for wages, and in practice this often means attempting to regulate the amount of work being exchanged for an already agreed upon amount of wages. Efforts to establish a normal day were intimately connected with this problem because of a belief that irregular work, or ultimately casual labour, were the surest roads to the individual bargain and wage cutting. Similarly payment by the piece, ostensibly the easiest way to fix the exchange rate of work for labour, was opposed because it led to competition amongst workmen and hence inevitably to rate cutting, particularly because the size of the 'piece' was usually difficult to measure and define. For this reason unions in trades where summer and winter hours differed were often torn between the two conflicting motives of reducing hours of work or of establishing regular hours. A problem arose only with regard to changes in winter hours, for attempts to reduce summer hours naturally satisfied both of these aims. It was often pointed out that an additional benefit of a reduction of summer hours was that this 'will equalise the winter with the summer'.[28] On the other hand attitudes to changes in winter hours were as a result of this conflict highly erratic, and in a period when the masons as a whole were consistently pressing for a reduction of normal hours, there were substantial numbers of lodges seeking permission to strike for a reduction in winter hours or against their extension through the introduction of work by artificial light, while at the same time there were numerous lodges seeking the equalization of winter with summer hours through the use of artificial light or striking against the introduction of short time in the winter.[29]

More generally the source of resistance to 'share-the-work' arrangements was that they involved the reduction of hours at the same hourly rate of pay, and it was the consequent loss of pay that often forfeited the support of the men. How the men would react in any particular case would of course depend on the extent to which those in employment identified with those out of work, as well as on how directly their sacrifice would assist the unemployed. But probably the most important determinant of their reaction was the extent to which they themselves felt threatened by unemployment. When in 1833 a mill-owner called his operatives together 'and stated . . . (he) would either stop half of the mill or divide the work among them all . . . they all said they would rather divide the work'.[30] It is certain that if this mill had first laid off one half of its labour force and then after some time had asked those remaining at work whether they would agree to work half time for the sake of the unemployed, who could then be employed again, the answer of the workmen would have been more equivocal. This makes the point that the likelihood of getting the agreement of men for a reduction of hours when this involves a reduction of earnings is greater when the men in question are themselves threatened by unemployment. This is not to deny that there were many instances of men accepting short time in order to alleviate the pressure on others in their trade who were out of employment, but in cases where this was the only inducement such sacrifice was more likely to be rejected. Here one can point to the great difficulty of the mining unions to induce their members to observe restrictions that would bring others into employment, and there is more general evidence to show that the unions themselves were aware of the problem. Thus one masons' lodge expressed the opinion that the 'unwillingness to work overtime ... to benefit their own class by securing permanent employment to a larger number of their own class ... is a noble proof of self-denial and disinterestedness'.[31]

If an imminent threat of unemployment sharply increased the workman's willingness to give up current income, this was no less true of his willingness to give up an increase in income for a reduction of hours to forestall future unemployment. Here also pressure was most intense when it could be said that 'the job you save may be your own' and this was true whenever employment was high, but there was a great fear of impending unemployment. To argue this one need not go as far as the trade unionist who wrote that 'as Trade Unionists we do not attempt to solve the problem of unemployment. We are selfish and the most bigoted of protectionists',[32] but one must recognize the element of truth in it. The unionist will be more willing to accept sacrifice to alleviate unemployment if that problem either threatens his job or his bargaining position. Thus unemployment existing within a union's immediate labour market might lead to action like the attempts of the miners to enforce the stint in bad times, and the many other examples of the acceptance of short time during periods of depression, but it is significant that these attempts often met with non-cooperation from the membership, while it is a matter of record that the effective movements for short hours always took place with the support of the membership and often with the non-union workmen even in advance of the organization.

The solution to our paradox now becomes clear. Not only were the unions in the best position to press for a reduction of hours during periods of boom, but also their demand for short hours to prevent unemployment was likely to be strongest at such times if there was a general fear of future unemployment. The three major sources of the fear of future unemployment were the fluctuations of the trade cycle; the seemingly unlimited possibilities of technological change; and fear of a rise in labour supply. We must now see whether these were particularly in evidence at the time of the four reductions on record.

The trade cycle came increasingly to be accepted by the working man after the middle of the century, and this had the obvious effect of leading him to expect that both boom and slump were transitory. As early as 1844 Shaftesbury wrote of the Lancashire textile districts that 'the operatives, poor fellows, to a man, distrust this present prosperity',[33] and time only reinforced these views. In 1857 a mason refuted a charge that the building depression was due to the activities of the union by saying that 'there is nothing unusual in the present depression, seeing that a similar state of things is of periodical occurrence'.[34] By 1870 the belief was fully established. When the first signs of a revival of trade appeared in 1870, *The Bee Hive* summed up this feeling when it stated that 'it is not enough to tell us that the evil at present is being diminished. We have a right to demand that its recurrence should be prevented',[35] and it was echoed by the bookbinders in 1873, when they wrote: 'Our trade during the three months just passed has been, as we anticipated, brisk. . . . But it cannot be expected that such a good state of trade will be lasting (and) we would . . . impress upon your minds the . . . necessity of making provision for a slack season': they pointed out that the members of Liverpool 'have done so, in their recent attempt to shorten the hours of labour'.[36] In short, each boom was seen as a prelude to a slump and increasingly the working man accepted the need to use his strength in the boom to soften the blow of the next downturn.

Both great wars brought with them powerful demands that the blight of unemployment should not be allowed to recur. In a speech early in 1919, the Prime Minister gave an indication of the strength of this demand, when he said:

'During the war, the workers have been removed for four and a-half years from the terrible dread of unemployment, and it is only those who have lived in industrial homes who can realise what a horror that prospect is. For four and a-half years that has been eliminated from their lives; it has been taken away from the horizon. Now peace has been established and the spectre re-appears, and there is a general feeling that something must be done to suppress it, to destroy it, to eliminate it for ever out of the lives of the workers'.[37]

The strength and pervasiveness of this feeling was striking, and the issue preoccupied most trades and every Labour Party conference during the second half of the war. During the Second World War the same feelings were in evidence, only this time they were possibly even more intense, if only because the problem of unemployment had been so much more intractable during the decades preceding that conflict. Once more it could be said that 'everyone is agreed that the mass unemployment which defaced the period between the wars . . . must not be allowed to return', and the problem of how to achieve this became a major preoccupation of government, of unions, and of many academics.[38]

With full employment after 1945 the fear of the trade cycle receded,[39] though a fear that this extraordinary boom will come to an end lingers, and is revived by any sign of growing unemployment: it is significant that the reductions of 1960-1 and 1964-6 came immediately after the two highest unemployment peaks since 1947. Throughout 1958 the trade-union world became very restive about the growing unemployment, and the printing unions only reflected a general feeling when they issued a statement to their membership late in the year warning them that there was 'increasing evidence . . . to show that we are likely to move into harder times'.[40] By early 1959 when the success of the government's wage restraint became evident it was reported that 'the emphasis in most unions now is on the question of redundancy and how it can be fought',[41] though more generally the problem of redundancy seems to have been growing more serious since 1956.[42]

The second major source of the fear of future unemployment is the expectation of drastic technological change.[43] This can be even more pervasive than fear of the trade cycle, because technological change may affect anyone, whereas many men are safe from cyclical unemployment. Each of the four reductions in hours came at a time when this issue was of particular concern.

From early in the nineteenth century technological change had been an important feature of industrial growth, and increasingly the implications of these changes were becoming a matter of great public interest. The riches promised by these developments seemed borne out by the rapid rise of money wages after 1853,[44] but the very uneven growth of the economy tempered the optimism that resulted. The severe and prolonged slump of the late 1860s was felt the more acutely because it confirmed people's secret fears about the future. Thus a book published in 1870,[45] which asserted that 'the class of people who "would work", and who cannot obtain it, are seriously and permanently on the increase' fell on receptive ears. Was not the upswing in trade which came in 1870 accompanied by an increase in pauperism? Did such a paradox not point to the pernicious effect of 'the extension of machinery'? Grant's book thought that this was the case, and *The Bee Hive* commented: 'however scouted the idea a few years ago, and however triumphantly disproved, as they thought, by McCulloch and others, the idea still gains ground as the facts bear and accumulate'. Thus while 'no man in his senses would at this time of day lay an arrest upon inventions and adaptions of machinery increasing productiveness and diminishing the amount of human labour', the fact that 'the mechanical productive powers have been increasing rapidly from year to year in a continually increasing ratio' and were 'capable of being increased to an extent to which no limit can be assigned', was contrasted with the feeling that 'at no period during the present century was there more prevalent distress than at this moment'. The result was a determination to remove this paradox for 'it is not an immutable law of nature that superabundant manual and mechanical means for the production of wealth and happiness for all, should become most influential causes of widespread poverty and misery'. The remedies to the problem were a matter of constant debate, and included the increasing of home demand by a redistribution of income; the opening up of the waste-lands of Britain; and the reduction of the supply of labour, either through emigration or the reduction of hours of work. 'The wide-spread desire for emigration was a natural result of the two . . . evils (of) the most disastrous increase in the number of able-bodied paupers (and) the cry for want of employment', and recent meetings had shown 'how strongly the movement in favour of emigration to the colonies takes hold of the sympathies of our artisans'. In this setting 'the Nine Hours' movement is reported to be steadily progressing, 'North, South, East and West'.[46]

The two World Wars undoubtedly saw great advances in the industrial application of technology. Thus, although the years 1890 to 1914 saw many important discoveries, 'not till during and after the First World War did they reach the stage of widespread application',[47] and the effects of the Second War were similar. At that time it was recognized that to avoid unemployment after the war it was not enough 'merely to prevent a decrease in total expenditure', but that the aim must also be 'to ensure its continuous increase, so as to absorb and take advantage of the increasing productivity of industry',[48] that the war's technological advances would make possible.

Since 1945 an apprehension has persisted regarding the uncharted possibilities of automated processes,[49] which has led some experts to make predictions such as that 'in the end (unemployment) is likely to reach a very high figure, say 90 per cent of the labour force, unless radical changes are made in the present pattern of working', or again, that the introduction of automated processes 'will produce an unemployment situation, in comparison with which the . . . depression of the thirties will seem a pleasant joke'.[50] Whatever one may think of the validity of such statements they do create and reflect an atmosphere in which the industrial application of technological advances is watched with some apprehension by the trade unions.

The hours reductions of 1960-1 came at a time when 'the heavy investment in a number of industries in recent years' was expected to 'yield its benefits in increasing productivity during 1961-66'. The belief in a generally accelerating growth of productivity was further documented in a weighty government publication which pointed out that: 'In the inter-war years, and in the 50 or 60 years before 1914, output per worker rose at an average rate of some 1½ per cent per annum. From 1951 to 1961 the average underlying rate of growth of productivity was faster, at more like 2½ per cent per annum. It seems quite probable that it has now risen further and may be nearer 3 per cent per annum'.[51] This circumstance partly explains the revival of trade-union interest in the 40-hour week in the late 1950s. The 1957 Annual Conference of the Transport and General Union thus resolved 'that full consultation should take place when it is proposed to introduce automated processes and in addition that there should be a progressive reduction in the hours of work',[52] and two years later the issue was still in the forefront of union demands. At that time the shipbuilding and engineering trades decreed that 'unemployment and mechanisation made this question (of a "shorter working week") acute', and the Transport and General Union urged that the 42½-hour week of the motor industry be challenged in the light of the 15 per cent increase in productivity that this industry had achieved in one year. This convinced the union that a reduction of hours must be achieved and they declared that 'the unions must fight for it and the time is now ripe'.[53] Later in that year the reduction of hours began, and spread to the rest of the economy one year later.

The third and final potential source of the fear of future unemployment is the prospect of a rapidly increasing labour force. Once more it is true that each of the four periods of hours reduction had special reasons to be concerned with this problem.

At the time of the changes in hours in the 1870s there was good cause for the workman to be concerned about the growth of the labour force. Population growth in the 1860s had reached a new high of 13.2 per cent, a rate which was to be surpassed only once, namely in the 1870s when it rose to 14.4 per cent.[54] But this was combined with the fact that this was a period of very rapid urbanization which was a development of more immediate significance to the labouring man. Whereas in 1851 the proportion of the total population living in urban areas was 50.2 per cent, only twenty years later this had risen to 61.6 per cent.[55] As *The Times* pointed out in 1870 the net consequence of these shifts was that 'the whole pressure of a population increasing at the rate of 1,000 a day was concentrated upon 20 large towns'.[56]

Both World Wars brought their own special problems with regard to the growth of the supply of labour. Here the fears concerned demobilization, the shut-down of war industries, and the possible continuation of the high labour force participation rates induced by the war. While the first two 'fears' were of course inevitable, the third focused on the possibility that the many people, and in particular the many women, who had entered the labour force for the first time during the war would not return to their 'not in the labour force' status after the peace. In the event this 'fear' proved justified for female participation rates did remain above their pre-war level.

table 11
Great Britain 1954-1961: young persons entering the labour force (000s)

year	number	year	number
1954	505	1958	514
1955	508	1959	572
1956	482	1960	548
1957	504	1961	588

Source: *see* Notes to figures and tables

Even at the time of the 1960-1 reductions there was concern about the growth of the labour force, although the problem was less serious than it had been on the previous three occasions. 1959 saw the beginning of the entry into the labour force of the Second World War baby bulge which had now come of age. Table 11 shows that the annual number of labour force entrants remained virtually static around 500,000 per annum from 1954 to 1957, rose slightly in 1958, and then rose sharply to new high levels of 572, 548 and 588 thousand in the next three years. This was a significant increase and was added to the fact that, as *The Economist* pointed out, 'for the first peacetime year since 1938, there has probably been a net inward balance of migrants to Britain in 1958'.[57] Taken together these two circumstances constituted a source of concern for the labour movement.

That the reduction of hours was an anti-unemployment measure, even though its introduction was usually associated with very low unemployment, is supported by other evidence as well. Only thus can one explain the insistence on the 54-hour week by the engineers in 1871, even though this meant a loss of pay and an agreement to do any amount of overtime demanded. Demands for hours reductions to forestall unemployment are compatible with the general trade-union willingness to work overtime at the times of full employment when the reductions were achieved. This motivation is also suggested by the fact that those few industries that did achieve significant reductions of hours outside the general periods of change were often found to be particularly subject to technological change just at that time.

How do these various factors, that account for the workman's fear of unemployment, affect the employer's resistance to hours demands? In so far as he fears the downturn of the trade cycle he will be particularly vulnerable to union pressure as he will wish to take advantage of his business opportunities while they are available. In addition, the usual willingness of the men to do overtime during the boom removes one of his major sources of opposition. That the reductions were often granted under such temporary duress is suggested by the observation that where they were followed by a slump it was usual for the employers to try to reverse this concession, though usually with little success.

The effect of technological change is to increase the employer's resistance to reductions of hours, since it usually increases his capital/labour ratio. This effect may be offset, however, by his greater vulnerability due to the heavy capital outlay involved[58] and, more significantly, by the prospect of productivity increases. We have seen that, to the extent that these increases result from the reduction in hours, they tend to reduce the employer's resistance to reductions, and it is significant that the earliest reductions were achieved at times when their potential effects on productivity were coming to be widely recognized by employers.

Employer opinion on the subject of hours underwent a major change around the middle of the nineteenth century. Hobsbawm has shown that in the 1840s employers began gradually to move from the extensive to the intensive use of labour, and as this change proceeded the question of the efficient utilization of labour time came to be analysed more rationally. The original belief that output was determined solely by the speed of machines and the number of hours they ran,[59] was slowly displaced by a recognition that the intensity of the labour input could substantially affect the rate of production. Thus, although the 1833 Royal Commission still reported that 'the majority of witnesses agree' with the Committee, that a reduction of hours 'must be attended . . . with a corresponding diminution of production',[60] by 1846 Sir George Strickland was able to tell the House of Commons that 'a great change had taken place in the minds of the master manufacturers. Many of them had adopted the eleven-hours day with the most gratifying results'.[61] This change of heart had been brought about at least in part by progressive employers who had tried the 'new system' and reported favourably on it. As early as 1841 a large Yorkshire manufacturer had written to the Home Secretary stating that 'some think, that the cost of production would not be at all increased by a reduction in the hours from twelve to ten',[62] and these views gained ground as the evidence accumulated. By 1871, what had once been believed about a reduction from twelve to ten hours was thought possible for a reduction from ten to nine hours. In commenting on the great engineering strike of that year, *The Times* thought that 'it is indeed doubtful whether masters gain anything by exacting longer working hours . . . whether nine hours' active work does not represent the MAXIMUM of an average workman's daily labour',[63] and they were supported in that view by the master builders of Newcastle who reported that 'after the nine hours had been conceded by them . . . they were benefited'.[64] Thus both the passage of the Factory Act of 1847 and the hours reductions of the 1870s were facilitated by this change in employer attitudes.

In later years when the hours to be reduced were less excessive, and hence when the productivity gains resulting directly from the reduction of hours were less clear,[65] employer opposition to such reductions intensified once again. Even so this opposition varied in intensity and could always be reduced if hours reductions were bartered in return for the relinquishing of some 'restrictive practice', thus bringing about the productivity increase that was no longer the direct result of the reductions themselves. Such *quid pro quo* arrangements ranged from the crude early efforts of the master builders to impose payments by the hour on the men after they had had to concede a reduction in hours, or the widespread 'destruction of restrictive trades union regulations relating to apprenticeship, piece-work, and shop routine'[66] which followed the hours reductions of 1872-3, to the modern productivity agreement where this exchange takes place with the consent of both parties and is part of the agreement reducing hours.

More generally, as has been pointed out, employer opposition to hours reductions was effectively reduced by the willingness of the men to do overtime. Thus in cases where there were no restrictions on overtime work the determination of the hours of work was in effect returned to the individual bargain where each individual's leisure was purchasable at some premium rate of pay. Thus the overtime rate became one of the means through which the employer could undermine the union attempts to restrict supply. Ironically the unions had originally pressed for its introduction as part of their effort to restrict supply. Hence the major purpose of such rates had been to act 'as a prohibitive tariff to the master and a protection to the men against overwork'. From the beginning the unions had recognized that such rates also affected their members but they had seen this as merely an added benefit which served 'if extra work was unavoidable, to compensate the workman . . . for the sacrifice of a portion of that leisure which becomes more valuable to him the less of it he has left'.[67] In time it was this second effect of the rate that came to predominate and so its role shifted from being a deterrent to the employer, to being a means of inducing employees to spend longer hours at work.[68]

The most striking diminution in employer opposition to reductions in hours occurred whenever shifts were introduced or became possible because of a reduction in hours. Under such circumstances employer opposition at times turned into outright support, so that as early as the 1840s we saw the masters of the iron furnaces attempting to introduce the eight-hour shift over the opposition of their employees. Although somewhat less dramatically, the introduction of shifts also made shorter hours acceptable to the gas industry in 1890, and accounts for the atypical reductions of hours that took place in the cotton industry in 1956. This latter reduction was atypical in that it occurred at a time when there was no general adjustment of hours. It was made possible because the unions had 'approved in principle an agreement which opens the way to the wider adoption of shift-working, a more rational wage structure and improved working conditions'. In return 'the unions have accepted the principle of two shifts based on a 38¾ hour working week . . . for the same wage as for the present 45 hour week'.[69] Finally on a more general level it is worth noting that the ten years ending in 1964, which witnessed one of the major reductions in normal hours, also saw the proportion of employees working shifts rise from twelve to eighteen per cent.[70]

5 Institutional factors

Institutional factors and their underlying ownership relations were of the greatest importance in determining the pattern of change in normal hours. Once the contract of hire stipulates the number of hours a man is to work using equipment that belongs to someone else, a conflict of interests results. When the resolution of that conflict occurs through the collective bargain a certain pattern emerges. Would this pattern or the final result have differed had the employer been free to determine the hours? It is our contention that both would have differed, so that by implication the unions were influential in the reductions which did take place.

It has been said that 'while employers, under non-union conditions, may raise wages in response to economic pressures, they would be unlikely to initiate a reduction in hours'.[71] Our evidence supports this view, though with important qualifications. In the early textile mills the introduction of machinery led to the extension of hours, and here as in virtually all similar instances attempts to reduce them met the strongest opposition. This was 'natural' while the employers retained the simple belief that the output of their equipment was a constant multiple of the time it was worked. But why did they not initiate reductions of hours when they came to realize that this might result in productivity increases?[72] A few did of course. In numerous industries there were a few progressive firms that introduced short hours from an early date and it is noteworthy that most of these early experiments involved the use of shifts in some form or another, for shifts represent the solution to that conflict of interest that demanded long hours for the machines at the same time as short hours for the men. Apart from these isolated instances of hours reduction by progressive firms, there were a few regionally concentrated sectors of industry which introduced short hours of their own accord, and this too was invariably combined with the use of shifts. This group included the coal-mines of the north-east with their short double day shifts, the machine lace workers of Nottingham, and some of the iron furnaces and gas-works. Nevertheless such occurrences were sufficiently rare for their general absence to require explanation.

The reasons why shifts were not more widely used are not entirely clear. On the one hand shift work was unpopular and this was the more true since the labour force had not yet been fully integrated into the structure of industrial society. Nevertheless such dislike would not have been a sufficient deterrent to the introduction of shifts, just as the workman's dislike of child labour or the rigours of factory labour were unable to stop the introduction of these practices. A more important reason for the unpopularity of shifts was probably the difficulty of introducing shifts into small factories, because of the difficulty and the inconvenience of duplicating the supervisory skills of the owner/ managers,[73] as well as the greater hazard and lower productivity of night-shift work. Whatever the reason we do know that shifts were not very widely used, except in those industries working by continuous process for technical reasons.

Without the compensation of shifts, hours reductions became, for the capitalist, a risky experiment fraught with many imponderables and promising him at best a meagre reward. Hence in the early textile mills, for example, under conditions of intense competition between relatively small units the position of each firm was too precarious to allow it to risk an experiment with shorter hours, especially when even the most optimistic forecasts promised that they would at best 'not lose output' by such a change.

Once large firms rose in the industry they developed an interest in maintaining the *status quo*. This meant, among other things, restricting the extent of competition and one important way of doing this was to standardize the hours of work for the industry. Thus even when a view was gaining ground which held that long hours did not necessarily confer a great benefit on the employer such restriction was considered a useful safeguard against the entry into the industry of small manufacturers who might establish themselves through the short-run advantage they might derive from the use of long hours. The important point for us is that when standardized hours for an entire industry were being considered, somewhat shorter hours were no longer such a risky undertaking since all manufacturers would suffer the same advantage or disadvantage as the case might be. This made it possible to consider the issue more rationally.

Certainly this feeling assisted the passage of the Textile Factory Acts, brought about the regulation of the workshops and factories in other industries, and helped to spread the effects of the reductions of the early 1870s through the united front presented by many employers on this issue. The fact that employers would consider a joint reduction in hours, while in most cases being unwilling to contemplate a unilateral reduction, accounted for the 922 firms 'which forwarded petitions in support of ten hours' labour per day'[74] in 1847, while more generally the demand for the standardization of hours was spelled out perfectly clearly in a report from the Royal Commission on the Factory and Workshop Acts. They wrote in 1876 that: 'There are very great grievances urged on the part of owners of factories which come in competition with workshops, those owners of factories complaining that the owners of workshops should be placed under more lenient restrictions than they are', and that 'from the point of view of the occupiers of factories, the argument is very strongly urged that they are subjected to unfair competition'.[75] The regulation of the hours of workshops followed soon after.

Finally, the lack of standardization of hours in the building industry, in spite of the strength of their unions, is an exception that proves the rule. Thus in 1871 the master builders argued that they could not grant reductions in hours because the intense competition in their industry made the standardization of hours impossible. The engineers had been able to do this they said, because

'an engineering business requires more capital than a builder's and therefore there is less competition between engineers. If all builders were in the front rank of contractors, this question of short time would not as much affect them as it does the engineers. But the great bulk of the . . . trade . . . in building is carried on under a competition the keenness of which is unknown in other trades, and one part of it is competition between little masters and big masters'.[76]

To the unions this problem presented itself in the form of an absence of a meaningful bargaining partner, so that the Sheffield painters lamented 'that masters have no union which makes it very difficult to deal with them', while the Blackburn masons complained of 'a large number of petty employers (who) are generally far more troublesome to the society than the large employers'.[77]

On balance it appears that employer initiative played only a very limited role in the reduction of hours. Though their opposition weakened once they accepted that a reduction would not necessarily reduce output in proportion, it rarely changed to support except in a few cases where shifts could be employed. This means hours changed in the way they did not simply because of the decisions of employers to introduce such changes. Rather the changes must be seen as the outcome of the continuous struggle between employer and employee. Hence it is right to seek the causes for these changes amongst the various factors that determine the outcome of that conflict.

The conclusion that the initiative for hours reduction came generally from the unions and not from the employers is strengthened by our previous finding that early hours reductions were concentrated in trades and in areas where unions were relatively strong. This and the fact that the major reduction in hours were associated with sharp increases in union membership suggest strongly that the unions played a decisive role in bringing about the reductions of normal hours.

The relation between strong unions and the early introduction of shorter hours has been amply demonstrated with reference to the changes of the nineteenth century. The relation between hours reductions and the growth of union membership was equally strong. Thus the very same years that witnessed the first two major reductions in hours — the early 1870s and 1919 — also saw by far the largest and most striking increases in membership ever recorded in the British trade-union movement. The likelihood that this was a coincidence is reduced by the fact that the two later hours reductions — those of the late 1940s and the end of the 1950s — were also associated with significant upward shifts in the growth rate of trade-union membership, although these latter changes were very much smaller than those referred to earlier. Nevertheless the years 1946 and 1960 saw increases that can be readily distinguished as rising above the then prevailing trend. On balance there is little doubt that the issue of hours was one of the most effective in inducing men to join the trade unions and this reflected the fact that on this issue more than most others men were readily convinced of the need for unionization.

table 12
Great Britain 1943-1947 and 1954-1961: annual percentage increases in the membership of trade unions

year	percentage increase	year	percentage increase
1943	3.9	1954	0.4
1944	1.1	1955	1.8
1945	2.6	1956	0.4
1946	11.8	1957	0.5
1947	3.9	1958	1.9
		1959	0.2
		1960	2.2
		1961	0.6

Source: *see* Notes to figures and tables

This role of the issue of hours as a catalyst for the trade-union movement has been substantiated by a variety of evidence. Thus it was shown that the establishment of the great amalgamated societies that changed the face of trade unionism in the middle of the nineteenth century, was directly related to the issue of hours via the workman's concern over job security. Again in the 1880s, when the 'new trade unionism' swept up the ranks of the unskilled industrial workers, it marched under the banner of the eight-hour day. Equally significant in this respect were the repeated statements by the early building trades to the effect that it was on the hours issue that the union most readily received the support of the non-union men, and that at times the non-members had been in advance of the union. If there is little doubt that the question of hours reductions played a role in fostering unionism, it is almost as certain that the major reason for this was the fact that while the market might under certain circumstances bring about a rise in wages without union pressure, it was most unlikely to bring about a reduction of hours of its own accord.

Finally it is noteworthy that while the nature and timing of hours reductions were to a large extent determined by the institutional context in which they were established they also played a role in shaping that context itself. Quite apart from the issue's role in attracting men into the unions, it also contributed directly to the progressive increase in the size of the bargaining unit that has taken place. On the one hand, the comparability of the hours of work over wide areas meant that trade unions were able to achieve an unusual degree of cohesion and unanimity on this issue, so that unions with extremely autonomous branches often found this one of the few areas in which they could agree to present a common front. On the other hand the employers, in their general desire to standardize hours if reductions could not be prevented altogether, were often induced by trade-union offensives on this front to form bigger and stronger employers' organizations designed to prevent or to reverse reductions in hours. Thus the Lancashire master builders formed an association in 1857-8; the London builders followed this example in 1859 and they in turn were followed by masters in 'the North', who organized themselves between 1864 and 1868. In all cases these organizations sprang up specifically in response to agitation for reduced hours by the building unions at that time. In 1873 the 'National Federation of Associated Employers of Labour' was formed following the major reductions of the previous two years. This body included masters from coal, iron and steel, textiles, engineering, shipbuilding and the boot and shoe trades and 'its object was to protect capital and to prevent any further reduction of hours'.[78] Although the organization of engineering employers that sprang up in response to the demand by their employees for reduced hours in 1897 managed to defeat the men in the ensuing struggle, most of the above bodies did not stop or reverse the hours reductions that had called them into being. Indeed, in many cases they became agencies for the enforcement of the newly established hours amongst their members.

A careful analysis of the reduction of working hours in Great Britain leaves little doubt that the trade unions were instrumental in bringing about such reductions over the opposition of the employers. What motivated the unions to seek such reductions?

6 Motives of the unions

In order to explain finally why it was that changes in hours came about in the particular way and at the particular time they did, it is necessary to clarify why it was that the unions sought reduced hours. What light can the foregoing analysis throw on the unions' motives? From the evidence so far presented it would appear that the motive of 'job security' was the strongest and provided the most consistent explanation of the changes that have taken place, though leisure preference may have played a part on the assumption of the existence of money illusion. There are generally three motives imputed to a union seeking shorter hours. It is said to seek leisure, to seek to combat unemployment, or to seek to increase incomes.

The charge that hours are reduced merely to obtain an indirect increase in income is as old as the movement for such reductions. In 1786 it was said of the bookbinders that their general willingness to do overtime 'amounts to a direct contradiction' of the 'pretence of fatigue and hardship of labour' and showed that their ultimate aim was an increase in income.[79] One hundred and seventy-two years later the engineering employers rejected a claim for the 40-hour week because they said 'it was merely a claim for higher overtime rates, and not a real demand for a serious cut in the working week'.[80] How plausible is this claim?

It does not stand up to closer inspection. A union may sometimes submit a claim on these grounds, but the likelihood of its succeeding is extremely small, for the simple reason that an employer could buy it off by offering a rise in wages with an equivalent income effect. Although the hours worked and earnings levels might remain the same in both cases, there are reasons why the employer should prefer the case involving more 'normal' hours and fewer 'overtime' hours. Overtime makes production planning more difficult as its voluntary nature makes full regular attendance less likely; a high level of habitual overtime tends to eliminate the major benefit of overtime, namely the provision of some short-run flexibility in output levels; and overtime has notoriously adverse effects on worker morale, in that its earnings come to be incorporated in the employee's expenditure plans, and the only way in which he can assure himself of the continued receipt of this 'necessary bonus' is by going slow all day in order to ensure the necessity of overtime.

The advantages to be weighed against these disadvantages are quite insignificant by comparison. It is true that an employer who expected that production would have to be cut back in the foreseeable future might prefer shorter normal hours and more overtime for two reasons: he might feel that in as far as such future reductions in output were to be brought about by reductions in the actual hours, this might be more easily achieved if it meant eliminating overtime; or the financial advantage might lie with this alternative. The first consideration is undermined by the fact that unions have proven remarkably willing (or resigned) to accept short-time arrangements once they are convinced that output must be reduced. Secondly the financial advantage may lie with either alternative, depending on the size of the reduction in actual hours; if one assumes, not unreasonably, that some overtime is being worked at the time of the bargain, then this advantage lies with the reduced normal hours only if the required reduction in actual hours is large.[81] In any event, unless production runs are entirely continuous, a reduction in employment may often provide a better alternative from the employer's point of view.

This leaves only the possibility that wage increases are for some reason blocked, say by a government wage freeze. There is then a greater chance that a demand for shorter hours will really be one for an indirect increase in income, but even here there are alternatives such as bonus or incentive payment schemes, upgrading and in general all the fringe benefits that cost the employer less than they are worth to the employee. The employer will prefer all of these to a reduction of hours, and all may be used to raise the union's real income by some equivalent amount. In any event this external constraint on wage increases existed only for the 1960-1 reduction and, as we have seen, other pressures to reduce hours were very strong at this time. At best then this factor may have played a minor role in the 1960-1 reductions.

The normal reason given for the persistent claim that these reductions are designed merely to increase income has been, at least since 1786, the observation that union men were willing to work overtime before and after these changes. This observation does indeed weaken the case for leisure preference as the source of the pressure for shorter hours, but it does not therefore show that income preference was the motive. The desire to forestall future unemployment is perfectly compatible with the working of overtime during boom conditions. Indeed it makes it likely, for the expectation of a slump which induces the hours reduction will also induce the desire, common to casual labour and the early miners, to work as much as possible while the work is to be had. Here there is another reason why boom conditions will make a reduction of normal hours more likely, namely the availability of overtime which in the short run weakens the resistance of those union members who are income preferrers.[82]

The only situation in which a reduction of hours may indeed have been sought with the intention of raising income appears in the nineteenth century when narrow craft unions sought such reductions with the intention of restricting supply within their own protected labour markets, or in the case of the miners with the intention of reducing the output of the industry. The prevalence of this motive, especially among the strong building unions, goes a long way towards explaining the more continuous nature of the changes in this industry in the years before 1879. Paradoxically, it also explains their greater preoccupation with the elimination of overtime, a demand which is generally confined to periods of depression.

This brings us to the role of leisure preference. The argument that a willingness to work overtime shows that leisure is not in demand has been tentatively accepted above, but it needs qualification. It is absurd to expect that a man who works eight regular hours and two overtime hours, and who wishes to work one hour less, should try to eliminate one of the overtime hours.[83] It is therefore not possible to conclude from a willingness in the short term to work overtime that it was not a demand for leisure that led to a reduction in hours, unless overtime increased after the reduction so as to keep actual hours unchanged, or, as was the case with the engineers in 1872, the union agreed to work all the overtime demanded of it. Even where this happened, however, there is still the possibility that the demand for leisure was for the long run and the willingness in the short run to work overtime reflected merely the desire to take advantage of high incomes while they were available. Indeed, by the terms of this argument the long-run reduction of actual hours which has accompanied the reduction of normal hours is a sign of leisure preference.

If the frequent willingness to work extra overtime in the short run makes it unlikely that the immediate cause of the reductions in hours is a demand for leisure, and the long-run reduction of actual hours leaves open the possibility that it was a significant factor in the long run, what other evidence is there for the existence of this demand? Over the very long run we have identified a tendency for the amount of time spent at work to be reduced during prolonged periods of high real wages. Furthermore, we were able to identify a similar tendency among the domestic labourers who had discretion over their own time.

Most modern studies have confirmed the inverse relationship between the rate of pay and hours worked.[84] But these studies have a number of grave short-comings. The most serious are the assumptions that the actual hours of work represent positions of labour market equilibrium, and the well known problem of identifying the kinds of movements in the supply and demand curves that account for the observed movements of this 'equilibrium'. Hence the locus of a series of 'equilibrium' points will describe a supply curve only if the supply curve has remained stationary over the period of observation and all of the movement is due to shifts in the demand curve. This is clearly unlikely. It has been suggested that it could be more realistically assumed to apply in cross-sectional studies dealing with a number of closely related labour markets where supply curves could be assumed identical. However, such studies would normally suffer from a lack of dispersion in the data, once more making it difficult to establish the desired relationships.[85] In any event it is very doubtful whether it is sensible to expect the amount of work an individual is prepared to do to be determined by a wage rate. Quite apart from the undoubted weakness of the *ceteris paribus* assumption, it is clear that, to the extent that this willingness to work is related to wages, it is related to the rate of change of wages rather than to a particular rate.

It has been usual procedure to seek a relationship between the rate of pay and actual hours worked. Studies relating the rate of pay to the normal hours of work have been rare, although it could be assumed that shortly after a reduction in normal hours a settlement would reflect the collective leisure/income preferences of the bargainers. This would raise the possibility of seeking a correlation between normal hours and basic pay in various separate collective agreements. Barbara Wootton has presented evidence from a wide range of British industries between 1946 and 1951 suggesting a negative correlation between these two variables,[86] and our own cursory examination of some cross-sectional data relating to carpenters in 1877 suggested that further research in this area might well turn up additional support for this view. The existence of such a relationship would tend to discount the extent to which hours reductions and wage increases are considered as substitutes, while focusing attention on the possibility that short hours, like high wages, are the result of some common cause affecting the bargaining strength of the union.

For all the above reasons it is difficult to derive information about leisure preferences from the relationships between real wages and working hours. The most useful comparison is between reductions in hours and the rate of change of real wages and at a macro-economic level there did not appear to be a relationship between these two variables, a result which conforms to the results of a previous study done of the American experience.[87] It follows from this that for the rise in real wages to have precipitated the observed reductions in hours, it would have to be possible to treat the demand for leisure as cumulative over time.

The fact that the period from 1875 to 1895 experienced an enormous rise in the real-wage index but was not followed by a major reduction in hours suggests that the demand for leisure cannot be treated as simply cumulative, and this confirms the earlier hypothesis that the workman's conception of his normal income adjusts rapidly to higher levels of income. It was pointed out earlier that this together with the nature of the interests of employer and employee raised the possibility that the demand for leisure could be permanently thwarted, and it is now time to look more closely at the way in which this would happen.

Whereas the domestic worker might well respond to an increase in his potential income by taking advantage of a slight increase in both his earnings and his leisure, the industrial worker is unable to do this. He is faced by a series of small potential increases in income which may in each case generate a small demand for leisure but this is easily bought off by the employer's opposition which induces him to exact a high price for such a concession. Now if there is any positive relation between income and the demand for leisure then it follows that the larger the increase in potential income being considered at any one time the stronger is the demand that some of that increase be taken in the form of leisure. It is for this reason that the issue of cumulative versus non-cumulative leisure preference becomes crucial. If one considers a group of workmen earning £20 per week working 48 hours in Year 0, and receiving an annual increase of £1, the question is what happens in Year 3 when they are earning £23 per week and considering a further one-pound increase. If the demand for leisure is not cumulative they will regard themselves as men who normally earn £23 per week and are considering a one-pound per week increase. In this case the demand for leisure will be weak and easily subverted since the increase being considered is small. If however the demand for leisure was cumulative then the men would not yet have adjusted their conception of their normal incomes. They would regard themselves as men who normally earn £20 per week, who are considering an increase in income of £4 per week. They have taken three pounds of this increase in the form of higher wages and must now decide how to divide the fourth between income and leisure. It is suggested that under such circumstances the demand for leisure would be much stronger and would in time come to the fore, so long as there was a consistent upward trend in real wages.

It has been argued that under normal circumstances men do revise their conceptions of their normal incomes upwards and thus undermine their demands for leisure. In this connection it is interesting that two of the major reductions in hours occurred at times when extraordinary events can be said to have slowed down or stopped this process of upward revision. Thus during both World Wars people's incomes rose but the increased incomes could not be spent. As a result it was reported that by 1944 'the aggregate of "small" savings from September 1, 1939, to December 31, 1943, was £2,547 millions', while at the same time 'there was hardly a family in the country which was not short, in some cases desperately short, of consumer goods such as clothing, footwear, furniture . . . '.[88] This could be described as a classic case, where the effects of income rises were felt in a cumulative manner. There is little doubt that this contributed to the success of the movements for shorter hours that followed the end of both wars. At other times, however, the substitution of leisure for income rises could be identified as a factor bringing about hours reductions only on the assumption of the existence of a money illusion, an assumption that was supported by the observed association between hours reductions and the rate of rise of money wages and prices.

Finally it is necessary to consider the extent to which factors other than income may be influential in determining the workman's demand for leisure. That there are such factors is not in doubt, though they are often ignored because they are difficult to quantify. Nevertheless their potential effects can be discussed. Foremost amongst these is the 'disutility of work'. As this increases so does the demand for leisure, though in practice this has been a double-edged sword. Some analysts have argued, with reference to particular instances, that the increasing intensity of work was a major cause of pressure for short hours,[89] but this has not been borne out by the general picture. Although it is true that one major aim of most trade unions has always been to define and protect the pace of work, increases in that pace have not usually been combated by reduced hours primarily because hours reductions themselves often were the cause of an increased intensity of work. The iron-furnace workers refused to accept the eight-hour shift in the 1840s because they wished to retain their traditional pace of work, and in the 1890s the gas workers complained to the Trades Union Congress that the reduction in hours had gained them little because the pace of work had been increased at least in proportion to the reduction. It is relevant to note in this connection that a recent study of workers' attitudes in West Germany revealed that 45 per cent of a large sample were actually opposed to a further reduction in hours because they felt this would inevitably lead to a further intensification of work.[90] With these reservations in mind it is still possible that occasionally a sudden and large increase in the intensity of work, such as occurred during the two wars, may well be responsible for an increased demand for leisure.

A further point that will affect the demand for leisure is the time spent going to and from work. If this increases it is likely to provide some impetus to demands for shorter hours on the job. At early dates this was often explicitly considered in the provision for hours, possibly because it was unusual while the 'reference group' was still the dominant domestic industry. Thus the builders often subtracted 'walking time' from their regular hours, and in one area the miners 'reckon hours by the time "out of the house". What employers called 12 hours they called 14 hours.'[91] In time it was the employers' definition which prevailed although it is well to remember that the domestic worker not only worked shorter hours than the factory hand but also had a commuting time of nil. What has happened to commuting time since the early move into the factories is not clear. At first the growing size of towns must have increased the time spent travelling to work. This was in time reduced once more by the development of new urban transport systems. Now there has been another reversal and the transport systems seem to have lagged behind the growing need for transport so that in most cities commuting times are once more lengthening. On balance it is not possible to say that this factor has exerted a consistent influence on the issue of hours.

Yet another factor influencing the demand for leisure concerns the related effects of the kinds of goods acquired and the kinds of leisure activities pursued. These can affect the issue in an infinite variety of ways and there is only one that seems to deserve special comment at this stage. There is a basic difference between what might be called 'communal' and 'individualistic' leisure-time activities. Communal activities would include such events as fairs or races. Such activities tend to be confined to particular periods of time and hence require limited amounts of free time. Individualistic activities on the other hand have no such self-contained limitation on the amount of time required for their pursuit. In this connection it may well be significant that the 1960 hours reductions were immediately preceded by the introduction in Britain of the automobile and television as mass consumption goods, while the reductions of the 1870s were similarly preceded by the introduction of cheap excursion train fares.[92]

While the foregoing factors have been working to increase the workman's demand for leisure, there have also been other factors working in an opposite direction. Thus the pressures of advertising; the compulsory 'income preference' imposed on people by their hire-purchase commitments; and the increasing use of incentive payment systems, all exert a steady pressure to reduce the demand for leisure. The end result can be a kind of vicious circle where the demand for income nullifies the demand for leisure in yet another manner, so that one study found a marked lack of enthusiasm for additional leisure because the respondents repeatedly stated that 'more leisure costs more money'.[93]

On balance the net effect of all of these 'exogenous' factors influencing the demand for leisure is indeterminate and very much variable over time.

The third motive which has induced the unions to seek shorter hours is the fear of unemployment. This has been established as probably the major source of union concern with this issue. Only thus can the pattern of change be adequately explained and the apparently paradoxical fact that reductions were achieved at times of extremely low unemployment found its explanation in the relative strength of the trade unions at such times and their continued interest in the issue of hours at such times because of the threat to job security presented by the business cycle, technological change, and the growth of the labour force. It might be added here that on this assumption it also becomes clear why the reductions of hours when they did come were substantial, since only a sizeable reduction could possibly contribute meaningfully to the prevention of future unemployment. In this connection it may be significant that the four major changes in hours that have taken place all reduced hours by a similar proportion. The changes were from 60 to 54 hours per week; then from 54 to 48 hours; then from 48 to 44 hours; and finally from 44 to 40 hours per week. This represents changes of ten, eleven, eight and nine per cent.

7 Summary and conclusions

Over the very long run the evidence suggests that there were three major periods in which a desire to spend less time at work took effect. Each of these periods coincided roughly with one of the three great waves of prosperity that have been experienced by the working man. Here there was evidence of a fundamental and permanent relationship between income and leisure. From such a historical perspective it appears that whatever may be the short-term relationships between these two variables there is an underlying tendency for an inverse relationship between them which asserts itself in spite of extreme changes in the employee's way of life, terms of contract, leisure activities and labour content.

With the arrival of the nineteenth century the evidence began to yield some more detailed information. The rapid introduction of machinery, the geographic dislocation of industries, the destruction of traditional practices and the insecurity of small-unit competition caused an extension of actual hours in most industries, in spite of rising real wages. Meanwhile the domestic trades gave every indication of having maintained the traditional inverse relationship between income and leisure. Nevertheless as wages fell in many of these some displayed great reluctance to extend hours beyond the customary limit of a working day extending over twelve hours. Indeed, the outstanding feature of this entire period was the extent of the support which this customary limit enjoyed. Although actual hours ranged widely, by 1843 the only major industries to have lost this customary limit on their normal day were textiles and mining.

From the 1830s the tide turned and the workers in certain industries were able to make their employers recognize their interest in the determination of the hours of work. In textiles they were able to invoke the public interest to have the extension of their hours reversed. From the 1850s the customary day changed imperceptibly into the normal day as the unions were able to have the terms of contracts specified.

From this point forward there is a constant pressure to reduce normal hours accompanied by a virtually unbroken increase in real wages. Thus far, all is as we might expect on the basis of our long-term observations and we might agree that 'the hour-line, if drawn, would be steadily downward'[94] from 1850 on. Instead we found very little change in hours, except for four major readjustments.

The explanation for this was found to be the conflict of interests that arises when the contract of hire requires a man to work so many hours at someone else's machine. To the extent that the workman was able to attain a meaningful bargaining position at all, the nature of this conflict meant that hours were not reduced because the employer placed more value on the employee's attendance, than the employee on his absence. If this explained the absence of changes under normal conditions, how could we account for the sudden shifts and why were these as general as they were?

It was argued that the occasional interest in hours was due to changes in the relative preferences of the bargainers, while the widespread nature of the changes suggested that the factors responsible were general to the economy.

Analysis of the evidence suggested that the unions were instrumental in bringing about the reductions in hours, and that their dominant motive appeared to be that of 'job security' for their members, aided by a leisure preference founded on a money illusion. After the two wars this preference was particularly strong, and based on an accumulation of real income and the exhaustion induced by the war effort.

It was shown that the four periods during which there were reductions of hours were marked by a configuration of economic factors that distinguished them from other periods. They were periods of particularly rapid rises in money wages; they were periods of great prosperity, hence low unemployment, and hence great union bargaining power; finally, they were periods when unemployment was felt to be a serious threat.

This last statement was based on the proposition that the fear of unemployment stemmed from the expectations arising out of the trade cycle; the apprehension regarding the potential scope of technological advance; and the rate of growth of the labour force. Each of these was a particular problem at each of the four times when hours were reduced, but the issue of technological change stood out above the others. By common consent the four periods when hours were reduced were the thresholds of those 'spontaneous and discontinuous changes in the channel of the circular flow'[95] of which Schumpeter spoke, or those periods when the economy 'lurched forward in a highly discontinuous way, with a high concentration of decisions to expand, or to improve technique'.[96]

While all this points to great union pressure for reduced hours it was also shown that employers' resistance would be reduced at such times because of their vulnerability to strikes and because of the increases in productivity which were then in prospect and which offset the effect of an increasing capital/labour ratio. The point that only productivity increases resulting from the reduction in hours can be used to offset the cost of shorter hours, as argued in chapter six, is not applicable, because, in practice, it is notoriously impossible to tell what is the source of an increase in productivity.

It is one thing to show that each of these periods displayed certain features that made a reduction of hours possible. It is another to show that these conditions did not also exist at any other time. The closest one can come to duplicating the circumstances of the periods of change is probably in the late 1890s, when the net ten-year rise in the money-wage begins to approach the levels achieved in the early 1870s. But in the '1890s . . . there was some check . . . to the rate at which the British wage-earner was getting the benefit of technical advance'[97] and when the engineers struck for the eight-hour day in 1897 they met totally intransigent employers who could not look forward to great productivity increases, while the employees gave little support, at least in part because not enough of them were threatened by unemployment at this time.[98] That the failure to reduce hours was not only due to a lack of bargaining strength is of course obvious from the substantial wage increases that were negotiated at this time. Finally, the great reluctance of the 'old unionists' to support the 'new unionists' with their demand for the eight-hour day could well have been due to the fact that at this time they did not feel themselves threatened by rising unemployment nearly to the same extent as the unskilled, for the greatest threat to the job of the skilled artisan is technology, not the business cycle.

These were the global similarities of the changes in hours since 1850. There were also some differences. The hours in the nineteenth century were more dispersed and changed less discontinuously than those that came later. The regional and industrial pattern of these changes suggest that these differences were due to the wide variation in the degree of unionization and to the fact that the economy was much less national for most industries than it was to be later.

These patterns and differences emerged also in the data for the building industries in particular. Indeed here the changes were most continuous. The explanation lies both in the motivation of the union and the nature of the industry. It was during this period that it does seem that hours reductions were designed as ways of increasing income, and the strong and protected building crafts seem to have had this end in view. As a result their pressure for shorter hours was almost continuous from 1845 to 1877, although their successes were still clustered around 1864-5 and 1872. In addition the capital/labour ratio in the industry was low so that reductions became less costly and there was less incentive for the employers to try to standardize hours. Nevertheless employer resistance was formidable at all times. Finally we have shown that the nature of the work makes those employed in this industry particularly prone to the idea that reduced hours mean more employment.

In the long run it is a rising real income that induces people to wish for leisure. Under industrial conditions this wish is, however, apt to remain unfulfilled because of the nature of the bargain. Occasionally there is added to this latent leisure preference the fear of losing one's job. When this fear comes at a time when it reinforces an already high leisure preference and when the union's position is strong then it leads to a reduction of normal hours. The coming together of all these circumstances is not, however, mere chance. Those periods when the economy 'lurches forward' bring them all in their train: the rising prices; the technological changes; the instability of rapid change; the vulnerability of the employer; and the strength of the union. Here lies the source of reductions in the normal week.

In the final analysis it has been the insecurity of employment that has been the major focus of the workman's discontent in the market economy. It was this issue, rather than changes in his absolute or relative material condition, that led to his most concentrated offensives and that consistently allowed him to achieve very high levels of solidarity, just as it had earlier contributed greatly to the process of unionization itself. Repeatedly when the unions mounted their drives to ban the spectre of unemployment they hoped to achieve their end by the reduction of working hours.

Certainly, if the employees' real wages continue to rise in future, the threat of unemployment will become even more unacceptable than it has been in the past. As a result it must be expected that at some future date if circumstances are again such that both the fear of massive unemployment and the strength of the trade unions reach very high levels at one and the same time, the working man will once more rally his forces and demand relief from the perpetual insecurity of employment. He may well seek relief again through a reduction in hours, but if confidence is lost in this 'solution', he will at such times demand more fundamental changes in the system. Possibly it is here that the long lost revolutionary potential of the modern labour force is to be found.

Notes

Chapter two

1. S. L. Thrupp, 'The Gilds', ch. V in the *Cambridge Economic History of Europe,* (1963) III, pp. 231-3.

2. L. Brentano, 'On the History and Development of Gilds', in *English Gilds*, ed. Toulmin Smith, (1870), p. CXXXI.

3. S. L. Thrupp, *Cambridge History* op.cit., pp. 253-60. It is explained here that those gilds working for local markets tended to be much more restrictive than others, p. 271.

4. Ibid., pp. 263-75.

5. Ordinance of the Coopers at Hull (1598), cited in J. M. Lambert, *Two Thousand Years of Gild Life*, (1891), p. 287.

6. B. H. Putnam, *Enforcement of the Statute of Labourers,* (1908), p. 2.

7. L. Brentano, op.cit., p. CXLVII, citing a London ordinance of 1383.

8. 23 Edward III, c.I-VIII, (1349).

9. N. Ritchie, 'Labour Conditions in Essex in the Reign of Richard III', in *Essays in Economic History,* ed. E. M. Carus Wilson, (1962) II, p. 91.

10. Ibid., p. 93.

11. Ibid., p. 93, and D. Knoop and G. P. Jones, *The Mediaeval Mason,* 3rd ed. (1967), p. 105. These were summer hours and winter hours were said to be eight and three quarter hours, i.e. daylight to dark with one and one-quarter hours for meals. Elsewhere it is said that these short hours were worked from 1 November (All Saints') to 2 February (Purification) and that even these short hours were not always observed for 'often work practically ceased' at that time. See, L. F. Salzman, *Building in England down to 1540,* (1952), pp. 58-9.

12. Evidence to this effect occurs in J. Stow, *Survey of London,* (1598), pp. 229-30, and in J. R. Green (Mrs), *Town Life in the Fifteenth Century,* (1894), p. 104.

13. 11 Henry VII, c. 22, (1495).

14.   In the winter the hours are from the 'springing of the day . . . till night of the same day' and this applied from mid-September to mid-March. Meal hours were: two and a half hours from mid-May to mid-August; two hours from mid-August to mid-May. K. Marx, *Capital,* (1887) I, p. 272, claims the Act provides for three hours for meals but this is not the case. The actual wording on the subject is as follows: 'And that he have but half an hour for his breakfast, and an hour and a half for his dinner at such time as he has season for sleep to him appointed (mid-May to mid-August) by this statute . . . (otherwise) he to have but an hour for his dinner and half an hour for his nonemete'.

15.   6 Henry VIII, c. 3, (1515).

16.   R. A. Brown, H. M. Colven, A. J. Taylor, *The History of the King's Works,* (1963), pp. 428-33; L. F. Salzman, op.cit., pp. 62-5; 'Statute Anent the government of the Maister Maisonn of the College Kirk of St. Giles, 1491', Edinburgh Burgh Record as cited in J. Cruickshank, *Sketch of the Corporation of Masons* (Glasgow 1879); R. S. Mylne, *Master Masons to the Crown of Scotland,* pp. 63-4. In general the remarkable mobility of the masons meant that their conditions of work were quite uniform over the whole country. See D. Knoop and G. P. Jones, op.cit., p. 154.

17.   E. H. Phelps Brown and S. Hopkins, 'Seven Centuries of the Prices of Consumables, compared with Builders' Wage-rates', in *Essays in Economic History,* (1962) II, ed. E. M. Carus Wilson, p. 186.

18.   G. Unwin, *Studies in Economic History*, (1958), p. 320 – There certainly were attempts made to protect trades from the downturn in real wages which set in after the first quarter of the sixteenth century. An Act of 1548 notes these attempts and outlaws them. 'Artificers, Handicraftsmen, and Labourers have made Confederacies and Promises, and have sworn mutual oaths not only that they should not meddle one with another's Work, and perform and finish that another has begun, but also to constitute and appoint how much Work they shall do in a Day, and *what Hours and Times they shall work,* contrary to the Law . . .'. 2 & 3 Edward VI, c. XV, (1548).

19.   *Cambridge Economic History of Europe,* II, p. 514.

20.   5 Elizabeth I, c. 4, (1563).

21.   J. E. Thorold Rogers, *Six Centuries of Work and Wages,* (1906), p. 394; and H. L. Smith, 'Chapters in the History of London Waterside Labour', *Economic Journal,* December 1892.

22.   L. Brentano, op.cit., p. CXXXI.

23.   D. Knoop and G. P. Jones, op.cit., p. 108.

24.   4 Henry IV, c. 14, (1402).

25.   11 Henry VII, c. 22, (1495).

26.   L. F. Salzman, op.cit., pp. 56-7; 60-1; 64-5.

27.   D. C. Coleman, 'Labour in the English Economy of the Seventeenth Century', in E. M. Carus Wilson, op.cit., II, p. 304.

28.   L. Brentano, op.cit., p. CXXI; Hunter, *History of Sheffield*, (1869), p. 119; J. Strutt, *The Sports and Pastimes of the People of England*, (1801), p. XLIV.

29.   Prior to the sixteenth century the practice of tradesmen ceasing work for the harvest was all but universal. Thus 'the activity of the townsfolk was not confined to their special crafts or trades. In harvest time they poured out of the towns into the country', and the long vacations of the courts and universities were designed to provide 'ample leisure for the all-important work of the harvest', (J. E. Thorold Rogers, op.cit., p. 122). The Statute of Artificers (1563) provided that men could be compelled to help with the harvests, even if it meant they had to go to neighbouring counties (5 Eliz., c. 4), and there are many instances of individual trades whose rules forbid work for the harvest period (Hunter, op.cit., p. 119, and K. J. Allison, 'The Norfolk Worsted Industry in the Sixteenth and Seventeenth Centuries', *Yorkshire Bulletin*, vols. 12-13). But even at the time of the Statute of Artificers it was coming to be recognized that the uninterrupted working of the urban economy was also important and so apprenticed tradesmen were exempted from this obligation. After this some trades ceased to work during this time for other reasons, though some who pursued agriculture as a secondary employment continued to go out to harvest. This diversity inevitably caused some problems. Thus the Norfolk weavers had to cease work between 15 August and 15 September, because the domestic spinners went out to harvest at that time. The fact that the weavers induced Parliament to pass an Act to forbid work during that time suggests however that not all of their number considered this free time as leisure, but saw it rather as unemployment or idleness (13 & 14 Car. II, c. 5 (1662), 'An Act for regulating the making of Stuffs in Norfolk and Norwich').

30.   D. Knoop and G. P. Jones, op.cit., p. 106. The specific records refer to masons at Vale Royal in 1279 (27 holidays); and in 1280

(22 holidays); and at Beaumaris Castle in 1319-20 (20 holidays). The fact that most of the variation can be explained by other than regional differences is suggested by the five-day difference between the two years at Vale Royal.

31.   11 Henry VII, c. 22 (1495). The practice of paying for holidays was never generally established and there appear to have been a great variety of arrangements. In some cases all men were paid, in others none, and in yet others only some of the men or only some of the holidays were paid. *Cambridge Economic History,* II, p. 513; D. Knoop and G. P. Jones, op.cit., pp. 106-8; R. A. Brown et al, op.cit., p. 185.

32.   A. L. Rowse, *Tudor Cornwall,* (1941), pp. 232-3.

33.   5 and 6 Edward VI, c. 3 (1552).

34.   17 Car. I, in the *Journal of the House of Commons,* II, (December 24, 1641), p. 356.

35.   January 4, 1645, *Acts and Ordinances of the Interregnum,* I, p. 607.

36.   'An Act for setting Apart a Day of Solemn Fasting and Humiliation And Repealing the former Monthly Fast', April 23, 1649, *Acts and Ordinances of the Interregnum.*

37.   This is a broad category that includes most of the ancient crafts except those that had moved out of the towns and were now carried on under the domestic system. It might best be regarded as a residual category including all trades and industries except the domestic trades and those like coal, iron and steel, or glass, that were working under factory conditions from an early date.

38.   F. W. Galton, *The Tailoring Trade* (1896), p.v. ff.

39.   *The Sheffield Iris,* Aug. 20, 1820.

40.   'The Case of the Master Taylors Residing Within the Cities of London and Westminster, in Relation to the Great Abuses Committed by their Journeymen, Humbly offered to the Consideration of Parliament', 1721. (See F. W. Galton, op.cit. pp. 1-4).

41.   *The Forfar Review,* Summer 1892.

42.   There is reason to believe that this day from six to six was granted without a strike or combination, thus increasing the likelihood that it was part of a general reduction. Thus the masters' reply stressed that the demand of the journeymen for more wages in 1764 could not be entertained since there was no 'security against a demand of a second and third augmentation when the journeymen think

proper'. If the previous reduction of hours had been achieved by such means this would surely have been used to emphasize this point.

43.   R. Campbell, *The London Tradesman*, (1747), p. 331 ff.

44.   The day laid down in the statutes was from 5 am to 7 or 8 pm while these trades were all working a day from 6 am to 8 or 9 pm. It seems that the adverse period of the sixteenth and seventeenth centuries had however left its mark in at least some of these, since the time set aside for meals had been reduced in the case of the tailors, from the old two and a half hours to but one hour per day – though they got extra money for the breakfast half hour, which they no longer observed.

45.   Bricklayer, Cabinet Maker, Carver of Houses, etc., Carpenter, Mason, Pavior, Plasterer, Plumber, Sawyer.

46.   Anon., *The Case of the Journeymen Tailors and Journeymen Staymakers*, (1752).

47.   E. Howe and J. Child, *The Society of London Bookbinders*, (1952), p. 13. Use of shifts at this time almost always entailed two twelve-hour shifts and thus a day from six to six. In these trades this was, however, a rare occurrence.

48.   M. D. George, *Johnson's England*, I, p. 167, cited in T. S. Ashton, *Economic Fluctuations in England 1700-1800*, (1959), p. 149.

49.   F. W. Galton, op.cit., pp. 61-3.

50.   Anon., *An Essay on Trade and Commerce*, (1770); see also K. Marx, *Capital*, I, p. 262.

51.   R. Campbell, op.cit., p. 331 ff.; E. Howe and J. Child, op.cit., p. 13.

52.   T. J. Dunning, 'Some Account of the London Consolidated Society of Bookbinders' in *Trade Societies and Strikes*, National Association for the Promotion of Social Sciences, 4th Meeting, Glasgow, (1860), p. 93.

53.   E. Howe and J. Child, op.cit., pp. 24-5; 51-7; and 69-73.

54.   J. Langlands (Secretary) to H. Hobhouse, August 20, 1821 writes of the coopers that 'those employed are . . . from 6 in the morning to 6 in the evening'. A. Aspinall, *The Early English Trade Unions* 1949, p. 351.

55.   W. A. D. Englefield, 'Early History of the Painting Trade in London' in the *Journal of Decorative Art*, (June 1919).

56.   E. H. Phelps Brown, op.cit., pp.185-6.

57.   Virtually the only two Acts against combinations among workmen

passed before 1450 were both aimed specifically at builders. 34 Edward III, c. 9, (1361); 3 Henry VI, c. 1, (1425).

58. T. S. Ashton, *Economic Fluctuations in England,* 1700-1800, (1959), pp. 92-93; 143.

59. The account of the strike of 1786 in T.. J. Dunning, op.cit., emphasizes the extent of this mobility by showing that most of the leaders of the strike soon afterwards became masters in their own right.

60. T. S. Ashton, *Economic Fluctuations,* op.cit., pp. 145-50.

61. The word Industries refers to those trades that worked under conditions which are akin to those of the factory, in that considerable numbers of individuals work interdependently at the same place of work. This is of course not a precise definition but it will suit our purpose.

62. T. Guest (prop.) to Mr. Hornblower, Dowlais Furnace, June 13, 1785, from *Iron in the Making: Dowlais Iron Co. Letters, 1782-1860,* ed. M. Elsas, (1960), p. 4.

63. D. R. Guttery, *From Broad-Glass to Cut Crystal,* (1956), pp. 9 and 117.

64. J. Wedgwood, pottery prop., Evidence before the 'Select Committee on the State of the Children employed in the manufactories of the United Kingdom', (hence referred to as SCC), *BPP,* 1816, III, p. 304.

65. R. W. Cooke Taylor, *The Factory System,* (1891), p. 116.

66. SCC, op.cit., pp. 295-305, evidence by J. Wedgwood.

67. In 1747 the author of a book of trades feels compelled to explain that 'by engineer I do not mean the Military Engineer, but the Tradesman who is employed on making engines for raising of Water, etc.' (R. Campbell, op.cit., p. 248).

68. P. Mantoux, *The Industrial Revolution in the Eighteenth Century,* (1928), p. 216, tells us that around the middle of the century 'there were no professional engineers (and) their place was more or less filled by carpenters, locksmiths, or clockmakers . . . (though) a special place must be given to millwrights'.

69. Glasgow machinists and blacksmiths are said to work the ten-hour day in 1810 and after. (*Tables of the Revenue, etc. of the United Kingdom,* Part XVIII, (1850), cited in *BPP,* (1887), Vol. LXXXIX, p. 28). In Birmingham where there are a good number of engineers the hours of work were ten hours and ten hours and a half in 1816, and this was true 'uniformly . . . throughout the manufactures of

the town . . . and throughout the year'. (T. Price, Birmingham magistrate, in Evidence to SCC, op.cit., pp. 360-1).

70. M. P. Ashley, *England in the Seventeenth Century,* (1956), pp. 14-15.

71. A. Smith, *The Wealth of Nations,* (1776), Bk. I, Ch. XI, Pt. 1.

72. G. Jars, *Metallürgische Reisen,* I, p. 320; II, p. 438.

73. Arthur Young, *Tour in the North of England,* (1772), p. 262.

74. K. T. Weetch, 'The Dowlais Ironworks and Its Industrial Community, 1760-1850' (unpublished M Sc Econ., LSE), p. 106. It is pointed out here that the miners working directly for iron-works were subject to much less fluctuation in trade. It is significant that these miners generally worked regular twelve-hour days, though this latter finding stems from M. Elsas, op.cit., p. 4.

75. This stems from the fact that coal is not further processed and often sold in local markets, especially at this time. It is for the same reasons that this industry was one of the first to try sliding scale wage arrangements in the nineteenth century. (See Board of Trade, 'Report on Strikes and Lockouts', (1889), in *BPP,* (1890), LXVIII.)

76. M. P. Ashley, op.cit., p. 14-15.

77. 'We should be mistaken if we thought that "manufacture" (i.e. workshop production) was the characteristic and dominant form of industry during the period immediately preceding the advent of the factory system'. P. Mantoux, op.cit., p. 89.

78. T. Manly, *Usurie at Six Per Cent,* (1669), cited in D. C. Coleman, op.cit., p. 303.

79. Evidence to the 'Report of the Factories Commission, 1833', cited in J. Rae, *Eight Hours for Work,* (1894), p. 5.

80. This implies that they are working less time since the usual practice was to do so many pieces a week.

81. T. S. Ashton, op.cit., p. 149.

82. All of this evidence comes from witnesses to the Select Commission of 1816, in particular a Liverpool ironmonger and a Preston cotton-mill manager, SCC, op.cit., pp. 539, 512 and 497.

83. J. Rae, op.cit., p. 5; there is a wealth of evidence of this point in all the Commissions cited here and in most of the works of contemporary chroniclers, like Baines, Cooke Taylor, Gaskell, etc.

84. J. Moss, Governor of Preston workhouse, originally a shoemaker's apprentice, in evidence to SCC, op.cit., p. 416.

85. Parliamentary Committee on Manufactures, 1832, cited in E.

Baines, *History of the Cotton Manufacture in Great Britain,* (1835), pp. 485-6.

86. W. Merriott, Prestwich Justice of the Peace, to H. Hobhouse, August 17, 1818. Home Office Papers (HO 42/179).

87. While D. C. Coleman, op.cit., p. 303, says of the seventeenth century that 'the domestic industrial workers became increasingly dependent on industry and in many cases was an agriculturalist only nominally', it is certain that this transition lasted into the nineteenth century in many of these trades. Thus Samuel Crompton's 'father held a farm of small extent, and, as was customary in those days, employed a portion of his time in weaving, carding, and spinning'. ('Brief Memoir of Samuel Crompton' in *Memoirs of the Literary and Philosophical Society of Manchester,* Second Series, Pt. V, p. 319). For the same point see D. Defoe, *A Tour through the Whole Island of Great Britain, 1724-1727,* III, pp. 97-9. Even as late as 1806 it was reported that 'the greater part of the domestic clothiers live in villages and detached houses . . . (and) . . . a great proportion of the manufacturers occupy a little land, from 3 to 12 or 15 acres each. ('Report from the Select Committee on Woollen Manufacture', *BPP,* (1806), p. 9).

88. A good deal of evidence exists on this point and it is all summarized in J. Rae, op.cit., pp. 2-7. The hours cited here from a great variety of contemporary sources vary between seven and ten per day, though some of these do not include the chores that had to be done after work in the fields was finished. One contemporary source (W. Marshall, *Agriculture of Southern England,* p. 434) expresses the belief that these short hours were the result 'partly of the scarcity of workmen who well know that if one master will not give them their hire for a short day another will'.

89. 'Report to the Board of Agriculture on the County of Hampshire', by Vancouver, cited in J. Rae, op.cit., pp. 3-4.

90. R. W. Cooke Taylor, op.cit., p. 78 — states that by 1790 there were 150 water-frame cotton factories in England and Wales.

91. Anon., *The Book of Trades,* (1804), p. 11 — the author does point out that Arkwright's machines have achieved some success in this branch of the industry.

92. Sir Robert Peel, evidence to SCC, op.cit., p. 105.

93. One scheme was to work a day shift from 6 to 7 and an eleven-hour night shift. This was done at the original Arkwright

mill (SCC, p. 259) and at mills around Manchester, as well as Drinkwater's mill in Northwich, Cheshire (SCC, p. 594). Another scheme was to work six to six, but to give a one-hour meal break only to the day shift. This was done by W. Sidgwick's mill in Skipton from 1784. SCC, p. 349).

94. Evidence of two cotton mill proprietors to the 1816 Select Commission. The latter comment relates to the years between 1795 and 1799. SCC, op.cit., pp. 594 and 472.

95. All witnesses agree on this point. In SCC, op.cit., see evidence of R. Arkwright, p. 259; G. Gould, p. 340; W. Sidgwick, p. 348-9.

96. Question to G. Gould, Manchester merchant, SCC, op.cit., p. 340. The answer to the question was, yes.

97. G. A. Lee, of Phillips and Lee, Salford (a cotton mill employing 937 people in 1816), in evidence to SCC, op.cit., pp. 581-2.

98. Sir R. Peel, SCC, op.cit., p. 375.

99. These figures come from two submissions to the Select Commission of 1816, one from the employers (SCC, p. 612-13) and one from G. Gould, an advocate of restrictive legislation (SCC, pp. 330-1). The essential agreement of these two submissions lends credence to them.

100. The Scottish hours are basically the same as those in Lancashire but they generally allowed 1½ hours for meals, so that the day from six to seven was an 11½-hour day, and that from six to eight a 12½-hour day. The evidence for the Lancashire mills is in SCC, op.cit., pp. 612-13, while that for Scotland can be found in ibid., pp. 478-9, 406 and 404.

101. Evidence from a Wiltshire woollen-mill proprietor. SCC, op.cit., pp. 546-7 and 308-10.

102. The evidence regarding Leeds comes from two large manufacturers from there, Mr Gott, SCC, pp. 324-5, and Mr Marshall, SCC, p. 363. The latter witness indicates that the pressures for longer hours seem to be operative here as well, except that the nominal day of twelve hours has been preserved. Thus 'extensive overtime' is worked when trade is brisk.

103. It is suggested that this is the only such mill in Scotland, SCC, p. 475.

104. W. Sidgwick, SCC, p. 354. This is not entirely reliable since he is a cotton manufacturer who has just 'admitted' to working these hours and is then justifying it by saying 'in the Woollen factories they work the same hours'.

105.   Indeed the first textile mill in England, a silk mill established in Derby around 1718, (P. Mantoux, op.cit., p. 194) had worked these hours from its inception (SCC, op.cit., p. 455).

106.   Evidence from two silk-mill owners. SCC, op.cit., pp. 309-11.

107.   Evidence re Scottish mills, SCC, pp. 480-1; re flax spinning in West Riding, SCC, p. 323.

108.   Figures from Tables presented by H. Houldsworth to SCC, pp. 240-3.

109.   Committee to G. Gould, SCC, pp. 337-8.

110.   It was also true that the woollen mills in this area were much less capital intensive than most of the cotton mills.

111.   Evidence from Preston cotton mill owner. SCC, op.cit., p. 511.

112.   By 'ten-hour day' we mean here the day from six to six, which in practice sometimes was a ten-and-a-half-hour day, or occasionally even an eleven-hour day, depending on the amount of time allowed for meals.

113.   Although the first mills were established in the country, Manchester was the heart of the area in which they sprang up. Thus it was from Manchester that the inquiry into the fever outbreak in Radcliffe was undertaken.

114.   B. L. Hutchins and A. Harrison, *A History of Factory Legislation*, (1926), pp. 8-10.

115.   Dr Percival, 'Resolutions for the Consideration of the Manchester Board of Health', January 25, 1796, cited in SCC, pp. 377-8.

116.   'An Act for the Preservation of the Health and Morals of Apprentices and others employed in Cotton and other Mills, and Cotton and other Factories', 42 George III, c. 73, (1802).

117.   R. Arkwright, SCC, p. 515, testifies that 'these thirteen years, I think they (the magistrates who were to enforce the Act) visited my mills at Cromford twice'. See also M. W. Thomas, *The Early Factory Legislation*, (1948), pp. 12-13; and B. L. Hutchins and A. Harrison, op.cit., p. 17; or H. A. Mess, *Factory Legislation and its Administration'*, (1926), p. 3.

118.   Sir R. Peel, evidence to SCC, p. 133.

119.   59 George III, c. 66, (1819), 'An Act to make further Provisions for the Regulation of Cotton Mills and Factories, and for the better Preservation of the Health of young Persons employed therein'.

120.   The relevant provisions were: no employment of children under 9; employment of those between 9 and 16 only between 5 am and 9 pm and during this time for a maximum of twelve hours with 1½

hours for meals in addition; one hour extra could be worked to make up for lost time.

121. See M. W. Thomas, op.cit., pp. 22-7, and G. D. H. Cole, *Robert Owen*, (1925), p. 75.

122. For the early cotton shops see above, note 94; for the potteries see evidence of J. Wedgwood to SCC, p. 295. He estimates that 'our people . . . on an average lose one day a week'.

123. J. Bush, proprietor woollen mill, Bradford, Wiltshire, to SCC, p. 549.

124. D. R. Guttery, op.cit., pp. 9, 38.

125. H. Houldsworth to SCC, p. 473.

126. Select Committee to witness, SCC, p. 573.

127. SCC, op.cit., pp. 449-67, 401-2, and 468.

128. A Preston employer states that 'the people prefer working longer five days in the week, in order that they may have Saturday afternoon to themselves; many of them have small gardens and potato-grounds, which they wish to attend to on that day, or go to market, Saturday being the market-day in Preston'. (SCC, p. 496). Another states that a limitation on hours, if instituted, should be on weekly rather than daily hours, since 'it is desirable that the poor should have sufficient time to go to market on Saturday, and not be compelled to buy their meat from hucksters'. (SCC, p. 512).

129. See J. Strutt, op.cit., pp. XXVII-XXVIII and 271-2, and D. Hughson, *London and its Environs to Thirty Miles Extent*, (1810), p. 392.

130. Evidence of cotton mill owner. SCC, op.cit., pp. 578-96.

131. SCC, pp. 612-13. One of the Manchester mills reports 21 days, but this may be explained if one includes the quarter day that is granted on every Saturday. This would leave eight other days and would conform to the general evidence. For the mills outside Manchester the figures are more erratic, including two which report 28 and 33 days. These must have been water-driven mills which would lose a number of days due to shortage of water every year.

132. SCC, op.cit., pp. 508, 316 and 548.

133. SCC, op.cit., p. 570.

Chapter three

1. A. J. Taylor, 'Progress and Poverty in Britain, 1780-1850', in E. M. Carus Wilson, op.cit., III, p. 393.

2. From here onwards we shall discuss daily and weekly hours together since such a very large number of different arrangements of hours were introduced over the next decades. Only occasionally, when for example a reduction of hours on Saturday is specifically preferred to a reduction of daily hours and when there is a significant reason for this preference, will the problems be discussed separately.

3. Hence we drop the distinction between 'crafts' and industries, a vague distinction at the best of times, but increasingly meaningless as wage employment without prospects of upward mobility becomes more widespread.

4. We shall henceforth ignore the fact that this legislation applied only to women, young persons and children. In practice the hours of women and young persons were invariably the hours of the mills. The only minor exception to this were a few mills which tried to use relays or overlapping shifts for women and children to evade the restrictions of some of the later legislation.

5. 6 George IV, c. 63, (1825).

6. In 1813 there were in Britain 'not more than 100 powerlooms in use. . . . In 1820 there were already fourteen thousand and in 1829 nearly sixty thousand' while in 1833 there were over 100,000. R. W. Cooke Taylor, op.cit., p. 95.

7. 'Factory Commission: Report', *BPP*, (1833), XX. Henceforth referred to as FCR.

8. H. W. Sefton, cotton-mill proprietor, in 'Minutes of Evidence before Select Committee on Manufactures, Commerce, and Shipping', *BPP*, (1833), VI (hence referred to as EMCS), pp. 625-37.

9. *Leeds Mercury,* October 16, 1830.

10. *Leeds Intelligencer,* October 23, 1830. Letter by S. Townend.

11. *Leeds Mercury,* October 30, 1830.

12. R. Webster, Halifax manufacturer, cited in C. Driver, *Richard Oastler: Tory Radical,* (New York, 1946). pp. 56-7.

13. FCR, op.cit., pp. 59 and 9.

14. FCR, op.cit., p. 8.

15. They proposed for children under 14, and thus in effect for the mills in general, a reduction 'to 11 hours a day (exclusive of two hours for meals) and 8 hours on Saturday'. C. Driver, op.cit., p. 59.

16. FCR, op.cit., p. 59.

17. 'Evidence to the Factory Commission', *BPP*, (1833), XX, (hence referred to as EFC), pp. 99-185.

18.   3 & 4 William IV, c. 103, (1833).
19.   'Act to Limit the Hours of Labour of young Persons and Females in Factories', 10 & 11 Victoria, c. 29, (1847).
20.   The use of relays had enabled many mills to employ men and machines beyond the ten-hour limit, and to force children in many cases to work their hours discontinuously. To avoid this possibility it was decreed that the mills should work only between 6 am and 6 pm and should stop for one and one-half hours for meals.
21.   It appears now that the death rate was indeed rising between 1822 and 1841. (See T. H. Marshall, 'Population and the Industrial Revolution' in E. M. Carus Wilson, op.cit., I.) The point was never fully accepted at the time.
22.   This point will be elaborated later. Essentially it would have increased over this period because of the changed nature of the business cycle and the increased degree of specialization in the labour market.
23.   E. Hodder, *The Life and Work of the Seventh Earl of Shaftesbury,* (1888), pp. 390-2.
24.   The general categories refered to are those of the 1911 census, and the employment figures given for these groups are from B. R. Mitchell, *Abstract of British Historical Statistics,* (1962), Statistics on the Labour Force, Pt. B.
25.   'Royal Commission on the Employment of Children' (hence referred to as RCC), *BPP,* (1843), XIII and XIV.
26.   'Reports to the Commissioners of the Royal Commission on the Employment of Children, 1843', *BPP,* 1843, XIV, p. E33. See also pp. e43; e56. These Reports and the Evidence to the Commission will henceforth be referred to as R-RCC. References from the Reports to the Commissioners are identified by page references preceded by a capital letter; references to the evidence are preceded by lower case letters.
27.   For evidence regarding the various areas see R-RCC, op.cit., pp. B41; M38, 46, 51, 57 and 64 for Lancashire; pp. 02; S4 and d45 for the West of England including South Gloucestershire; pp. Q4 and C21 for the Midlands; pp. f290-3 for the North-East and Scotland; and p. K6 for the London area.
28.   This refers to the practice of working irregularly during each week, often not working, or 'playing', on Monday and/or Tuesday, as was common in most domestic trades. The system was carried over into many of the new industries.

29.   'First Report of the Commissioners for inquiring into the Employment and Condition of Children in Mines and Manufactories: Mines', *BPP*, (1842), XV, (hence referred to as RCC-R1), p. 200.

30.   One of the works reporting on the effects of ceasing work for a few hours on Sunday, stated that they first experimented with the idea '25 years ago'. Evidence from Madeley Wood Iron Works, RCC-R1, op.cit., pp. 201-2.

31.   Mr Best, manager British Iron Co. speaking to the Midland Mining Commission. 'First Report: Midland Mining Commission', *BPP*, (1843), XIII, (hence referred to as MMC), pp. CXLII-CXLIII.

32.   H. Scrivenor, *A Comprehensive History of the Iron Trade*, (1841), pp. 291-2.

33.   See RCC-R1, op.cit., pp. 202-3; MMC, op.cit., p. CXLIV.

34.   R-RCC, op.cit., p. 02, states that in the iron-works of South Gloucestershire 'Sunday labour does not prevail to any great extent' and suggests that 'such infractions of the Sabbath should be altogether dispensed with'. This statement is of course compatible with a situation where only the blast furnaces are working on Sunday, since they would represent only a small proportion of employees in an iron-works. More difficult to explain is the note attached to the 'Wage Tables for Staffordshire iron works' in *Tables of Revenue, etc. of the United Kingdom*, Pt. XVIII, (1850), p. 198, reprinted in 'Labour Statistics: Returns of Wages Published between 1830 and 1886', *BPP*, (1887), LXXXIX, p. 28, which suggests that to obtain the weekly earnings for the occupations listed one should multiply the daily wage by six in the case of 'the furnace men (blast-furnace men) who work every day regularly'.

35.   The list of those pressing for the adoption of this change includes the British Iron Company (MMC, op.cit., p. CXLII) and the great works of Coalbrookdale, Dowlais, and Madeley Wood (RCC-R1, op.cit., pp. 200-2).

36.   See S. Homfray of the Tredegar Iron Works to Guest, Lewis & Co. on April 22, 1840: 'I beg to inform you that I have received answers to my letters respecting the reduction of Wages from the different Iron-masters and all *concur* in the proposition and *necessity* of reducing wages . . . it is essential that unanimity should be preserved', in M. Elsas, op.cit., p. 13. More generally, 'Iron-masters colluded openly when trade was bad. They met in Dec. 1836 and again in 1840 and agreed to restrict production to

keep up the price – compensating by blowing out some furnaces as well'. H. Scrivenor, op.cit., p. 314.

37. R-RCC, op.cit., p. S4.

38. In Scotland 'it is customary to leave off work on Saturdays . . . one and . . . two hours earlier than on the other days'. 'Second Report of the Royal Commission on the Employment and Condition of Children in Mines and Manufactories', *BPP,* (1843), XIII, (hence referred to as RCC-R2), p. 7.

39. In Warrington the other metal trades all enjoyed a four-o'clock Saturday, R-RCC, op.cit., pp. M7, 30 and 31.

40. J. S. Hodgson, 'The Movements for Shorter Hours, 1840-1875' (unpublished D.Phil.Oxon.), (1940), pp. 218-22.

41. See figure 1 which shows the frequency distributions of normal hours in a number of industries including ironfounding.

42. H. Scrivenor, op.cit., p. 121.

43. J. J. Guest, proprietor of the Dowlais iron works, South Wales, to his confidential clerk in London, May 26, 1826. (in M. Elsas, op.cit., p. 24).

44. R-RCC, op.cit., pp. E34 and f293.

45. This is the same report described in note 34. There it was seen to claim, almost certainly falsely, that the blast furnaces worked only six days a week. The present claim is also suspect, if only because it is difficult to see how these works could operate on the sixth day each week with only the carpenters, labourers, etc., in attendance but without the furnace men.

46. H. Scrivenor, op.cit., pp. 291-2.

47. MMC, op.cit., pp. CXLIV-CXLV.

48. Ibid., p. CXLIV.

49. R-RCC, op.cit., p. B41.

50. RCC-R2, op.cit., p. 50.

51. See R-RCC, op.cit., pp. f153-6 for Birmingham; pp. e47-50 for the West Riding; p. c46 for Bristol; pp. 43-4 for Leeds; p. K6 for Scotland; p. L5 for Northumberland and Durham; p. M56-8, 64 for Lancashire; p. 02 for South Gloucestershire; p. S4 for the West of England; p. F27 for London.

52. J. Brown, proprietor flax-spinning mill in Dundee, to EFC, op.cit., p. 124.

53. B. Clarke, of the firm of Clarke & Sons, Lancashire, in FCR, op.cit., p. 61.

54.   H. Houldsworth, proprietor of cotton mills, Glasgow, to EMCS, op.cit., p. 324.

55.   S. & B. Webb, *History of Trade Unionism,* (1906), p. 206; see also J. S. Hodgson, op.cit., pp. 114-16.

56.   W. H. Beveridge, *Full Employment in a Free Society,* (1944), The index of industrial activity cited here rises above 110 only three times between 1830 and 1910: once in 1845-6; once in 1874; and again in 1882-3.

57.   *The Northern Star,* March 7, 1846.

58.   Board of Trade, 'Report of Trades (Hours of Work)', *BPP,* (1890), LXVIII. (hence referred to as BTH).

59.   W. H. Beveridge, op.cit., pp. 277 and 310-13. The index of the activity of the 'Construction and Instrument' sector reached 137 in 1846, a figure that was not surpassed again until 1920.

60.   The 1842 depression was attended by very high unemployment rates, although exact figures are not available. E. J. Hobsbawm 'The British Standard of Living, 1790-1850', in E. J. Hobsbawm *Labouring Men* (1964), pp. 72-6.

61.   EMCS, op.cit., p. 276.

62.   R-RCC, op.cit., p. E4.

63.   Evidence from R-RCC, op.cit., p. e34, and from S. Pollard, *A History of Labour in Sheffield,* (1959), p. 61.

64.   In Warrington the file-cutters generally enjoy a four-o'clock Saturday, R-RCC, op.cit., pp. M7, 30 and 31. Interestingly one of these shops has made a concession to the former habits of the domestic workers by working one hour less on Monday. In the Sheffield trades generally 'the Saturday half-day was introduced in the 1840's. By 1850 work generally finished at 3 pm or 4 pm'. (S. Pollard, op.cit., p. 62).

65.   In all trades where steam was not used hours tended to be irregular, and in 1843 'it often results, especially when trade is brisk, that the workman will do no work on the Monday and Tuesday'. (R-RCC, p. E4). One of the 'five or six' large employers who were in a position to enforce regular hours in the Sheffield cutlery trade complained that 'sometimes the grinders won't work even for witness (i.e. employer). Tuesday is often a 'Natty day' with grinders, when nothing will persuade them to work — not even a barrel of ale, and yet they (the said employers) have more control over this class of workmen than any other manufacturers'. (R-RCC, op.cit., p. e15).

66.   BTH, op.cit., The figures from that report make up figure 1.

67.   RCC-R2, op.cit., pp. 74-5. In these trades it is usually two hours per day, with a few exceptions at 1½ hours, and one or two cases of but one hour being allowed.

68.   RCC-R1, op.cit., pp. 106-18.

69.   The Commission states that regular meals were observed only in South Staffordshire and in the Forest of Dean, where they were one hour in each case. With regard to North Wales they say that they do not have enough evidence to decide whether meal times were actually set aside. Ibid., pp. 119-21.

70.   Forest of Dean (8 hours, some 12); South Gloucester (8 to 10 hours); Halifax (8 or 9 hours). The hours of the mines in the Forest of Dean and South Gloucestershire explain the comment by the inspector to the Second Report of the Royal Commission (RRC-R2, op.cit., p. D2) to the effect that 'the very numerous body of colliers is particularly favoured, as far as mere time and leisure go, as their 'turn', or day's work, is seldom more than eight hours at a time'.

71.   Derbyshire (except Chesterfield area) worked from 6 am to 8 pm; East of Scotland worked over twelve hours much of the time.

72.   Bradford and Leeds (10 to 11 hours); Oldham (9, 10 or 11 hours); North Lancashire (8 to 12 hours); North Somerset (8 to 12 hours); West Riding (10 to 11 hours).

73.   MMC, op.cit., p. CXIV.

74.   Ibid, pp. CVII-CVIII.

75.   Ibid., pp. XXXVII and LXXII.

76.   Ibid., pp. LXXIV and CXXI.

77.   J. S. Hodgson, op.cit., p. 17.

78.   A. T. Penson, *Traité de l'exploitation des mines de houille,* (Liège, 1854), I, pp. 320-1 and IV, p. 120, as cited by E. J. Hobsbawm, 'Custom, Wages and Work-load', in E. J. Hobsbawm, *Labouring Men,* (1964), p. 353.

79.   Those pits directly supplying iron-works 'give the most regular employment' but even they work no more than five days a week on average. MMC, op.cit., pp. LXXV and CXIV.

80.   Two mines in the potteries are reported as working Saturday 5 am to 1 pm and 6 am to 4 pm respectively (Ibid., p. LXXXI) while in South Staffordshire two pits that close at 5 pm on Saturday are mentioned as exceptional cases (Ibid., pp. XLV, LXXIII). Some

mines in the North-East apparently have every second Saturday off. (J. S. Hodgson, op.cit.).

81.   See *The Northern Star,* May 1843; February, August, 1844; January 1845; August 1849. For a detailed description of the 1842 strike in the Midlands for '4s. per day, and eight hours' work' see MMC, op.cit. See also S. & B. Webb, *History of Trade Unionism* (1898), pp. 280-9.

82.   The Miners' Advocate, November 16, 1844.

83.   RCC-R1, op.cit., p. 216-218.

84.   This can be inferred from the fact that earlier hours had been of this magnitude, and later in the late 1850s the building trades were invariably found to be working these hours.

85.   R. W. Postgate, *The Builder's History,* (1923), pp. 136-8.

86.   From 'Manuscripts to the Webb History of Trade Unionism', Coll. E, Section A, (hence referred to as MWH, EA), XIII, p. 179.

87.   The exact date seems to be lost, although it is known to be between 1828 and 1831. At its peak in 1833-4 this federation included masons, carpenters, bricklayers, plasterers, plumbers, glaziers, and slaters.

88.   R. W. Postgate, op.cit., pp. 72-3.

89.   MWH, EA op.cit., X, p. 76. In general these strikes attempted to establish formally customary practices of all kinds. The rules that were to be established included the elimination of overtime, the regulation of piece work, wage differentials and of apprenticeship schemes. There was only one instance of concern over normal hours and that came from the Manchester plumbers whose working day had recently been extended to twelve hours. They demanded a return to the ten-hour day and although all the strikes were utterly defeated this one demand was granted. MWH, EA, X, pp. 79-80, 95, 191, and MWH, EA, XII, p. 297.

90.   R. W. Postgate, op.cit., p. 97.

91.   This was of course also the year of the death of the Grand National Consolidated Trades' Union.

92.   Fortnightly Returns of the Operative Masons' Society, July 1837.

93.   'Resolution of Delegate Meeting, Operative Society of Masons, 1838' cited in MWH, EA, XIII, p. 121.

94.   The strike had begun after the plumbers of Manchester and area had in 1845 'published . . . a proclamation that too many apprentices were being kept and that the limit was to be "any

master keeping his men regular winter and summer to be allowed two apprentices" '. (R. W. Postgate, op.cit., p. 134).

95. J. S. Hodgson, op.cit., p. 214; and *The Northern Star,* November 1, 1845.

96. R-RCC, op.cit., pp. A1-A2, and RCC-R2, op.cit., p. 63, where one witness states that she 'would rather not work that way (constant overtime) but I must, or mistress would have some one else'.

97. R-RCC, op.cit., pp. r11-r12 (a mill near London works 12-hour shifts); pp. b59, 142, and M67 (Lancashire hours 'from ten to twelve'); pp. L4 (Durham and Northumberland hours ten to twelve); p. I53 (West of Scotland hours 10½ to twelve); p. K1 (East of Scotland hours are twelve). For source of quotations see ibid., p. K1, and RCC-R2, op.cit., p. 78.

98. J. Child, *Industrial Relations in the British Printing Industry,* (1967), p. 73.

99. E. Howe and H. E. Waite, *The London Society of Compositors,* (1948), pp. 98-100.

100. R-RCC, op.cit., pp. f246-52, and RCC-R2, op.cit., pp. 133-5. Within each city there was sometimes some variation in hours. In general the newspaper shops worked more irregular hours, though it appears that on average they were no longer.

101. R-RCC, op.cit., p. f251.

102. 'Printers Strikes and Trade Unions' in *Trades Societies and Strikes: Report of the Committee on Trades' Societies,* National Association for the promotion of Social Sciences, Fourth Annual Meeting, Glasgow, (1860), p. 82.

103. J. S. Hodgson, op.cit., p. 15.

104. R-RCC, op.cit., pp. f238-46.

105. Ibid., p. f238. The statement regarding the division of labour and its effects is submitted by a workman who has been '50 years' in the trade. The statement regarding the influx of women comes from RCC-R2, op.cit., p. 134.

106. E. Howe and J. Child, op.cit., pp. 114 and 135.

107. See figure 1. The one town working 54 hours at this date was Hull.

108. This evidence comes from one of the largest London shops employing 250 to 300 journeymen in the season. R-RCC, op.cit., p. f237.

109. S. & B. Webb, *History of . . .* op.cit., pp. 149-50.

110. R-RCC, op.cit., p. F30. The hours inclusive of meals at normal times are twelve in Birmingham, Nottingham and Leicester and

13½ to 14 in Leamington and Bristol. RCC-R2, p. 120.

111. In machine lace these short hours were not exceeded. If it was 'necessary to work a machine for 24 hours' three sets of men were used. Only the boys who threaded the machines worked very long hours. RCC-R2, pp. 55-9.

112. Ibid., p. 66.

113. RCC-R2, op.cit., pp. 54, 75 and 77; R-RCC, op.cit., pp. c15-c54; pp. C4-C10 (for hours in Staffordshire); p. P1 (for hours in Derbyshire); p. E34 (hours in Yorkshire); p. L3 (hours in Durham and Northumberland); p. K7 (hours in Scotland).

114. R-RCC, op.cit., pp. F24, L1, and K7; and RCC-R2, op.cit., p. 54 and 78.

115. D. R. Guttery, op.cit., p. 117; see also R-RCC, op.cit., p. d48 (in Bristol they worked 13 hours minus two hours for meals); elsewhere they worked 10 and 10½ hours per day, pp. M37 and f147.

116. See figure 1. Seven towns were working 60 hours per week, and one worked 59 indicating a short Saturday. Two towns worked eleven hours per day, one with a short Saturday, so that their hours were 66 and 65. One worked 70 hours indicating a twelve-hour day with a short Saturday.

117. See figure 1. The sixth town in the group worked 54½ hours.

118. The first statement as to daily hours refers specifically to hours in Scotland (R-RCC, op.cit., p. 14); but the same was true of the other areas. Thus 'in . . . Lancashire, Cheshire and Derbyshire, the nominal hours of work are twelve' (ibid., p. B13). Summary as to the two hours allowed for meals to be found in RCC-R2, op.cit., p. 75.

119. See R-RCC, op.cit., p. I4.

120. RCC-R2, op.cit., pp. 59, 69-70, and 73. Generally for conditions in this industry see also R-RCC, op.cit., pp. B13-B14, B30 and a8. The need to get orders out quickly was 'to get your pattern out before it is stolen'. Nevertheless a few firms had introduced regular hours.

121. EMCS, op.cit., pp. 276 and 296.

122. S. Pollard, op.cit., p. 61.

123. FCR. op.cit., p. 7.

124. EMCS, op.cit., pp. 248 and 703-4. The witness who referred to the relatively good position of some of the Lancashire weavers believed that this was so because they do not compete with the power looms.

125. W. R. Greg, proprietor of numerous cotton mills in Lancashire, to EMCS, op.cit., p. 686.
126. J. Milne, proprietor of a textile mill, Crompton, Lancs, to ibid., p. 663. This apparently conflicting evidence suggests that the hours of these weavers were shorter than 10½ per day before the onset of depression. Thus they can say that they work 10½ hours *now*.
127. S. Jackson, manufacturer of saws, Sheffield, to EMCS, op.cit., p. 176.
128. RCC-R2, op.cit., pp. 50-1.
129. E. Baines, op.cit., p. 485.
130. RCC-R2, op.cit., pp. 51, 52, 53, 65 and 68.
131. W. Graham, Glasgow cotton mill proprietor to EMCS, op.cit., p. 332.
132. FCR, Evidence p. C1, pp. 36-7. The long hours of this trade were ascribed to 'the expensiveness of the lace-machinery and its peculiar liability to depreciation'. It was also reported that the owners of 3,253 machines signed the agreement to restrict hours worked.
133. W. Stocks, Huddersfield cotton mill proprietor to EMCS, op.cit., p. 620.
134. In one area in the late eighteenth century the weavers 'used to walk about the streets "with a five pound Bank of England note spread out under their hatbands"; they would smoke none but long "churchwarden" pipes, and objected to the intrusion of any other handicraftsmen into the particular rooms in public houses which they frequented'. (R. W. Cooke Taylor, op.cit., p. 92).
135. P. Mantoux, op.cit., p. 423.
136. There is much evidence for these claims. Thus one hand-loom weaver, when asked whether many of their number had gone into the factories, replied: 'No, the whole of the (factory) trades have combined, and it is impossible for a weaver to break in upon them; but their children, especially young girls, are taken in to work at the power-loom' (EMCS, op.cit., p. 701). There are many witnesses who state that only a very few hand-loom weavers, if any, could find employment in the factories, or anywhere else for that matter. 'Are the majority of them (hand-loom weavers) able to obtain any other employment? Not the majority.' (EMCS, op.cit., p. 688). For other witnesses who state this opinion see ibid., pp. 670, 612, 570 and 161.
137. Evidence from a Lancashire cotton-mill owner and a Lancashire

calico printer. (EMCS, op.cit., pp. 605 and 246).

138. E. Baines, op.cit., p. 494. See also the evidence by a young female witness before a government commission. She worked in domestic embroidery and stated that she 'liked it better than the factory, though we can't get so much. We have our liberty at home, and get our meals comfortable, such as they are'. (cited by Dr Ure, from P. Gaskell, *Artisans and Machinery,* (1836), p. 40).

139. RCC-R2, op.cit., p. 77.

140. It was of course stipulated by the Factory Act of 1825 which laid down a nine-hour Saturday. Furthermore the adult male spinners of Manchester 'seem (in 1825) for the most part to be dismissed on Saturday about 4 o'clock, pm'. (Anon., 'Hours of Work in Manchester', Pamphlet, 1825).

141. RCC-R1, op.cit., p. 122.

142. In many cases the practice was to 'make up' for holidays by working overtime before and after the event without extra pay. Operatives who refused to do such work were not paid for the holiday'. (FCR, op.cit., p. 11). See also: ibid., pp. 107 and 121; R-RCC, op.cit., for Kent see pp. a3-a4, for other areas in the South-East pp. a27-a41. More generally for practices regarding paid holidays in England and Scotland, see RCC-R2, op.cit., pp. 78, and R-RCC, op.cit., pp. B16, D5, S5.

143. Evidence of mill owners. (FCR, op.cit., pp. 124, 128 and 61).

144. E. Baines, op.cit., p. 456.

145. H. Sefton, clerk of Stockport to EMCS, op.cit., p. 637.

146. B. Clarke, of Clarke & Sons, Lancashire, FCR, op.cit., p. 61.

147. S. & B. Webb, *History of . . .* op.cit., p. 168.

148. FCR, op.cit., pp. 12-14.

149. Though there were a few isolated cases during this period such agreements do not become common until the 1850s, and even then they are restricted to a very few trades.

150. Board of Trade, BTH, op.cit.

151. Between 1810 and 1847, the index of industrial activity for the textile trades fell below 90 only three times: to 82.3 in 1816, to 89.5 in 1920, and to 80.6 in 1926. In 1847 this index stood at 77.1 (W. H. Beveridge, op.cit., p. 311).

152. A. J. Taylor, 'Progress and Poverty in Britain, 1780-1850', in E. M. Carus Wilson, op.cit., III, p. 391.

153. E. J. Hobsbawm, 'Custom, Wages and Work-Load', in E. J. Hobsbawm, op.cit., p. 356.

154.   Ibid., p. 356.
155.   S. & B. Webb, 'History of . . .', op.cit., p. 183.
156.   Figures for coal exports from Britain are: ('000 tons)

      1829 = 371   1832 = 588   1835 = 729   1838 = 1303
      1830 = 504   1833 = 629   1836 = 911   1839 = 1432
      1831 = 511   1834 = 610   1837 = 1106   1840 = 1592

      From B. R. Mitchell, op. cit., Ch. IV, 'Coal', Series 5, p. 121.

Chapter four

1.   E. J. Hobsbawm, 'Trends in the British Labour Movement', in E. J. Hobsbawm, op.cit., p. 323.

2.   In 1875 about half of the then union members came from traditional crafts, many of which had not yet been affected very severely by the industrial revolution. They included the builders, printers, cabinet-makers, tailors, glass-bottle makers, bookbinders and coach-makers. The engineers and shipbuilders (iron) had of course been 'created' by the industrial revolution, but once established they had not undergone any great changes by this time. The rest were to be found in mining, iron and steel, and skilled textile trades. See E. J. Hobsbawm, 'The Labour Aristocracy' in E. J. Hobsbawm, op.cit., pp. 280-1.

3.   Ibid., p. 279, 'aristocrats' are here defined as men earning over 28s per week.

4.   The division of time into decades is entirely artificial and is designed only to break the narrative into manageable pieces. Since any such chronological sub-division would have been artificial to some extent, it was deemed an advantage to choose periods for which it is clear that there is no further significance. Furthermore, such a division was convenient because the figures of the Board of Trade that were used to corroborate and complement our findings refer to every tenth year beginning in 1850.

5.   Statistics for figures 3, 4 and 5 stem from BTH, op.cit. Each statistic refers to a town or area, and the graphs show the proportion of such towns or areas that work certain hours. Occasionally this may be misleading because at this stage – 1850 – there are some industries for which there are only very few readings. This problem is lessened for those industries that are concentrated in a few areas since then the large percentage change in the hours of the industry as a whole occasioned by a change in hours in one town will be an accurate indicator of change. In

general these statistics should be used to corroborate other evidence or to indicate major trends or changes. Minor changes are not significant.

6.   MWH, EA, op.cit., XIII, pp. 233 and 193, and Operative Society of Masons, Fortnightly Returns (Hence OSM-FR), July 1850.

7.   See *The Builder,* December 31, 1853, and *The Bricklayers' Trade Circular,* No. 9, May 1, 1862 as cited in MWH, EA, X, p. 210.

8.   ASE (Amalgamated Society of Engineers, etc), 'Jubilee Souvenir', (1926), p. 22, cited in J. S. Hodgson, op.cit., p. 255.

9.   For an account of the strike see, *Social Science Association, Report,* (1860), p. 172; *The Times,* Jan. 9-14, 1852; J. S. Hodgson, op.cit., pp. 245-62.

10. OSM-FR, op.cit., March and May 1853, as cited in MWH, EA, XIII, pp. 235 and 240. The agitation was for the nine-hour day, together with an 8½-hour Saturday for a 53½-hour week.

11. G. Shaw Lefevre and T. R. Bennet, *Account of the Strike and Lock-out in the Building Trades of London in 1859-60,* Pamphlet, (Br. Mus).

12. A builder writing to OSM-FR, March 5, 1857.

13. Shaftesbury's letter in *The Times* of May 21, 1856, also refers to a great meeting on the subject held by the Early Closing Association in April. The two firms writing letters were Truman's Breweries and a saw mill. *The Times,* March 27 and April 22, 1856.

14. *The Times,* May 14 and 17, 1856.

15. E. A. Johns, *The Social Structure of Modern Britain,* (1965), p. 123.

16. G. Howell, *Bricklayers' Trade Circular,* I, No. 3, November 1, 1861, p. 4.

17. Descriptions of these events are to be found in OSM-FR, op.cit., October 16, 1856 and April 30 and July 9, 1857.

18. OSM-FR, op.cit., July 23, 1857 and September 15, 1859. The 61-hour week was worked in Liverpool and Huddersfield until 1857 (ibid., July 9, 1857), and in Newcastle-upon-Tyne until 1859 (ibid., February 17, 1859).

19. MWH, EA, XIII, pp. 231-5.

20. OSM-FR, op.cit., December 10, 1857 and March 17, 1859.

21. In Lancashire it spread to Bolton, Preston, Blackburn and Ashton-under-Lyne, though some of these did not change until 1860. In Cheshire it applied to Altrincham, Stalybridge, Stockport and Macclesfield by the end of 1860 (OSM-FR, 1856-60). For

Scotland the information is more spotty, and the masons here were not so strongly unionized at this time; it appears, however, that the 57-hour week — i.e. 2 pm Saturday — had become common in the building trades around Glasgow and Edinburgh by the end of the decade, and that it had been introduced during the decade. See MWH, EA, XI, p. 231, where one is told that Glasgow joiners struck in 1854 for a reduction from 60 to 57 hours; ibid., p. 268, for declaration to the same effect by Edinburgh and Leith Operative Joiners; ibid., XIII, p. 420 for reduction from 60 to 57 hours for Glasgow plasterers, p. 361 for the same change for the Glasgow masons in 1853. In another place we are told that the Scottish builders in general reduced hours to 57 in this decade (BTH, op.cit.).

22. Here too there had been 'for some time past an agitation among the trades' for a Saturday half-holiday. The strike began August 2 1856, and was abandoned in October of that year. See OSM-FR, August 21, September 4, October 2 and 30, 1856.

23. Masons at Keel Hall, by Newcastle-under-Lyme, see OSM-FR, April 30, 1857.

24. Reports of all of these events are to be found in OSM-FR, op.cit., March 29, 1860 and June 21, 1860.

25. These London events are described in OSM-FR, op.cit., June 24 and November 11, 1858, and September 2 and 15, 1859.

26. For the 1859-60 strike see OSM-FR, August 18, 1859 to February 16, 1860, or a summary of it in G. Shaw Lefevre and T. R. Bennet, op.cit. The clearest summary of the confused events of the 1861-2 strike is to be found in *The Operative Bricklayer's Society Trade Circular and General Reporter,* July 1862, in an article entitled 'Report and Balance Sheet of the Dispute relating to the Attempt to introduce the System of Hiring and Paying by the Hour', (Pamphlet — Br. Mus.).

27. OSM-FR, op.cit., August 20, 1857 and May 13, 1858.

28. These figures are from OSM-FR, and refer in almost all cases to hours laid down in collective agreements.

29. This was a fairly common practice, making Monday a day of nine or nine and a half hours. It meant starting one hour late on that day.

30. Table 2 summarizes the statistics in figure 3 by showing the unweighted mean average of the distributions of normal hours in each industry. It is thus subject to the same qualifications as that figure. It shows that no changes of any significance were recorded

in 1850-60, except in building and in the boot and shoe trade. This latter result is highly suspect however, as there is no corroborating evidence and much of this trade was still domestic at this time. Moreover the 1850 average is based on only six towns, while that of 1860 includes eleven.

31. S. Pollard, op.cit., p. 62; and BTH, op.cit.

32. OSM-FR, op.cit., May 14, 1857.

33. *Report of the Social Science Association,* (1860), pp. 19-21, 37, 302.

34. BTH, op.cit. Hours of hewers were reduced between 1850 and 1860 from 60 to 54 in Newcastle, from 66 to 45-66 in Northumberland county, and from 50 to 42½ in South Northumberland, while in Seaham in 1860 the hours were 44. (All hours bank to bank.)

35. *The Times,* May 9, 1956. For report on end of strike see *The Times,* June 11, 1856.

36. Although the actual magnitudes of these figures are of little importance they do show the beginning of a trend towards shorter hours in most industries. The figures for all employees would probably show the same trend, although the reductions would be smaller since all the subsidiary evidence indicates that the changes did not extend to the smaller places during this period.

37. OSM-FR, op.cit., March 31, June 9, December 8 and 22, 1859 and March 1, 1860.

38. Ibid., July 19, 1860. For accounts of how the nine-hour day was established in Huddersfield see ibid., January 19, February 2 and March 29, 1860; for Bradford see ibid., June 7 and 21, 1860; and for Halifax ibid., July 19, August 30, September 13 and November 8, 1860. The Halifax strike lasted until 1862 and its end was reported in ibid., February 28, 1862.

39. The Scottish events are described in MWH, EA, op.cit., XIII, p. 252, and in T. F. Connelly, *The Woodworkers, 1860-1960,* (1960), p. 22.

40. OSM-FR, March 27, 1862.

41. J. S. Hodgson, op.cit., p. 328.

42. For a report of this strike see OSM-FR, July 3, 1862.

43. Paper to the Social Science Association reprinted in OSM-FR, July 3, 1862.

44. These views stem from the Bradford lodge (OSM-FR, op.cit., May 10, 1860) and from the Halifax lodge (ibid., July 19, 1860). With

effective barriers to entry this may of course have been a rational
position depending on the elasticity of product demand and the
labour intensity of the industry.

45. See index of industrial activity by Sir W. Beveridge, *Full Employment in a Free Society*, (1944), pp. 277, 310-13.

	Construction and Instrument	Textiles	All
1861	92.2	107.0	100.2
1862	93.4	65.1	88.6
1863	110.1	67.5	95.5
1864	115.6	70.0	99.1
1865	114.7	86.2	101.9
1866	100.2	92.7	98.9
1867	90.5	93.0	95.9
1868	91.7	98.8	97.2

46. *The Bee Hive*, April 7, 14, 21 and May 5, 1866.

47. The main source for all of these changes in the metal trades is BTH, op.cit. It shows the following reductions: Liverpool whitesmiths 58 to 56 hours; London boilermakers 63 to 60; Willenhall locksmiths from 70 to 65; Swansea tin-plate workers 70 to 60; Aberavon tin-plate workers 78 to 72. For evidence regarding the coach-makers from Lancs. and Yorks. and Clyde shipbuilders see J. S. Hodgson, op.cit., pp. 330 and 334, while for the Sheffield trades see S. Pollard, op.cit., pp. 130-1.

48. *Transactions and Results of the National Association of Coal, Lime and Ironstone Miners of Great Britain, held at Leeds, November 9, 10, 11, 12, 13 and 14, 1863*, p. 14.

49. 'Royal Commission on Trade Unions', *BPP*, (1867), Q, pp. 13, 467.

50. The miners (general) of Barnsley and Shipley reduced their hours from 60 to 54, those from Sheffield from 72 to 49 hours. The miners of Wigan (miners generally) reduced their hours from 72 to 60½ hours; those of Manchester from 55 to 50 (BTH, op.cit.).

51. *Scottish Typographical Circular*, I, April 5, 1862.

52. E. Howe and J. Child, op.cit., p. 192.

53. MWH, EA, op.cit., XXX, and see also '1866 Addenda to the London Scale of Prices for Compositors', cited in E. Howe and H. E. Waite, *The London Society of Compositors*, (1948), p. 177.

54. J. S. Hodgson, op.cit., p. 334 and 373.

55. The troubles of the Scottish tailors are described in the reports of their first two national conferences in 1865 and 1866. Most of it

comes from the *Report of the First National Conference of the Operative Tailors of Scotland, 1865.* Copies of these are in the Trades Union Congress Library.

56. These events are reported in detail in R. W. Postgate, op.cit. and are also described in S. & B. Webb, *History of . . .* , op.cit. Some additional details were found in OSM-FR, May 1852, and MWH, EA, op.cit., XIII, pp. 233-4.

57. *The Financial Report of the Amalgamated Society of Carpenters and Joiners,* (June to December 1860), p. 6.

58. In addition part 6 of this chapter will discuss the statistical evidence for the building trades available for the period 1860 to 1890. Since these figures refer only to England and Wales a separate word about Scotland is called for. In 1866 the Scottish masons met 'to celebrate the success of their efforts to obtain the 9 hour day . . . the first great step toward the thorough emancipation of labour from the chains of capital'. (MWH, EA, XIII, p. 433). The Scottish building trades generally are said to have observed a 55- to 57-hour week in 1870 (BTH, op.cit.). It is clear, however, that some had obtained the 51-hour week.

59. OSM-FR, op.cit., May 1866 and February 1867, as cited in MWH, EA, XIII, pp. 298 and 261.

60. MWH, EA, op.cit., XIII, pp. 261-9.

61. See A.S.C.J. Annual Reports for the years in question.

62. MWH, EA, op.cit., XIII, pp. 210-17 and 269.

63. Operative Bricklayers Society (OBS), *Annual Report,* June 1870.

64. 'The Perseverance Society of Carpenters and Joiners' from MWH, EA, op.cit., XI, p. 320.

65. Report prepared by Mr Redgrave, factory inspector, March 1870 and presented in the 'Report of the Commissioners appointed to inquire into the working of the Factory and Workshop Acts', I, *BPP,* (1876), XXIX (hence CFW), p. 100. A totally incomprehensible thing about this report is that it is presented in 1875 to a government commission by an assistant factory inspector with the comment that he is 'not aware of any alteration in the hours of work since' 1870. There is no explanation for this but it is too fantastic to believe that a London factory inspector should not know about the universal changes in hours which we know occurred in 1872 in building, engineering, printing and bookbinding among many other trades.

66. *The London Illustrated News,* May 4 and June 15, 1872.

67.   The nine-hour day refers to a day of nine working hours but, as was the case with the ten-hour day, the term is often used to refer to a day of nine and one-half actual working hours per day which was often worked in conjunction with a short Saturday to make a fifty-four-hour week.

68.   The carpenters and joiners obtained the nine-hour day in 1870 in Glasgow. MWH, EA, XI, p. 59.

69.   *The Bee Hive*, April 8, 1871.

70.   J. S. Hodgson, op.cit., pp. 389-91.

71.   OSM-FR, August 1851, cited in MWH, EA, XI, p. 216.

72.   ASCJ, *Annual Report*, 1872. These include Leeds, Middlesborough, Sunderland, Gateshead, Stockton, Darlington and Huddersfield.

73.   J. S. Hodgson, op.cit., p. 394.

74.   *The Bee Hive*, March 28, 1874.

75.   S. Pollard, op.cit., pp. 130-1.

76.   H. J. Fyrth and H. Collins, *The Foundry Workers: A Trade Union History*, (1959), p. 41.

77.   BTH, op.cit., Boilermakers of Leeds, Manchester, London all adopt 54-hour week (two from 60, Manchester from 57½). The brassworkers of Tyne and Wear go from 59 to 54, those of Birmingham work 54 by 1870; the smiths from all nine cities and areas listed adopt a 54-hour week; Liverpool whitesmiths go from 56 to 54, while the tin-plate workers adopt 54 hours in Birmingham (from 60), 50 hours in Swansea (from 60), and 48 to 58 in Aberavon (from 72).

78.   BTH, op.cit.

79.   BTH, op.cit.

80.   *The Bee Hive*, May 11, 1872, cited in MWH, EA, XXIII, p. 24.

81.   MWH, EA, op.cit., XII, p. 433. In 1871 Glasgow and Paisley plumbers reduced hours from 57 to 51 (ibid., XII, p. 335); 1870-4 the Scottish carpenters got the nine-hour day (ibid., XI, pp. 59, 239, 275 and 279); 1872 the marble and slate masons of Edinburgh and Leith got the 51-hour week (ibid., XIII, p. 423); 1873-4 the Edinburgh paviors got a 54-hour week (ibid., XIII, p. 450).

82.   The general depression that began in 1874 did not affect the building trades until 1877. Thus the ASCJ Annual Report of 1875 complained that arbitrators 'imagine that a general inflation or depression of trade affects the building trade immediately, whereas

they follow very slowly after. Hence the present depression in general trade has been considered inopportune for advances whereas the building trade is just beginning to be brisk'. Cited in MWH, EA, XI, p. 62.

83. MWH, EA, XI, p. 154.

84. The evidence relating to the printing and allied trades stems from a variety of sources. E. Howe and J. Child, op.cit., pp. 192-4; *Bookbinders and Machine Rulers' Consolidated Union Trade Circular,* IV, Nos. 28 (December 1877) and 6 (March 1873); MWH, EA, op.cit., V, p. 147 and ibid., XXXI, p. 268; and E. Howe and H. E. Waite, op.cit., p. 208.

85. *The Bee Hive,* November 11 and December 9, 1871 and March 16, 1872.

86. *Report of the Fifth National Conference of the Operative Tailors of Scotland,* March 1870, p. 7, and also the *Report of the Seventh . .* , ibid., February 1873, p. 6.

87. CFW, op.cit., p. XXIX.

88. *The Bee Hive,* September-December 1870, February 11, April 28 and May 13, 1871.

89. S. & B. Webb, *Industrial Democracy,* pp. 250-1, and *The Penny Bee Hive,* January 6, 1872.

90. *The London Illustrated News,* April 6, 1872.

91. For a detailed account of the agitation in the textile trades see J. S. Hodgson, op.cit., pp. 413-20, and also MWH, EA, op.cit., XXXV, p. 164.

92. *Capital and Labour* (Journal), April 7, 1875.

93. In Gateshead the glass houses granted the nine hours in November 1871 and by December 1872 they were common throughout Britain for the non-shift workers. (*The Bee Hive,* January 18, 1873).

94. Evidence relating to these trades comes from CFW, op.cit., pp. XXXII and 99, and from *The Bee Hive,* January 6, 1872.

95. W. H. Warburton, *History of Trade Union Organisation in the Potteries,* (1931), pp. 42-3. He quotes from the 'Potteries Board of Arbitration, Award by Mr Brassey, 1880'.

96. A. L. Bowley, *Wages and Incomes in Nineteenth Century Britain,* (1900), p. 199.

97. Most of the evidence for miners' hours at this time comes from BTH, op.cit. It shows the following hours: Newcastle 35½; Durham 43½; Seaham 41½; Northumberland County 44; (all the foregoing

for hewers) and South Northumberland 32½ hours for miners generally. Other hours for hewers stem from BTH, op.cit., pp. 35-9. For surface workers hours were longer. According to BTH, op.cit., pp. 38-9, in Northumberland County these men achieved a shift from 10 to 11 hours, while some places in Lancashire, the Midlands, Somerset and North Wales received weekly reductions of from two to six hours. Meanwhile non-hewers working underground received the ten-hour day in Nottingham, Derby, Leicester, Warwick and North Wales ('Royal Commission on Coal, 1873', Q. 3,754, as cited in J. S. Hodgson, op.cit.).

98. All the hours that follow are taken from CFW, op.cit., pp. 10, 12, 14, 16, 51-8, and 100.

99. G. Howell, *Labour Legislation, Labour Movements, Labour Leaders,* (1902), p. 394, and also *The Bee Hive,* April 10, 1875.

100. J. S. Hodgson, op.cit., pp. 446-50, describes this process in detail for miners and engineers, with some information on builders. In Merthyr the miners chose a wage cut instead of an increase of hours by 22,560 to 755 votes (*Capital & Labour,* December 18, 1878). Hodgson stated that in general between 1876 and 1879 'men worked part time or suffered wage reductions'.

101. Lancashire and Cheshire coach-builders had their hours increased from 54 to 56½ in 1879; Northumberland and Durham miners had their hours increased, ½ hour per day for hewers and one hour per day for others; S. Staffordshire miners had to accept a nine-hour day instead of the eight hours they had adopted. J. S. Hodgson, op.cit. In fact the coach-builders of Lancashire had reduced hours to 54 in 1871 and to 53 in 1875, and these were increased to 56½ in 1879 (BTH, op.cit.). The hours of Scottish engineers were 51 from 1873 to 1879, when they returned to 54 (BTH, op.cit.).

102. *Report on the First Edinburgh Trades Union Congress, 1879.*

103. MWH, EA, XIII, pp. 26-7, and ibid., XI, p. 342. It was the small 'Perseverance Society of Carpenters' of London that opposed the move because of the depression in trade.

104. OSM-FR, op.cit., March 1878 and January 1879, and also MWH, EA, op.cit., XIII, pp. 225-6, and ibid., XII, p. 256 for plumbers' report.

105. MWH, EA, X, p. 217, and ibid., XII, pp. 350-1.

106. G. D. H. Cole, *The British Working Class Movement,* (1947), p. 247.

107. H. M. Vernon, *The Shorter Working Week,* (1934), p. 39.

108.   Board of Trade 'Report on the Strikes and Lock-outs of 1889', *BPP*, (1890), LXVIII.

109.   *Report of Trades Union Congress, 1890,* Debate on Eight Hours Day, statement by Mr Fawn of London.

110.   Board of Trade, 'Reports on Strikes . . . ', 1890, op.cit., p. 12.

111.   Cited in Board of Trade, 'Report on Strikes . . . ', 1890. op.cit., p. 10.

112.   All the figures that follow relating to 1886 stem from Board of Trade, 'Report on Trade: Wages (General Report)', *BPP*, 1893-4, LXXXIII, Pt. II (hence BTW). The page references are: engineers pp. 25-7; iron and steel shipbuilding and brass and metal ware p. 95; railway-carriage builders p. 115; boot and shoe trades whose hours ranged from 52½ to 58½ 'but (were) generally 54' p. 105; printers and compositors, 75 per cent of whom worked 54 hours in large shops while 50 per cent worked those hours in the smaller ones, the rest working either 50 to 53 or 55 to 60 hours, pp. 117-21; coopers p. 101; chemical manure workers, who sometimes worked a seven-day week, p. 113; brickmaking p. 111; tin-plate workers of whom a few worked 44 to 48 hours, p. 93; furnace men who worked seven twelve-hour shifts almost everywhere except for a few Lancashire foundries where they worked seven eight-hour shifts and some South Staffs. establishments that worked but six hours on Sunday, pp. 5-16; and finally the foundry workers not on shift or on the furnaces who worked a variety of hours with 54 the most common, pp. 5-16.

113.   Board of Trade, 'Report on Rates of Wages, etc, . . . in Minor Textile Trades', *BPP*, (1890), LXVIII. This states that the shops in 'Jute, Hemp, Silk, Carpet, Hosiery, Lace, Smallwares, Flock and Shoddy, Hair and Elastic Web' all work 56-56½ hours, with the exception of the two instances cited.

114.   Board of Trade, 'Return of the Rates of Wages in the Mines and Quarries in the UK', *BPP*, (1890-1), LXXVIII. Those working 46 to 51 hours included Cumberland, Lancashire, Yorkshire, North Staffordshire, Somerset, Forest of Dean and Scotland, while 54 were worked in N. Wales, S. Wales, Monmouth, Shropshire, Leicester, Warwick, Mid and South Derbyshire, S. Staffordshire and N. Worcestershire.

115.   *The Eight Hours Movement. Proceedings at a Joint Conference of Representative Coal Owners and the Miners' Federation of Great Britain,* (London, 1891), p. 43.

116. This is true 'usually' but not 'always' because 'at many large collieries the men are raised and lowered up and down separate shafts, consequently no interference does now ... lessen the winding time (of coal)'. *Miners Federation of Great Britain. Rejoinder to the Coal Owners' Reply on the Eight Hour Question,* (Barnsley, March 12, 1891), p. 5.

117. Thus we may look at the bricklayers as an example. In 1872 they had relatively few collective agreements with their employers, but they published *A Collection of Schedules, Rights, Rules, Customs and Privileges of the United Operative Bricklayers Trade Protection Society* in that year. These rules had 'by the tacit compliance of those most interested in the matter' come to be established, 'custom having given its sanction' their 'preservation ... shall be the basis – the first principle of the Society – and any attempt to curtail, to infringe upon, or to deprive us of any, or any part of any one, of these said "rights, rules, customs, and privileges", shall at all times be resisted to the utmost extent of our power ... without the necessity of consulting, or obtaining any other opinion or authority for so doing'. It is clear that the normal hours would be as well protected by such an arrangement as by a collective agreement. (Title as above, printed by OBS Manchester Order, Sheffield 1872).

118. With masonry a declining trade, nevertheless, carpenters and masons together are said to make up 45 per cent of the skilled tradesmen in building in 1906. (Board of Trade 'Report ... on Earnings, etc.', *BPP*, (1910), LXXXIV).

119. London, Manchester, Birmingham, Huddersfield, Halifax, Bristol, Hull, Nottingham, Oldham, Portsmouth, Liverpool, Scarborough, West Bromwich, Wolverhampton, Coventry and Sheffield. (BTH, op.cit., p. 16-19).

120. Board of Trade, 'Report of an Inquiry into the Earnings and Hours of Labour', Vol. III, 'Building and Woodworking', *BPP,* (1910), LXXXIV.

121. Ibid., pp. XV-XVII.

122. In Manchester and Stockport in 1859 the issue became part of a collective agreement signed by the masons. For this purpose the hours of daylight, during which it was considered one 'could see to work' were computed. For the twelve shortest weeks these averaged 47 hours 34 minutes, while for the sixteen shortest weeks they were 49 hours 11 minutes. OSM-FR, April 15, 1859.

123.   In 1877, 166 of 224 towns – or 74 per cent – had carpenters who worked the same hours in winter as in summer. (From *Annual Report*, ASCJ, 1878).

Chapter five

1.   'The Weekly Hours of Young Persons under Sixteen in Factories (various Textile and Allied Industries) Regulations, 1940', which reduced hours for those specified to 48 per week. *Ministry of Labour Gazette* (hence *MLG*), January 1941.

2.   The figures for the numbers employed in this sector came from B. R. Mitchell, op.cit., 'Labour Force Statistics, Series 1', p. 60. The figures for this industry only are comparable for all censuses from 1891-1921. For weights, the figures for 1891 were used up to 1895, those for 1901 from 1896-1905; those for 1911 for 1906-15; and those for 1921 for 1916-20.

3.   Board of Trade, 'Report on Changes in Hours and Wages, 1900', *BPP*, (1901), LXXII.

4.   The comparison between hours in 1890 and 1906, made in figure 20, cannot be regarded as anything but a rough indication of the presence or absence of change. This is because the statistics for 1890 are based only on data for England and Wales and take no account of the number of people covered by any one entry, which refers simply to a town, or even a group of towns. The 1906 statistics, on the other hand, cover the whole UK, and provide frequency distributions of all workers in the sectors covered.

5.   Board of Trade, 'Report on Changes . . .', 1894, in *BPP*, (1894), LXXXI, Pt. II.

6.   E. H. Phelps Brown, *The Growth of British Industrial Relations*, (1965), pp. xv and 15-16.

7.   A. Fox, *A History of the National Union of Boot and Shoe Operatives, 1874-1957*, (1958) p. 141.

8.   A. E. Musson, *The Typographical Association*, (1954), p. 102.

9.   Board of Trade, 'Report and Statistical Tables Relating to Changes in Rates of Wages and Hours of Labour in the UK in 1897', *BPP*, (1898), LXXXVIII.

10.   E. J. Hobsbawm, *Custom, Wages . . .'*, op.cit., p. 356.

11.   E. J. Hobsbawm, 'British Gas-Workers, 1873-1914', in E. J. Hobsbawm, op.cit., pp. 160, 165-8 and 176.

12.   L. Brentano, *Hours and Wages in Relation to Production*, (1894), pp. 57-8.

13.   Mr Taylor (Leeds) to Trades Union Congress, 1890, in *TUC Report*.

14.   E. J. Hobsbawm, *British Gas* . . ., op.cit., pp. 158-78. This article which presents most of the evidence regarding these changes in hours rejects the claims by the union's founders and argues that the hours reduction 'caused' the technological changes which followed 1889. The major 'solid evidence' for this contention is the fact that expenditure on buildings and machinery in this industry rose from an average of £127,000 per year in 1880-4 to an average of £320,000 in 1890-2 in London. Unfortunately the figures for 1887-90 were not given and it is these that are needed to support the contention. In any event, even if the 1889 figures were very low, the speed of the reaction suggests strongly that plans for such expenditure must have been afoot at least as early as 1889. In addition it appears that while in the event the actual introduction of the inclined retort, the major new device, was slowed down until 1899 by patent difficulties, the increased labour costs are said to represent a major stimulus to innovation only immediately after their introduction. This alternative explanation seems at least equally consonant with the evidence, though no doubt higher wage costs would have done something to speed up the introduction of machinery.

15.   R. Page Arnot, *The Miners: A History of the Miners*, (1949), pp. 84-5.

16.   E. H. Phelps Brown, *The Growth* . . ., op.cit., p. 136.

17.   R. O. Clarke, 'The Dispute in the British Engineering Industry, 1897-8: An Evaluation', *Economica*, XXIV, No. 94, May 1957.

18.   The issues were: the eight-hour day, the necessity to work with non-unionists, the maintenance of skill levels in the face of new machines, the voluntary nature of overtime, apprentice restrictions and curbs on piece work. The one minor issue that does not conform to the pattern was the payment of a minimum wage to all. Ibid., p. 131.

19.   E. J. Hobsbawm, *Custom* . . ., op.cit., p. 360.

Chapter six

1.   *MLG*, (January 1965), pp. 9-10.

2.   We shall use the term leisure throughout as meaning time not spent working at the job in question. This circumvents the thorny problem of a pure definition of leisure in the sense of

non-productive time. For an interesting treatment of this problem see Gary Becker's article, 'A Theory of the Allocation of Time' – *Economic Journal* LXXV, (September 1965).

3.   For a full description of this traditional approach see H. G. Lewis, 'Hours of Work and Hours of Leisure', *Report of the Industrial Relations Research Association,* IX, (1956) – esp. pp. 196-9.

4.   The term 'normal hours' henceforth refers to the number of hours which are specified in the collective agreement as constituting a full week. The concept thus defined loses much of its significance if habitual overtime has produced a situation in which employers' long-term production plans and employees' long-term expenditure plans are based on the normal hours plus overtime. To the extent that overtime becomes thus established as a right to be demanded by employers or employees, it tends to lose its two most beneficial attributes: it no longer provides the employers with a degree of flexibility in their short-run operating decisions and on the other hand it reduces the extent to which the availability of overtime provides the employees with some scope for varying the amount of time they spend at work, because it becomes increasingly difficult to refuse to work overtime under such conditions. In fact, if the provision of overtime is specified in the contract, the 'normal week' becomes largely academic. Figure 26 represents such a situation. The axes are the same as in figure 23. The normal week is represented by *E*, and implies a work-week of *XH* hours with an income of £ *OW* per week. The working of habitual overtime however has brought about a situation where the actual working week is described by *A*, including *HH′* hours of overtime and a total weekly income of £ *OW′*. The wage rate for overtime work is described by the slope of *EY′*. Whether the bargainers in any particular case are primarily interested in moving *A* or *E* depends on their preferences. In most cases the bargain concerns movement in *E*, though this usually entails a related shift in *A*. The union will generally wish to bargain at *E*. From *E* they will either move to *E′* or *E″* or to some point between the axes *TES*. Any such move will produce a new actual working week described by *A′* or *A″* or some other point on *KA*. In the short run there will thus be no change in the hours worked and one is tempted to conclude that the only issue in the bargain will be how great the increase in actual weekly income will be, irrespective of whether it is occasioned by a change in the normal weekly hours or a change in the basic weekly wage.

When the settlement achieved at E entails a reduction in the length of the normal week this is usually regarded as an attempt to raise weekly income indirectly. To what extent this is true cannot be determined without more detailed knowledge of the particular union's motivation. In practice it has been the case that when the bargain specified a change in the normal week this has not moved A to a point on KA but to some point within quadrant KAL, or in other words the reduction in the normal week has usually led to some reduction in the actual hours worked. In this case the parties to the bargain would weigh the costs and benefits entailed by a move of A into quadrant KAL, in as far as they were concerned with the short run. In as far as they were concerned with the long run they would consider the cost-benefit implications of the shift of E. In both instances the calculation made either at A or at E would be consistent with the model set out below. If the bargain took place solely at A the application of this analysis would pose no special problems.

5. The straight line XY would have been a budget line if the hand-loom weaver had been paid by time, which would have been virtually impossible since he worked independently in his home. Since he was paid by output, a more realistic budget line would have been a decelerating curve reflecting the decreasing productivity of extended hours.

6. See in particular L. Brentano, *Hours and Wages in Relation to Production*, (1894), especially pp. 19-37; J. Rae, op.cit., and S. Webb and H. Cox, *The Eight Hours Day*, (1891).

7. Namely, in all cases except those where a reduction of hours makes it possible to introduce shift working.

8. For a discussion see W. J. Baumol, *Economic Theory and Operations Analysis*, (1962), pp. 198-9.

9. L. Moses, 'Income, Leisure and Wage Pressure', in the *Economic Journal*, LXXII, (June 1962).

Chapter seven

1. A. Flanders, *Industrial Relations*, (1965), p. 29.
2. *MLG*, op.cit., January 1965.
3. *MLG*, August 1919.
4. *The Times*, June 12, 1959.
5. Board of Trade, 'Second Annual Report on Changes in Wages and Hours of Labour in the UK, 1894', *BPP*, (1896), LXXX, Pt. I.

6.   H. G. Lewis, *Hours of Work and Hours of Leisure,* op.cit., IX, p. 199. In point of fact the author is using 'real wage and real property income prospects' as the relevant variable by which the individual adjusts his preferences.

7.   Ibid., p. 197.

8.   D. C. Coleman, 'Labour in the English Economy of the Seventeenth Century', in E. M. Carus Wilson, op.cit., II, p. 303.

9.   L. Brentano, *Hours and Wages in Relation to Production,* (1894), p. 46.

10.   W. v. Siemens, *Lebenserinnerungen,* (Berlin, 1892), p. 216.

11.   W. W. Rostow, *The British Economy of the Nineteenth Century,* (1949), pp. 52 and 96.

12.   *The Workers News Bulletin,* (hence *WNB*), July 6, 1957.

13.   *The Penny Bee Hive,* February 19, 1870. A letter by C. Neville (writing from the Athenaeum) on the role of unions.

14.   *WNB,* April 20, 1957.

15.   The foregoing statements are taken from OSM-FR, op.cit., May 10, 1860 (letter from Bradford Lodge), September 1, 1859 (letter from Salford Lodge), and March 14, 1861.

16.   A. Bullock, *Life of Bevin,* (1960), I, p. 218.

17.   *The Bee Hive,* September 23, 1871.

18.   W. W. Rostow, op.cit., p. 96.

19.   C. E. Dankert, 'Automation, Unemployment, and Shorter Hours', in C. E. Dankert, F. C. Mann, H. R. Northrup eds., *Hours of Work,* (1965), p. 161.

20.   Ibid., p. 166.

21.   The foregoing statements stem from OSM-FR, October 29 and April 30, 1857, and July 8, 1858.

22.   E. J. Hobsbawm, 'The Tramping Artisan', in E. J. Hobsbawm, op.cit., pp. 34-65. I am indebted for much of this particular argument to this article where it is applied to tramping. For indications of the extent of the 1842 slump, see ibid., pp. 74-5, and the 'Index of Industrial Activity' in W. H. Beveridge, op.cit., pp. 310-13.

23.   ASCJ, *First Annual Report,* (1860), address by J. Manders, Chairman.

24.   R. O. Clarke, *The Dispute . . .,* op.cit., p. 128.

25.   W. W. Rostow, op.cit., p. 79.

26.   Lord Althorp cited in *The Annual Review,* (1833), p. 208.

27.   SCC, op.cit., pp. 302 and 388.

28. OSM-FR, May 10, 1860.

29. In 1839 the Central Committee of the masons commented that 'the idea of working by candlelight seems to us preposterous in the extreme' (OSM-FR, op.cit., January 1839). There were many strikes against the introduction or use of the system. See OSM-FR, September 15, 1836, re Leicester; MWH, EA, op.cit., XI, pp. 243 and 257, re Glasgow carpenters' strikes in 1834 and 1836; OSM-FR, op.cit., October 10, 1861, re Newcastle-upon-Tyne; and the 'Minutes of the Annual Government Delegate Meeting of the Friendly Society of Operative House Carpenters and Joiners, 1839' whose Norwich delegates asked for support to 'return to the original rules of the town, which was not to use candle or gas'. On the other hand there were also numerous strikes against shorter winter hours. See *Bricklayers' Trade Circular,* I, No. 5, (January 1, 1862), pp. 46-8; OSM-FR, op.cit., (December 1868), for a report of several strikes by masons; MWH, EA, XII, p. 258, re Glasgow plumbers; and ibid., XI, pp. 290-1, re strikes by London carpenters in 1842 and 1846.

30. W. Greg, proprietor of several textile mills in Bury, Lancashire to EFC, op.cit., p. 688.

31. OSM-FR, August 15, 1861, Ashton-under-Lyme Lodge to Central Committee.

32. S. R. Compston, Secretary of the Macclesfield and District Trades and Labour Council, in a letter to Sidney Webb, dated December 3, 1892. (MWH, EA, XII, p. 298).

33. E. Hodder, *The Life and Work of the Seventh Earl of Shaftesbury,* op.cit., p. 318.

34. OSM-FR, op.cit., March 5, 1857.

35. *The Bee Hive,* June 11, 1870.

36. *Bookbinders' and Machine Rulers' Consolidated Union Trade Circular,* IV, No. 6, (March 1873).

37. Lloyd George in a speech to a special Conference of representatives of workers and employers on February 27, 1919, cited in 'Unemployment: A Labour Policy', *Report of the Joint Committee on Unemployment appointed by the Parliamentary Committee of the Trades Union Congress and the Labour Party Executive,* (1921), p. 13.

38. Sir W. Beveridge, *Full Employment in a Free Society: A Summary,* (1944), (pamphlet), p. 10. Two other interesting contributions to the debate were Beveridge's book to which reference has been

made and two PEP pamphlets published in 1944 and entitled, *Employment for All* and *Demobilisation and Employment.* These pamphlets include lists of other materials.

39. For example the pressure for shorter hours in the US in 1949 has been ascribed to the fear of recession. H. R. Northrup and H. R. Brinberg, *The Economics of the Work Week,* Conference Studies in Business Economics, No. 24, (1950).

40. Cited in *WNB,* October 22, 1958.

41. *WNB,* February 7, 1959.

42. H. R. Kahn, *Repercussions of Redundancy,* (1964), p. 24 and p. 243.

43. For a good discussion of the effect of this issue see J. Burtle, 'Automation, the Guaranteed Wage and Hours of Work', *International Labour Review,* LXXV, (June 1957); for an earlier view see A. G. B. Fisher, 'Technical Improvements, Unemployment and Reductions of Working Hours', *Economica,* 1937.

44. *Royal Commission on Gold and Silver,* (1888), Pt. II, para. 26, cited in E. H. Phelps Brown, *The Growth . . .* op.cit., p. 15.

45. D. Grant, *Home Politics,* (1870).

46. All of the quotations on these issues have been taken from *The Bee Hive* and *The Penny Bee Hive,* as it was known for some months. The specific issues from which we have quoted include for 1870: January 29, February 19 and 26, March 5, April 2 and 9, May 21 and 28, June 4, September 17; and for 1871: January 28, and June 17 and 24. The dread of unemployment and the experience of it led to constant debates over emigration, the opening up of the waste-lands, the creation of 'sufficient demand' and the reduction of hours. These debates are to be found in all issues of the paper.

47. E. H. Phelps Brown, *The Growth . . .,* op.cit., p. 16.

48. Liberal Party Committee on Full Employment, *The Government's Full Employment Policy Examined,* (1944).

49. There is a debate as to whether there is a generic difference between the kinds of changes promised by automated processes involving self-regulating plant with the ability to 'learn' and previous technological advances. This debate does not concern us here. Our interest is confined to the fact that both are felt by the working man to threaten his job. It is of course quite possible, indeed likely, that different jobs are threatened in each case. We shall use the term automation simply to refer to a form of technological change.

50. These statements come from Professor Crossman speaking to the OECD North American Joint Conference on 'The Requirements of Automated Jobs', *Final Report*, (1965), p. 21, and from Norman Wiener, *The Human Use of Human Beings*, (1950), p. 189.

51. NEDC, *Growth of the United Kingdom Economy, 1961-1966*, (1963), pp. 25 and 27.

52. T. & G. W. U., Annual Conference, 1957, cited in *WNB*, July 13, 1957.

53. *The Times*, June 24 and 25, 1959.

54. B. R. Mitchell, op.cit., p. 6.

55. J. Saville, *Rural Depopulation in England and Wales, 1851-1951*, (1957), p. 61.

56. *The Times*, June 20, 1870.

57. *The Economist*, January 3, 1959.

58. Thus one mason's lodge applying for a grant to strike said that it was a good time to do so 'as the employer has invested much in machines etc., for the job', OSM-FR, June 17 and 24, 1858.

59. This belief is nowhere better illustrated than by the 1816 Royal Commission whose incredulity at Robert Owen's suggestion that his output had dropped less than in proportion to the reduction in hours, knew no bounds. They repeated the same question about six times and clearly thought Owen mad or dishonest. They concluded the discussion with a sneering question that implied its own answer. 'Do you, as an experienced spinner, or a spinner of any kind, mean to inform the Committee, that the machines that you employ . . . can produce an additional quantity from any other cause whatever but the quickening of the motion of the machine?' (SCC, op.cit., pp. 326-9).

60. FCR, op.cit., as cited in M. W. Thomas, *The Early Factory Legislation*, (1948), p. 52.

61. M. W. Thomas, op.cit., p. 293.

62. Memorial by Messrs Walker and Rand, Yorkshire mill owners, to Sir James Graham, Home Secretary, cited in Alfred (S. G. Kydd), *The History of the Factory Movement*, II, pp. 173-85.

63. *The Times*, September 11, 1871.

64. *The Bee Hive*, September 16, 1871.

65. For a discussion of the relation between hours of work and fatigue the most systematic British studies were done during the war and are discussed in H. M. Vernon, *Hours of Work and their Influence on Health and Efficiency*, British Association for Labour

Legislation, (1943), and *The War and Women's Employment,* International Labour Organisation, Montreal, (1946). A comprehensive earlier study of the problem can be found in P. Sargent Florence, *The Economics of Fatigue and Unrest,* (1924).

66.   W. W. Rostow, op.cit., p. 93.

67.   OSM-FR, op.cit., July 18, 1861.

68.   This transformation of the overtime rate from deterrent to the employer to incentive to the employee is discussed in G. Brooks, *Monthly Labour Review,* November 1956.

69.   *The Economist,* October-December 1956, p. 449.

70.   *Statistics on Incomes, Prices, Employment and Production,* Ministry of Labour, (hence SIPEP), Series D. 16.

71.   H. D. Woods and S. Ostry, *Labour Policy and Labour Economics in Canada,* (1962), p. 334.

72.   Sir James Graham made this point in the Commons in answer to the many speakers and advocates of factory legislation who had provided evidence that the losses resulting from reduced hours were negligible or non-existent. He said that if their claims were true, then 'so far from legislation being necessary, it apears to me a conclusive argument against calling on the Government to interpose'. (*Hansard,* (1846), LXXXIII, p. 395).

73.   H. R. Kahn, op.cit., p. 239. In a study of the experiences of a group of redundant workers it was found that of those that had moved to new jobs a great proportion worked considerably longer hours than they had done in their original job. Nevertheless 54 per cent of them regarded these jobs as 'more convenient' because they did not entail shifts. Another explanation is possible in view of the fact that shifts are generally regarded as unsuitable for small enterprises. See F. Selliers, 'Les Mécanismes . . .', *Revue d'Action Populaire,* No. 170, Juillet-Août, 1963.

74.   S. G. Kydd, op.cit., II, p. 255. The idea that hours could be restricted only if all concurred appears time and again. As early as 1824 a leading manufacturer had petitioned the House of Commons to fix the hours of labour (MWH, EA, op.cit., V, p. 154). The *Leeds Mercury* wrote in the 1830s that legislation was necessary 'since the benevolent attempt by Wood and others in 1825 had shown how futile merely individual effort was: competition would always kill it', (C. Driver, op.cit., p. 55). Elsewhere it was said that regulation through unions would not be good enough either since that 'would have succeeded in reducing

the hours of Labour in towns' only hence bringing those Manufacturers 'to the brink of ruin', (S. G. Kydd, op.cit., pp. 310). Once legislation was passed this same feeling led to 'the formation of an association (of manufacturers) to prosecute those who violated its provisions'. See B. L. Hutchins and A. Harrison, *A History of Factory Legislation*, (1926), p. 47.

75. More than fifteen witnesses made this point in one form or another. *Royal Commission on the Factory and Workshop Acts*, op.cit., p. XV.

76. Builders Trade Circular, as cited in MWH, EA, XI, p. 154.

77. OSM-FR, op.cit., April 11, 1861 and MWH, EA, XII, p. 47.

78. G. Howell, op.cit., pp. 308-11. For other descriptions of the formation of these various bodies see: G. D. H. Cole, *Attempts at General Union*, (1953), p. 19; MWH, EA, XIII, p. 356 and p. 26; and R. O. Clarke, op.cit., p. 130.

79. *Morning Chronicle*, April 4, 1786, letter by the booksellers of London, cited in E. Howe and J. Child, op.cit., p. 12.

80. *WNB*, September 13, 1958.

81. A financial advantage accrues to the employer from that alternative which involves the lower wage costs after any specific reduction in actual hours. Figure 30 demonstrates that this advantage may lie with either alternative, depending on the size of the contemplated reduction. On the x axis we measure hours of work, from right to left, and on the y axis we plot weekly earnings. The diagram represents a hypothetical situation in which the actual hours of work are 48, and of these eight hours are overtime, for which the wage rate is double the basic rate. The original situation is represented by *AEO*, indicating that 40 hours are worked at x pence per hour and eight hours at $2x$ pence per hour. Now the employer is forced to choose between *BCO*, i.e. reducing the normal hours to 32 keeping the basic weekly wage rate unchanged, and *BDO*, i.e. raising the wage rate so that earnings for a 48-hour week are the same as in *BCO*. From figure 30 we can see that if actual hours are subsequently cut back, the financial advantage lies at first with *BDO* and not until the reduction exceeds the amount implied by point *F*, (which is always larger than the original amount of habitual overtime) does it come to lie with *BCO*. If we refer to the reduction in actual hours necessary to reach point *F* by the symbol a, then the financial advantage lies with *BDO* so long as the expected reduction in hours is smaller than a, while if it is

Income
(£/wk)

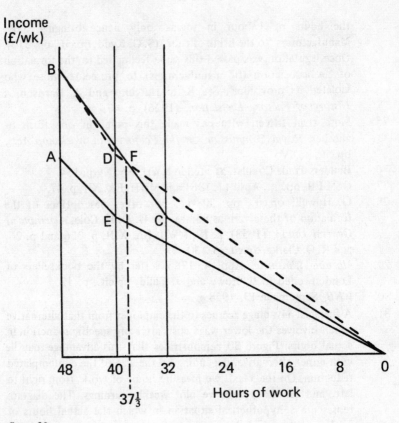

figure 30

larger than *a* the financial advantage lies with *BCO*. In the example hours would have to be reduced below 37 1/3 hours before the financial advantage reverts to *BCO*.

82.   L. Moses, op.cit., makes the point in his article. Namely that the availability of overtime tends to remove the resistance of the income preferrers in the union.

83.   It is reminiscent of the man who, given a walking stick with a beautiful carved head, found it too high for him. He insisted on cutting a foot off the top, because it was not too long at the bottom end.

271 Notes to chapter seven

84. A short resumé of the studies supporting this view, as well as a critique of them is to be found in M. S. Feldstein, 'Estimating the Supply Curve of Working Hours', *Oxford Economic Papers,* March 1968. This issue generally was the subject of a controversy between T. A. Finnegan, *Industrial Labour Relations Review,* January 1962 and H. G. Vatter, ibid., July 1961.

85. This problem is discussed in M. S. Feldstein, op.cit.

86. B. Wootton, *The Social Foundations of Wage Policy,* (1955), p. 59.

87. C. D. Long, *The Labour Force under Changing Income and Employment,* (1958).

88. Speech by Lord Kindersley, cited in PEP Pamphlet, *Demobilisation and Employment,* (1944), p. 23.

89. E. J. Hobsbawm, 'British Gas Workers', op.cit., p. 163.

90. *Arbeitszeit und Produktivität, Untersuchungsergebnisse Wissenschaftlicher Forschungsinstitute, Dritter Band,* (1962), pp. 121-2.

91. RCC-R1, op.cit., p. 109. The practice of walking time of the builders is discussed in MWH, EA, XI, p. 186.

92. *The Times,* June 23, 1870, and *The Penny Bee Hive,* May 28, 1870.

93. *Arbeitszeit und Produktivität,* op.cit., p. 122. *'Der immer wieder auftretende Hinweis, "mehr Freizeit kostet mehr Geld" '.*

94. Sir A. Bowley, *Wages in the United Kingdom in the Nineteenth Century,* (1900), p. 85.

95. J. A. Schumpeter, *The Theory of Economic Development,* (1949), p. 65.

96. W. W. Rostow, op.cit., p. 54.

97. E. H. Phelps Brown, *The Growth . . . ,* op.cit., p. 15.

98. The boilermakers told their men 'to take no part in the dispute' while 'the majority (of non-union engineers) stayed at work'. (R.O. Clarke, op.cit., pp. 130 and 133).

References

1 Books and Articles

Alfred (S. G. Kydd), *The Early Factory Legislation*, 2 vols, (1857).

Allison, K. J. 'The Norfolk Worsted Industry in the Sixteenth and Seventeenth Centuries' in E. M. Carus Wilson, vol. III.

Anon, *An Essay on Trade and Commerce* (1770).

Anon, *Hours of Work in Manchester* Pamphlet (1825).

Anon, *The Book of Trades* (1804). Patent Office Library.

Anon, *The Case of the Journeymen Tailors and Journeymen Staymakers* (1752). (British Museum).

'Arbeitszeit und Produktivität', Untersuchungsergebnisse Wissenschaftlicher Forschungsinstitute, Dritter Band (1962).

Ashley, M. P. 'England in the Seventeenth Century' (1956).

Ashton, T. S. *Economic Fluctuations in England 1700-1800* (1959).

Ashton, T. S. 'The Treatment of Capitalism by Historians' in F. A. Hayek ed. *Capitalism and the Historians* (1954).

Aspinall, A. *The Early English Trade Unions* (1949).

Baines, E. *History of the Cotton Manufacture in Great Britain* (1835).

Baumol, W. J., *Economic Theory and Operations Analysis* (1962).

Becker, Gary 'A Theory of the Allocation of Time' *Economic Journal*, LXXV, September 1965.

Beveridge, Sir W. *Full Employment in a Free Society: A Summary* (Pamphlet 1944).

Beveridge, W. H. *Full Employment in a Free Society* (1944).

Bowley, Sir A. *Wages in the United Kingdom in the Nineteenth Century*, (1900).

Bowley, A. L. *Wages and Income in the United Kingdom since 1860* (1937).

Brentano, L. *Hours and Wages in Relation to Production* (1894).

Brentano, L. 'On the History and Development of Gilds' in Toulmin Smith ed. *English Gilds* (1870).

Brown, R. A., Colven, H. M., Taylor, A. J. *The History of the King's Works* (1963).

Bullock, A. *The Life and Times of Ernest Bevin* 2 vols. (1960).

Burtle, J. 'Automation, the Guaranteed Wage and Hours of Work',

International Labour Review, LXXV, (June 1957).

Campbell, A. *The London Tradesman* (1747), Patent Office Library.

Carus Wilson, E. M. *Essays in Economic History* (3 vols.) (Vol. I, 1954; Vols. II and III, 1962).

Carus Wilson, E. M. 'Some Statistics of the Industrial Revolution, 1760-1830' in E. M. Carus Wilson ed., III.

Child, J. *Industrial Relations in the British Printing Industry* (1967).

Clarke, R. O. 'The Dispute in the British Engineering Industry 1897-8: An Evaluation' *Economica*, XXIV, No. 94, (May 1957).

Cole, G. D. H. *Attempts at General Union* (1953).

Cole, G. D. H. *Robert Owen* (1925).

Cole, G. D. H. *A Short History of the British Working Class Movement 1789-1927*, (1947).

Cole, M. *Robert Owen of New Lanark* (1953).

Coleman, D. C. 'Labour in the English Economy of the Seventeenth Century' in E. M. Carus Wilson, op.cit., II.

Cooke Taylor, R. H. *The Factory System* (1891).

Connelly, T. F. *The Woodworkers, 1860-1960* (1960).

Dankert, C. E., Mann, F. C., Northrup, H. R., eds., *Hours of Work* (1965).

Dankert, C. E. 'Automation, Unemployment and Shorter Hours' in C. E. Dankert, F. C. Mann, H. R. Northrup, *Hours of Work* (1965).

Defoe, D. *A Tour through the Whole Island of Great Britain, 1724-1727* (1778).

Driver, C. *Richard Oastler: Tory Radical* (1946).

Dunning, T. J. 'Some Account of the London Consolidated Society of Bookbinders' in National Association for the Promotion of Social Sciences, *Trade Societies and Strikes* (1860).

Elsas, M., ed., *Iron in the Making: Dowlais Iron Company Letters, 1782-1860* (1960).

Englefield, W. A. D. 'Early History of the Painting Trade in London' in *Journal of Decorative Art*, (June 1919).

Feldstein, M. S. 'Estimating the Supply Curve of Working Hours', *Oxford Economic Papers*, (March 1968).

Finnegan, T. A. 'Communication on the Backward Sloping Supply Curve', *Industrial Labour Relations Review*, (January 1962).

Fox, A. *A History of the National Union of Boot and Shoe Operatives 1874-1957* (1958).

Furniss, E. *The Position of the Labourer in a System of Nationalism* (1920).

Fyrth, H. J. and Collins, H. *The Foundry Workers: A Trade Union History* (1959).

Galton, F. W. *The Tailoring Trade* (1896).

Gaskell, P. *Artisans and Machinery* (1836).

Grant, D. *Home Politics* (1870).

Grazia, S. de *Of Time, Work and Leisure* (1962).

Green, J. R. (Mrs) *Town Life in the Fifteenth Century* (1894).

Guttery, D. R. *From Broad-Glass to Cut Crystal* (1956).

Hamilton, E. J. 'American Treasure and the Rise of Capitalism' in *Economica*, No. 27, (November 1, 1929).

Hammond, J. L. & B., *The Skilled Labourer 1760-1832* (1919).

Hammond, J. L. & B., *The Town Labourer 1760-1832* (1917).

Higenbottam, S. *Our Society's History: Amalgamated Society of Woodworkers,* (1939).

Hill, C. *Society and Puritanism in Pre-Revolutionary England* (1964).

Hobsbawm, E. J. *Labouring Men* (1964).

Hobsbawm, E. J. 'Custom, Wages and Work-load' in E. J. Hobsbawm, *Labouring Men* (1964).

Hobsbawm, E. J. 'British Gas Workers 1873-1914' in E. J. Hobsbawm, *Labouring Men,* (1964).

Hobsbawm, E. J. 'Trends in the British Labour Movement', in E. J. Hobsbawm, *Labouring Men,* (1964).

Hobsbawm, E. J. 'The Labour Aristocracy' in E. J. Hobsbawm, *Labouring Men,* (1964).

Hobsbawm, E. J. 'Economic Fluctuations' in E. J. Hobsbawm, *Labouring Men,* (1964).

Hobsbawm, E. J. 'The British Standard of Living 1790-1850' in E. J. Hobsbawm, *Labouring Men,* (1964).

Hobsbawm, E. J. 'The Tramping Artisan' in E. J. Hobsbawm, *Labouring Men,* (1964).

Hodder, E. *The Life and Work of the Seventh Earl of Shaftesbury* (1888).

Hodgson, J. S. 'The Movements for Shorter Hours, 1840-1875' (1940) unpublished Ph.D. (Oxon.).

Howe, E. & Child, J. *The Society of London Bookbinders,* (1952).

Howe, E. & Waite, H. E. *The London Society of Compositors,* (1948).

Howell, G. *Labour Legislation, Labour Movements, Labour Leaders* (1902).

Hutchins, B. L. & Harrison, A. *A History of Factory Legislation* (1926).

Johns, E. A. *The Social Structure of Modern Britain* (1965).

Kahn, H. R. *Repercussions of Redundancy* (1964).

Keynes, J. M. *A Treatise on Money,* 2 vols. (1930).

Knoop, D. & Jones, G. P. *The Mediaeval Mason* (1967).

Lambert, J. M. *Two Thousand Years of Gild Life* (1891).

Lewis, H. G. 'Hours of Work and Hours of Leisure' in *Report of the Industrial Relations Research Association* IX (1956).

Liberal Party Committee on Full Employment, *The Government's Full Employment Policy Examined* (1944).

Long, C. D. *The Labour Force under Changing Income and Employment* (1958).

Mantoux, P. *The Industrial Revolution in the Eighteenth Century* (1928).

Marshall, A. *Principles . . .*, (8th edition, 1930).

Marshall, T. H. 'Population and the Industrial Revolution' in E. M. Carus Wilson, I.

Marx, K. *Capital,* vol. I (based on 1887 English edition).

Mess, H. A. *Factory Legislation and its Administration* (1926).

Mitchell, B. R. *Abstract of British Historical Statistics* (1962).

Moses, L. 'Income, Leisure and Wage Pressure' in *Economic Journal,* LXXII, (June 1962).

Musson, A. E. *The Typographical Association* (1954).

NEDC, *Growth of the United Kingdom Economy, 1961-1966* (1963).

Nef, J. U. 'Prices and Industrial Capitalism in France and England, 1540-1640' in E. M. Carus Wilson, I.

Nef, J. U. 'The Progress of Technology and the Growth of Large-Scale Industry in Great Britain, 1540-1640' in E. M. Carus Wilson, I.

Nef, J. U. *The Rise of the British Coal Industry* 2 vols. (1932).

OECD, *The Requirements of Automated Jobs,* Report of Joint North American Conference (1965).

Page Arnot, R. *The Miners: A History of the Miners,* (1949).

Phelps Brown, E. H. *The Growth of British Industrial Relations* (1965).

Phelps Brown, E. H. & Hopkins, S. 'Seven Centuries of the Prices of Consumables, compared with Builders' Wage-rates' in E. M. Carus Wilson, II.

Podmore, F. *Robert Owen* (1924).

PEP (Political and Economic Planning) *Employment for All* (1944 – Pamphlet).

PEP (Political and Economic Planning), *Demobilisation and Employment* (1944 – Pamphlet).

Pollard, S. *A History of Labour in Sheffield* (1959).

Postgate, R. W. *The Builder's History* (1923).

Pugh, E. (pseud. D. Hughson) *London and its Environs to Thirty Miles Extent* (1810).

Putnam, B. H. *Enforcement of the Statute of Labourers* (1908).

Rae, J. *Eight Hours for Work* (1894).

Ritchie, N. 'Labour Conditions in Essex in the Reign of Richard II' in E. M. Carus Wilson, II.

Rogers, J. E. Thorold, *Six Centuries of Work and Wages* (1906).

Rostow, W. W. *The British Economy of the Nineteenth Century* (1949).

Salzman, L. F. *Building in England down to 1540* (1952).

Sargent, Florence P. *Economics of Fatigue and Unrest* (1924).

Saville, J. *Rural Depopulation of England and Wales, 1851-1951* (1957).

Schumpeter, J. A. *The Theory of Economic Development* (1949).

Scrivenor, H. *A Comprehensive History of the Iron Trade* (1841).

Shaw, G. Lefevre & Bennet, T. R. *Account of the Strike and Lock-out in the Building Trades of London in 1859-60,* Pamphlet, (British Museum).

Siemens, W. v. *Lebenserinnerungen,* (1892).

Smith, A. *The Wealth of Nations* (1776).

Smith, H. L. 'Chapters in the History of London Waterside Labour' in *Economic Journal* (December 1892).

Stow, J. *Survey of London* (1598).

Strutt, J. *The Sports and Pastimes of the People of England* (1801).

Tawney, R. H. *Religion and the Rise of Capitalism* (1927).

Taylor, A. J. 'Progress and Poverty in Britain, 1780-1850' in E. M. Carus Wilson, III.

Thomas, M. H. *The Early Factory Legislation* (1948).

Thrupp, S. L. 'The Gilds' in *Cambridge Economic History of Europe,* III (1963).

Trevelyan, G. M. *English Social History* (1964).

Unwin, G. *Studies in Economic History* (1958).

Vatter, H. G. 'On the Folklore of the Backward Sloping Supply Curve', *Industrial Labour Relations Review* (July 1961).

Vernon, H. M. *The Shorter Working Week* (1934).

Vernon, H. M. *Hours of Work and their influence on Health and Efficiency* (1943).

Warburton, W. M. *History of Trade Union Organization in the Potteries* (1931).

Ward-Perkins, C. N. 'The Commercial Crisis of 1847' *Oxford Economic Papers,* Vol. 2, No. 1 (January 1950).

Webb, S. *Labour in the Longest Reign* Fabian Tract No. 75 (1897).

Webb, S. & B. *Der Normalarbeitstag und die Englischen Gewerkschaften* (undated 1890s).

Webb, S. & B. *History of Trade Unionism* (1906).

Webb, S. & Cox, H. *The Eight Hours Day* (1891).

Weetch, K. T. 'The Dowlais Ironworks and its Industrial Community 1760-1850', LSE, (M.Sc. Econ. unpublished). (1963).

Wiener, N. *The Human Use of Human Beings* (1950).

Woods, H. D. & Ostry, S. *Labour Policy and Labour Economics in Canada* (1962).

Wootton, B. *The Social Foundations of Wage Policy* (1955).

Young, Arthur *Tour in the North of England* (1772).

2 Government Reports, etc.

1300-1820 *The Statutes of the Realm*, vol. I to VI.

The Statutes of the United Kingdom with Notes and References, vols. I to XXVI (some years).

1642-60 *Acts and Ordinances of the Interregnum 1642-1660*, vols. I and II, collected and edited by C. H. Firth and R. S. Rail (1911).

1547-1659 *Journal of the House of Commons*, vols. I to VII.

1816 'Report of the Minutes of Evidence taken before the Select Committee on the State of the Children employed in the Manufactories of the United Kingdom, 1816' *BPP* 1816, vol. III.

1830-8 *Hansard* (selected issues).

1833 'First Report from Commissioners appointed to collect information in the Manufacturing. Districts, relative to Employment of Children in Factories . . .; with Minutes of Evidence and Reports of District Commissioners', *BPP*, 1833, vol. XX.

'Second Report . . .', *BPP*, 1833, vol. XXI.

1842 'First Report of the Commissioners for inquiring into the Employment and Conditions of Children in Mines and Manufactories', *BPP*, 1842, vol. XV, Appendices vols. XVI and XVII.

1843 'Second Report of the Royal Commission on the Employment of Children', *BPP*, 1843, vol. XIII, Appendices vol. XIV.

1843 'Midland Mining Commission's Report', *BPP*, 1843, vol. XIII.

1871 'Report of the Inspector of Mines', *BPP*, 1872, vol. XVI.

1875 'Report of the Commissioners appointed to enquire into the working of the Factory and Workshops Acts, 1875', *BPP*, 1876, vol. XXIX.

1886 'Board of Trade, Report on Trade, Wages (General Report), 1886', *BPP*, 1893-4, vol. LXXXIII, Pt. II.

1888-93 'Board of Trade, Reports on Strikes and Lockouts' for 1888, *BPP*, 1889, vol. LXX.

1889, *BPP*, 1890, vol. LXVIII

1890, *BPP*, 1890-1, vol. LXXVIII

1891, *BPP*, 1893-4, vol. LXXXIII, Pt. I.

1892, *BPP*, 1894, vol. LXXXI, Pt. I.

1893, *BPP*, 1894, vol. LXXXI, Pt. I.

1886 'Report on Rates of Wages . . . in Minor Textile Trades', *BPP*, 1890, vol. LXVIII.

1886 'Return of the Rates of Wages in the Mines and Quarries in the UK', *BPP*, 1890-1, vol. LXXVIII.

1890 'Board of Trade: Report on trades (Hours of Work)', *BPP*, 1890, vol. LXVIII.

1893-1916 Board of Trade 'Changes in Rates of Wages and Hours of Labour in the UK'.

for 1893 *BPP*, 1894, vol. LXXXI – Pt. II

for 1894 *BPP*, 1896, vol. LXXX – Pt. I

for 1895 *BPP*, 1897, vol. LXXXIII

for 1896 *BPP*, 1897, vol. LXXXIII

for 1897 'Report and Statistical Tables relating to Changes in Rates of Wages and Hours of Labour in the UK in 1897' *BPP*, 1898, vol. LXXXVIII

for 1898 *BPP*, 1899, vol. XCI

for 1899 *BPP*, 1900, vol. LXXI

for 1900 *BPP*, 1901, vol. LXXII

for 1901 *BPP*, 1902, vol. XCVI

for 1902 *BPP*, 1903, vol. LXVI

for 1903 *BPP*, 1904, vol. LXXXIX

for 1904 *BPP*, 1905, vol. LXXVI

for 1905 *BPP*, 1906, vol. CXII

for 1906 *BPP*, 1907, vol. LXXX

for 1907 *BPP*, 1908, vol. XCVIII

for 1908 *BPP*, 1909, vol. LXXX

for 1909 *BPP*, 1910, vol. LXXXIV

for 1910 *BPP*, 1911, vol. LXXXIX

for 1911 *BPP*, 1912-13, vol. XCII

for 1912 *BPP*, 1912-13, vol. XCII

for 1913 *BPP*, 1914-16, vol. LXI

1906 'Report of an Enquiry by the Board of Trade into the Earnings and Hours of Labour'

Vol. I Textiles, *BPP*, 1909, vol. LXXX

Vol. II Clothing, *BPP,* 1909, vol. LXXX
Vol. III Building and Woodworking, *BPP,* 1910, vol. LXXXIV
Vol. VI Metal, Engineering etc. *BPP,* 1911, vol. LXXXVIII
Vol. VIII Paper, Printing . . .; Pottery, Brick, Glass . . .; Food, Drink;
Miscellaneous Trades, *BPP,* 1912-13, vol. CVIII
1921 *Unemployment etc. – A Labour Policy.* Report of the Joint
Committee on Unemployment appointed by the Parliamentary Committee
of the TUC and the Labour Party Executive.
1915-1965 *Ministry of Labour Gazette.*
1962-1965 Ministry of Labour *Statistics on Incomes, Prices, Employment and Production.*

3 Manuscripts
Webb Collection E, Section A
Vols. 1 to 9 General History
Vols. 10 to 13 Building Trades
Vol. 14 Clothing Trades
Vols. 15 to 20 Engineering and Metal Trades
Vol. 23 Iron and Steel Trades
Vols. 26 to 28 Miners
Vols. 29 to 31 Printing and Paper
Vols. 34 to 40 Textile Trades
Vols. 43 to 46 Miscellaneous Trades

4 Union Publications
1869-95 *Reports of the Trades Union Congress*
Bricklayers
1862-3 *Operative Bricklayers Trade Circular*
1872 OBS (Manchester Order) *A Collection of Schedules, Rights, Rules, Customs and Privileges of the United Operative Bricklayers Trade Protection Society*
1870-80 OBS (London Order) *Annual Reports* (selected issues)
Carpenters
1860-95 *Annual Reports* of the Amalgamated Society of Carpenters and Joiners (ASCJ)
1868-72 *Monthly Reports* of the ASCJ (selected issues)
Masons
1867-95 *Annual Reports* of the OSM
1856-64 *Fortnightly Review* of the OSM
1865-90 (selected issues) *Fortnightly Review* of the OSM

Printers and Bookbinders
1873-9 *Bookbinders and Machine Rulers* Consolidated Union Trade Circular
1862-4 *Scottish Typographical Circular*
Tailors
1865-90 *Report of the National Conferences of the Operative Tailors of Scotland*

5 Papers, Journals
1830-80 *The Annual Review*
1866-74 *The Bee Hive*
1873-8 *Capital and Labour* (Journal) (some issues)
1870-1965 *The Economist* (selected issues)
1860-75 *The London Illustrated News* (selected issues)
1843-9 *The Northern Star* (selected issues)
1870 *The Penny Bee Hive*
1830-1960 *The Times* (selected issues)
1956-61 *Workers News Bulletin*

Notes to figures and tables

1. Figures 1, 3 to 7 and 20
These figures present the information provided by the Board of Trade, *Report on Trades (Hours of Work)* of 1890. It was compiled by H. G. Calcraft and the introduction states: 'The Return has been mainly compiled from Returns made to the Board of Trade by employers on the one side, and workman's associations on the other, in response to circulars sent out by the Board of Trade. It should be understood that it relates to the "standard" hours of work in each trade, and that no account is taken of overtime'.

2. Figure 2
This is based on information collected from the Fortnightly Returns of the Operative Society of Masons from 1856 to 1861.

3. Figure 8
The statistics for this figure are taken from the Annual Reports of the ASCJ, 1865 to 1893.

4. Figures 9 to 13
Figures 9 to 11 present frequency distributions of the normal hours of masons weighted by population at the 1871 census. The weights were allocated as follows: 10 for towns below 20,000; 35 for towns between 20,000 and 50,000; 75 for towns between 50,000 and 100,000; 150 for towns between 100,000 and 200,000; and one unit weight per thousand of population for the six towns with populations above 200,000 in 1871 — i.e. London, Birmingham, Liverpool, Manchester, Leeds and Sheffield.
Figure 12 presents a weighted distribution of normal hours for carpenters and here the groupings were rather larger for the sake of convenience. Weights were allocated as follows: 10 for towns under 20,000; 35 for towns between 20,000 and 50,000; and 200 for all towns above 50,000.
In both cases the samples are extensive, including anything from 200 to over 300 towns in each year. Virtually all of the cities with a population over 50,000 in 1871 are included, and about 75 per cent of those between 20,000 and 50,000. In addition there are up to 200 towns with a population below 20,000 represented.

5. Figure 14
The information for carpenters and masons came from the same sources as

for figures 9 to 13 and is used without weights here.

The information for the bricklayers came from the OBS (Manchester Order), *A Collection of Schedules, Rights, Rules, Customs and Privileges of the United Operative Bricklayers Trade Protection Society* (1872).

In each case the distribution is based on an identical sample of towns – i.e. the comparison between bricklayers and each of the other trades is for the same towns – that between bricklayers and masons for 64 towns, that between bricklayers and carpenters for 76 towns.

6. Figure 15

The information for masons and carpenters came from their respective Annual Reports, while that for the other trades came from the Board of Trade, *Report on Trades (Hours of Work)*, 1890.

7. Figures 16 and 17

The information of both these figures comes from the Board of Trade *Changes in Rates of Wages and Hours of Labour* from 1893 to 1913. From 1914 to the present it was taken from the January issues of the *Ministry of Labour Gazette.*

For figure 16 the information for 1890 to 1893 was collected from the Board of Trade's *Reports on Strikes and Lockouts* for those years. It was the information in these Reports that was eventually organized and presented separately in the *Reports on Changes in Rates of Wages and Hours of Labour.* While these surveys are not as complete as subsequent ones, they do include all major changes in hours.

The first of the Reports stated that 'the field of employment covered more or less by the inquiry included the great majority of the wage-earning population, excepting domestic servants'. On the other hand agriculture, railways and seamen were reported on separately as the information for them was less complete (Board of Trade, 'Report on Changes . . . 1893', *BPP*, 1894, vol. LXXXI, pt. II, pp. XII-XIII).

In subsequent years the reports take on a more specified form. From the late 1890s they exclude agriculture, railway servants, seamen, police, government employees, domestic servants, shop assistants and clerks.

From 1920 railway servants were included, while after the Second World War the coverage was gradually extended to all manual wage earners.

8. Figure 18

The first three of these indices are given in the *Ministry of Labour Gazette* of September 1957.

The last index is the current one and can be found in the January issue of the *Gazette* in each year.

9. Figure 19

This index was compiled from the figures of aggregate changes in hours given in the Board of Trade Reports from 1893. These were spread over the number of people in the industry, taken from the successive census data presented in B. R. Mitchell, op.cit., in his section on the Labour Force. For construction the figures are comparable between 1891 and 1921.

The 1891 census was used up to 1895; the 1901 census from 1896 to 1905; the 1911 census from 1906 to 1915; and the 1921 census from 1916 to 1920.

The annual *per capita* change in normal hours was then expressed as a percentage of the Average Normal Hours given for this industry in the Board of Trade's comprehensive survey of 1906. This figure (51.0) was taken as the base of the index, so that 1906 = 100.0.

Figure 20 – see Section 1

10. Figure 21

These distributions are taken from the Board of Trade's *Enquiry into the Earning and Hours of Labour* of 1906 – vols. I, II, III, VI and VIII. The percentages in each case refer to the number of individuals working the given hours as a percentage of the total sample.

11. Figure 22

The comparison of these two sets of data is made difficult because the 1890 figures are unweighted by population, while those of 1906 refer to the number of individuals working the hours in any interval. Since large towns are therefore under-represented in the unweighted samples, and since in most trades hours in large centres tend to be shorter the reductions which appear to have occurred in the comparison must be largely discounted.

12. Figures 27 and 28

The series of Money Wages, Retail Prices and Real Wages all came from those prepared by A. L. Bowley and H. D. Wood for the years 1850 to 1902. These are cited in B. R. Mitchell, op.cit., in the section on 'Wages and the Standard of Living'.

For 1900-65 the series of Money Wages and Retail Prices is based on the London and Cambridge Economic Service Bulletin. Those for real wages were more difficult. For 1900-14 they are taken from a series by Bowley and Wood cited in B. R. Mitchell, op.cit. Cited in the same place was the series for the years 1920 to 1938 compiled by E. C. Ramsbottom. For the series 1936 to 1965 the money wages of the London and Cambridge Economic Service Bulletin were deflated by the retail prices in that same publication.

13. Figure 29
The unemployment figures from 1857 to 1920 were taken from Sir W. Beveridge, *Full Employment in a Free Society* (1944). From 1921 to the present they came from the London and Cambridge Economic Service Bulletin.

Before 1923 these figures refer to rates of unemployment in certain trade unions while after that date they are based on information derived from the government social insurance records.

It is almost certain that the early figures under-estimate the actual unemployment levels because they refer to unemployment among men in certain strong unions, who were normally in a favoured economic position. Nevertheless, it is accepted that the variations in this unemployment rate give a good indication of change in the national rate.

14. Tables 1 to 6 and table 8
These are based on the same information as figures 1 and 3 to 7.

15. Table 7
This table is taken as it is from the Board of Trade *Report on Trade: Wages (General Report)* for 1886.

16. Table 9
This is taken from the 1906 *Board of Trade Enquiry into Earnings and Hours,* vol. II.

17. Table 10
This is based on the Index of Money Wages used in figure 28.

18. Table 11
This is taken from SIPEP, series E. 13.

19. Table 12
This is taken from *MLG,* October 1955 and September 1965.

Index

References in italic figures are to the pages on which tables or diagrams appear.